To each of our families
and
To the students, faculty, and staff
of the
University of North Carolina School of Law.

* * *

Acknowledgments

The idea for a self-instructional workbook in legal research took seed more than two decades ago, and found form in the first edition of this workbook in 1996. The genesis for the workbook rests in the advantages of teaching legal research in a hands-on environment, where all students can learn at their own pace using their own learning styles. That idea grew into its present reality only through the direct help of many students, faculty, and staff members at the University of North Carolina School of Law over a number of years. Three entire classes of first-year students helped us experiment with the initial format, adding many editorial comments that remain in the present edition. Students serving on the RRWA Advisory Boards and students working as summer Research Assistants from 1992 through 2000 helped create the problem sets and concepts that developed in those early years and are now integrated in this work. Thanks to each of you individually for the contributions you made to our writing program, to each other, and to this publication.

In addition to the contributions of those special students, I want to expressly thank Shelley Lucas and Jeff Hudson who served as my primary Research Assistants during the first years of our experiment with this program design. Jeff Hudson deserves particular credit for having made major editorial contributions to both the original and final versions of this workbook. In addition, thanks go to Tracy Ward and Richard Norton who contributed significantly and creatively to the Assignment Sheets on state statutory law as well as the Guidelines for the early problem sets, and to Paul Meggett for his support of the RRWA Program during those years. I am also grateful to John Jaye for his work on Problem Sets D and I, and to Lara S. Nelson of the National Legal Defense Fund for the important ideas she contributed to Problem Set D. Thanks also to Keith Goodwin and Dameron Page for their creative and dedicated research that led to Problem Sets E and J, respectively, and to Diane Rupprecht and Amy Vukovitch for their follow-up research on those problems. Thanks to Chris Duerden for his work on Problem Set F, to Joe Dowdy for his work on Problem Set B, to Jaison Thomas for his work on Problem Set A, to Shannon Buckner for his work on Problem Set G, and to Kara McCraw for the addition of an index. A special thank you to the following students who added significantly to the fifth edition, both in editing help and substantive suggestions: Ryan Bliss, Jeremy Franklin, Caitlin Johnson, Drew Kifner, Luis Lluberas-Oliver, Eva Lorenz, Madlyn Morreale, Zach Orth, PJ Puryear, and Casey Winebarger. We are grateful also to Kevin Hunt of Loyola University Chicago School of Law and Carrie Wipplinger of Golden Gate University Law School for providing objective feedback outside of Carolina Law. Finally, thanks to our Research Assistants, Thad Woody, Claudia McClinton, Patrick Morgan, and Oni Seliski, for applying their exceptional research and editing skills, as well as unwavering good humor, to the second, fourth, and fifth editions.

We have the utmost gratitude for the support of the faculty of the UNC School of Law which consistently encouraged our experiment with this innovative approach to teaching the fundamentals of legal research, and am especially grateful to our past Dean and Professor Judith W. Wegner for the trust she placed in our experiment from the beginning, to Dean Gene R. Nichol for his support of the fourth edition, and to our current Dean, Professor John C. Boger, for his continued faith in this work. Similarly, Associate Dean of Academic Affairs and Professor Laura Gasaway, Professor Lissa Broome, Professor Rich Rosen, Professor and Dean Ken Broun, Professor Charles Daye, Professor Marilyn Yarbrough, Professor Andrew Chin, Professor John Conley, Professor and Interim Dean Gail Agrawal, and Professor Tom Kelley all helped in many concrete ways as this workbook moved from a vision, through early drafts, to its current form.

The members of the adjunct faculty for the Research, Reasoning, Writing, and Advocacy Program at UNC have all contributed significantly through their willingness to put the exercises into practice and to share their ideas on the importance of teaching strong research skills in a practical setting. We are also enormously grateful to Professor Anne Klinefelter, Director of the Kathrine R. Everett Law Library, and to the law library faculty past and present, including Professors Margaret Hall, Julie Kimbrough, Steve Melamut, Carol Nicholson, Nikki Perry, Nick Sexton, and Jim Sherwood and former Professors Anne-Marie Berti, Teresa Stanton, Donna Nixon, Marguerite Most, and Tom French who contributed their expertise in countless ways to the content of our early and later drafts. Debbie Webster of the Law Library staff, along with Martha Barefoot and Janice Hammet, who were formerly with the Law Library, made many valuable suggestions concerning the cognitive content and format of various editions of the workbooks. Terri Saye helped explain how students could use cataloguing systems with ease. Library staff members Dorothy Grant, Ed Beltz, Mosako Patrum, Steve Case, David Solar, and the many students who assisted them now or in the past – including especially Todd Venie, Stephen Chan, and Elliott Hibbler for this fifth edition – have earned our special thanks for their unwavering willingness to clarify details, seemingly at all hours of the day and night.

Thanks to Professor Tom Domonoske, formerly of the Duke University School of Law, for critically reading early drafts of the workbook; to Professor Kent Olson of the University of Virginia School of Law for critically reading later drafts of the workbook and for his continued advice; to Ray West and Dr. Mary Schweitzer for contributing editing suggestions to Chapters 2 and 3; to Dr. George W. McKinney III, for contributing his expertise in business to the fourth edition, to Dr. Ed Neal, Director of Faculty Development at the UNC Center for Teaching and Learning for unselfishly sharing his knowledge of the principles of active learning over the years; to George and Lucy McKinney for reading final drafts of the workbook and for contributing editing comments throughout; to the word processing staff at the UNC School of Law for their expertise and good humor in the face of a complex assignment; to Keith Page for his printing expertise and even disposition on early editions; to Dr. Buckner F. Melton, Jr. for naming our law firm; and to Ms. Esphur Foster for the countless ways she has cared for our students, faculty, and staff alike. The much-lauded Information Technology staff at the University of North Carolina School of Law has contributed to our work for many years, and special thanks go to Erin Jo Adair,

Instructional Technology Support Specialist, and Dawn Lynn, Computer Support Specialist, for their ongoing work in support of our accompanying website. We appreciate the input of our school's represenatives for LexisNexis and Westlaw, Danielle Eckelt and Greg Halbrook, respectively, who have each contributed to this fifth edition in creative ways. We would also like to expressly thank Professors Morris L. Cohen and Kent C. Olson, authors of *Legal Research in a Nutshell*, for their generosity in sharing the materials in their book as the background for much of the reading in this workbook.

We are grateful to Professor Bobbi Boyd, Deputy Director of UNC's Writing and Learning Resources Center, who shared her eye for detail and contributed significant editing suggestions. We are also most appreciative for the logistical support and encouragement offered by Patty Frey, Administrative Assistant to UNC's Writing and Learning Resources Center, and to Bonita Summers, supervisor for the Faculty Support Center.

In a work that has evolved over this much time, there are more individuals who contributed in large and small ways than can be named. Named or not, all of your contributions are significant and are woven into the fabric of the current work and the gratitude we feel for your help and support.

Table of Contents

Chapter 1: Introduction

A. WHAT IS ACTIVE LEARNING AND WHY DOES IT WORK?

Think back to the last time you learned how to do something – not intellectually *about* how to do it, but actually how to do it yourself. More times than not, we learn practical skills by rolling up our sleeves and trying them. Take a minute to visualize some skills that require hands-on experience. For us, some examples are swimming, knitting, carpentry, playing tennis, and writing. The skills people develop over the years vary widely, but almost always bring pride in accomplishment once we have acquired them. A common factor among all hands-on skills is that we learn how to do them through trial and error -- actual experience and practice – not just by reading about them or hearing someone else talk about them. Depending on your learning style preferences, reading about something or hearing about it is often useful, but practical skills are rarely mastered without actually trying them.

Doing legal research is the kind of skill that you can learn best when you roll up your sleeves and try it. While it is useful to read about it and to hear experts talk about it, there's no substitute for trying it yourself. Most of us know through experience that "learning by doing" is the way to go when developing a skill. Interestingly, educational experts agree. Statistics show that we retain only 10% of what we read, 26% of what we hear, 30% of what we see, but a full <u>90%</u> of what we do and say.[1] Your future employers and your future clients will depend on you to develop the critical lawyering skills of assessing a legal problem and conducting thorough, accurate research to find information with which to respond effectively to the problem. Acquiring those skills now – while you are a student – puts you at a distinct advantage in the early stages of your career and positions you to continue to develop those skills throughout your professional life.

This workbook is designed to facilitate your mastery of the knowledge and skills necessary to become an expert at legal research by applying active learning principles to the study of legal research through a simulated law firm setting. In this self-instructional workbook, you will be associated with our fictitious law firm, "Marshall, Story & Associates."[2] Our law firm is named after two of the most highly esteemed jurists in this nation's early history: Chief Justice John Marshall and his colleague, Justice Joseph Story, who served together on the United States Supreme Court in the first half of the nineteenth century. We chose Justice Marshall and Justice Story as our mentors because the seeds they planted in the early years of our country's history have grown into a powerful legal system that touches all our lives – and it is that wide-ranging influence that makes the ability to do accurate and efficient legal research such a valuable skill for you to develop today.

---

[1] James Stice, <u>Using Kolb's Learning Cycle to Improve Student Learning</u>, 77 Engineering Educ. 291 (1987). <u>See generally</u> Michael Hunter Schwartz, <u>Expert Learning for Law Students</u> (setting forth in readily understandable terms the learning behaviors that will lead to success in the study of law).

[2] The authors thank Dr. Buckner F. Melton, Jr., who combined his knowledge of history and of law to name our law firm.

We ask you to take on the role of a new associate at this firm. You will be working with a fictitious "assigning partner" who will introduce you (through a series of five assigning memos) to your client and to the legal questions you will need to research on that client's behalf. You will find these "assigning memos" at the beginning of each of five research lessons in the book. If you are using this book as part of a class exercise, you might want to visualize your professor as your "assigning partner."

As the authors of this self-instructional package, we see our roles as being your guides as you work your way through these five lessons. Years ago in many states, law was taught through individual apprenticeships. After enough years of study under a licensed attorney, the apprentice could sit for the bar exam. If the apprentice passed the exam, then he or she, too, could enter the practice of law. While these kinds of apprenticeships no longer exist in most states, we hope the design of this workbook will give you the same sense of direction and support you would get if we were actually working together.

Experts in educational theory have discovered that active learning takes place when three things are present in the classroom: *trust*, *motivation*, and *preparation*.[3] This book is expressly designed to be your classroom. We have tried to put *trust* in this classroom by drafting assignments that you can count on to be both coherent and accurate – assignments that will help you reach your personal goals for learning legal research skills. While you will provide the bulk of the *motivation* in our classroom based on your personal reasons for learning how to do legal research, this workbook is designed to add to your motivation by providing interesting lessons based on realistic client problems. Finally, concerning *preparation*, we have concentrated on creating lessons that will get the job done. If you do your part to follow each step and to keep thinking while you're doing so, you will have developed a new set of skills by the time you reach the end of the workbook.

B. HOW TO USE THIS WORKBOOK EFFICIENTLY

(1) <u>The best way to proceed</u>: After reading this introduction, read Chapter Two, "Fundamentals of Legal Reasoning," beginning on p. 11, and then read Chapter Three, "The Legal Research Process," beginning on p. 17. If you don't have much experience in law, you may want to read that chapter more than once and/or come back to it again as you gain more experience with legal research. Next, choose a client (or go to the first assigning memo for the client assigned to you) and move through each lesson in order (it's best not to jump around). Since you will be "learning by doing," it's important to actually write down your answers to each question along the way, rather than to just think about them. Don't skip steps unless you are already familiar with that resource or prefer to learn completely on your own.

---

[3] Edward M. Neal, Director of Faculty Development at the UNC Center for Teaching and Learning, first introduced us to the importance of making sure trust, motivation, and preparation are all present in every class. He also stressed the importance of separating what he called "nice" information from "critical" information when teaching a new skill. Dr. Neal, together with Professor Howard Aldrich of the UNC Department of Sociology, has also done extensive work with the writing faculty at UNC Law concerning other active learning techniques, and many of his ideas have been integrated into this workbook.

(2) **Integrating supplementary or advanced reading:** As you work through the assignments, you may find it helpful to supplement the steps you are following with more in-depth or detailed information from one of the several respected legal research textbooks available on the market today. Appendix A contains a detailed list of a number of such textbooks as well as cross-references to places in those texts that correspond to the hands-on lessons you will be following in this workbook. If you are using this workbook in conjunction with a class, you may already have one of those textbooks assigned or recommended by your professor. If not, and you are interested in supplementing these lessons with more in-depth information now or in the future, you may want to choose a supplementary text from those listed in Appendix A. You will find specific cross-references to *Legal Research in a Nutshell* (9th ed. 2007) by Morris L. Cohen and Kent C. Olson throughout your lessons.

(3) **Following proper citation format:** You will find references in the lessons to *The Bluebook: A Uniform System of Citation* (18th ed. 2005), published by the Harvard Law Review Association, and to *The ALWD Citation Manual: A Professional System of Citation* (3d ed. 2006). Until the first edition of the *ALWD Manual* was published in 2000, *The Bluebook* was the unquestioned giant in the field of legal citation. Today, the *ALWD Manual* is also widely recognized as a respected authority on proper citation form to follow in legal writing. If you are using this workbook in conjunction with a class, your professors will probably have assigned one of these citation manuals. If you are using this workbook on your own, you may find that the *ALWD Manual* is easier to follow. If you don't expect to read or write about law outside of your own work, you don't need to worry about either of these books and can skip those parts of the lessons.

(4) **Exploring with the right attitude:** Conducting legal research is always an adventure into the unknown. Embarking on such a trip is all the more daunting when you are just learning these new skills. As you explore the lessons in this workbook, we suggest that your ultimate goal while completing these assignments is *to learn about legal research sources and how they can help you.* You may be tempted to focus your attention instead on the substantive legal issues that your fictitious client may be facing. While it's useful to have a client question to explore to put your research efforts in a realistic context, be sure to pay close attention to the resources you are using and the process you are engaging in as you complete each assignment so that, ultimately, you can apply these skills to new assignments in the future. Also, try not to get sidetracked by the inevitable frustrations involved in all legal research. Experienced researchers have come to expect dead-ends and answers that lead to more questions. Remember that it is not possible to learn all the tricks and details of a complex skill like this by trying it just once. Rather, use this guided self-instructional method to lead you through the maze on this first adventure and then hold on to these lessons as a "map" you can return to many times in the future as you have more opportunities to do legal research. Each time you explore a legal question, you will find you learn something new.

(5) **Paying attention to necessary details:** You will save time and energy if you are careful to use the correct materials for each assignment. Using the correct materials

requires that you pay attention to at least these three things: (1) look at the EXACT title of the resource we refer to in the text and be sure you're using that EXACT document;[4] (2) especially if you're working in a large law library that stores lots of historical material, be sure you are working in current publications. Law changes rapidly and working with outdated material will net inaccurate results; (3) allow yourself time to become familiar with the lay-out of each different kind of material you're directed to use. Remember, the purpose of working through the lessons in this book is to learn how to use these important resources for now and in the future, not just to find answers to the specific legal question put before you.

(6) Using our "TIPS" and "BOMBS": There are "TIPS" and "BOMBS" marked throughout each lesson. It is helpful to read these before you answer related questions. We've put them there to help you distinguish critical information (such as the information contained in the text and the "bombs" in this workbook) from "nice" information (such as the supplemental information provided in the "tips" throughout this workbook). Educational experts emphasize that being able to separate "nice" information from "critical" information is an important part of learning a new skill where exposure to too much unsorted information can overwhelm you and interfere with your ability to absorb what you need to know.[5]

(7) Managing your time: Time is a valuable commodity to anyone working in, or thinking about working in, the field of law. To help you manage your time as you work through these lessons, you will find an estimated time of completion suggested at the beginning of each lesson. These time estimates are based on averages from students who have used this workbook in the past. Depending on your learning style and your personal goals, your times could be more or less than those estimated. If you find that you are taking considerably more time to complete a lesson than is suggested, you should seek help from your professor and/or a law librarian (unless you are deliberately taking more time and are enjoying doing so).

(8) Integrating TIPS about online research: This fifth edition includes "Online TIPS" designed to give you supplementary information about how online (computer-assisted) research materials might be used in addition to or instead of some of the hard copy materials you are being introduced to in each lesson. Competent researchers in the legal profession cannot rely exclusively on hard copy materials nor exclusively on online materials to achieve their research goals. Some information is more readily accessed in one format than another and some legal environments restrict your access exclusively to one format or another. Without question, learning to use both hard copy and online resources is critical to your success in the field of law. Many professors choose to introduce these resources in sequence. If you are using this workbook in conjunction with a class, do not become

---

[4] From time to time, publishers change the titles of their materials. If you are unable to locate the exact title referred to in a lesson, check with your law librarian to see if a change has occurred. You can also check www.LegalResearchWorkbook.com for updates. If you discover a change before we do, please contact Professor McKinney directly at ramckinn@email.unc.edu so we can update the website. Also, if we direct you to a resource that is not housed in your library, please ask your law librarian or your professor to show you an alternative resource you can use to complete the lesson.

[5] See references to Dr. Neal's work at the UNC Center for Teaching and Learning, supra n. 3.

distracted by "Online TIPS" until your professor has given you permission to begin to go online. If your professor prefers that you focus on hard copy materials in the beginning, you can go back later and review the Online TIPS after you have thoroughly mastered the hard copy materials.

(9) <u>Using the Supplement for Learning Online Research</u>: This workbook includes a separate supplement which contains online-specific assignments. These assignments are contained in a separate supplement because online materials change rapidly and introducing them through a supplement allows us to adapt to those changes annually. In the supplement, just as in the main body of this workbook, you will have an opportunity to engage in hands-on exercises as you seek answers to a legal question for a fictitious client – but the supplement will teach you how to use Lexis and Westlaw, the dominant fee-based legal research providers, to find your answers. The supplement also contains short exercises to introduce you to a number of free online resources and also to online tutorials that are offered by Westlaw and Lexis.

(10) <u>Seeking help from our website</u>: The website associated with this workbook contains two things that can help you with your assignments: (1) <u>UPDATES</u> on recent changes in the legal research process or in the workbook that you should be aware of before beginning each assignment; and (2) <u>GUIDELINES</u> to each lesson that may help you if you are stumped or confused at a particular step. The URL for the website is www.LegalResearchWorkbook.com, and the Guidelines section is password protected. If you are using this workbook in conjunction with a class, your professor may choose to supply you with any needed passwords to access that site. If you are using this workbook on your own, outside of a law school class, you can email Professor McKinney directly at ramckinn@email. unc.edu to obtain the password. Become familiar with your class rules and know your school's honor code before using the Guidelines available on the website associated with this workbook.

C. BECOMING FAMILIAR WITH YOUR LAW LIBRARY

Although finding an answer to a legal question is exciting, there are plenty of things about legal research that can be frustrating, too. Finding accurate answers to any legal question takes intelligence, patience, intuition, an eye for the big picture, and an eye for detail – all at the same time. In writing this self-instructional workbook, we have tried to keep to a minimum any unnecessary frustrations you might experience so you will have maximum energy left to deal with the natural frustrations that go along with mastering this challenging skill.

One of the ways you can nip a potential frustration in the bud is to become familiar with the resources that are available in the library you will be using. Ask at the reference desk for a map of the library and/or a key to your library's shelving system (some law libraries use the Library of Congress call number system, others use the Dewey Decimal System, others group materials by use). Wander around and see if you can find where your state's laws are shelved, where other state and regional materials are shelved, where federal materials are shelved, and where periodicals and journals are shelved.

As you explore your library, you can use the chart on the following pages to record the location of the main print resource materials you will need to use to complete the lessons in this workbook. While there are additional print materials included in the lessons from time to time, this chart contains the titles that you will rely on most frequently. As you work your way through the assignments in this workbook, continue to fill in the chart – including noting electronic research options to which you are introduced. By completing this chart as you go, you will end up with an excellent reference that you can use in the future when you take on new research projects.

Location of Legal Materials

Primary Sources

Resource by Title	Location in Your Law Library	Electronic Resource
Statutes by State *[state statutes are shelved together in a series of volumes, generally accessed by an Index]*		
United States Code (USC) *[the official publication of federal legislation, published by the U.S. Government Printing Office]*		
United States Code Annotated (USCA) *[unofficial private publication of federal legislation published by Thomson-West that contains annotations to relevant cases and other cross-references to help you find related law]*		
United States Code Service (USCS) *[unofficial private publication of federal legislation pubished by LexisNexis that contains annotations to relevant cases and other cross-references to help you find related law]*		
Code of Federal Regulations (CFR) *[publications for federal administrative regulations]*		
The Federal Register *[newspaper-type publication containing the most current federal administrative regulations]*		
Federal Court Reports *[published opinions from U.S. District Courts, U.S. Courts of Appeals, and the U.S. Supreme Court]* **Federal Reporter (F., F.2d, etc.)** **Federal Supplement (F. Supp.)** **Supreme Court Reporter (S. Ct.)** **U.S. Reports (U.S.)** **U.S. Supreme Court Reports, Lawyers' Edition (L. Ed.)**		
Reporters for Your State *[a reporter contains the published cases from a state's courts in chronological order]*		
West's Regional Reporters *[publications of written opinions from the state courts in a designated region of the country]*		

Secondary Sources

Resource by Title	Location in Your Law Library	Electronic Resource
American Jurisprudence 2d (Am. Jur. 2d) *[a legal encyclopedia]*		
Corpus Juris Secundum (C.J.S.) *[a legal encyclopedia]*		
State Encyclopedias *[if available]*		
American Law Reports (ALR) *[annotations of cases related to a selected lead case on a given topic]*		
Restatements of the Law *[on your topic]*		
Treatises *[on your topic]*		
United States Government Manual *[a listing of federal agencies, including a statement of their primary missions]*		

Finding Aids

West's Digest [by State] *[a compilation of annotated cases by state grouped by subject to help you locate cases to read on a given topic]*		
List of CFR Sections Affected (LSA) *[a tool to make sure your research in administrative regulations is current]*		
Shepard's Citators *[a research tool that allows you to update a statute or case, and also to find other resources that refer to that statute or case]* **Shepard's [your state's name] Citator: Case Edition** **Shepard's [your state's name] Citator: Statutes** **Shepard's U.S. Citator: Statutes**		
Current Law Index *[a guide for locating articles in legal journals]*		
Index to Legal Periodicals and Books *[a guide for locating articles in legal journals]*		
Legal Trac *[an electronic index to articles in legal journals]*		

D. WHAT YOU CAN EXPECT TO LEARN

As you work through these lessons seeking answers to the legal questions raised by your assigning partner, you will learn two things: (1) how *to find* specific kinds of materials used by lawyers and other legal researchers; and (2) how *to use* these materials to develop an answer to the legal question the partner raised.

You will learn to do research in five specific areas: (1) secondary resources (legal encyclopedias, journals, and treatises); (2) common law (court-initiated law expressed through written court opinions); (3) state statutory law; (4) federal statutory law; and (5) administrative regulations. These lessons are designed to introduce you to the fundamental sources of information that help lawyers and judges make decisions about how to answer legal questions. Learning to become a highly competent researcher (and legal thinker) takes time, practice, and experience. It's an ongoing process that lasts throughout a lawyer's career. As you become more advanced in your legal thinking, and as the questions you face become more complex, you will want to learn more about these resources, and others, in the years ahead.

To reduce the number of students using the same print resources at the same time, we have included two different sets ("sequences") of assignments in this workbook. Each "Sequence of Assignments" contains "assigning memos" for five different clients. These assigning memos appear at the beginning of each lesson and tell a story about your client, raising a legal question that you can begin to address by using the materials and techniques taught in the assignment that follows.

Sequence of Assignments #1 (beginning on page 27) introduces you to research sources in the following order: (1) secondary resources; (2) common law; (3) state statutory law; (4) federal statutory law; and (5) administrative regulations. Sequence of Assignments #2 (beginning on page 167) introduces you to these same resources in a slightly different order: (1) state statutory law; (2) federal statutory law; (3) administrative law; (4) common law; and (5) secondary resources.

<u>Sequence of Assignments #1</u> introduces you to five potential clients:

(1) "Client A" is Eric Arnold, a business person adjusting to life in a rural farm community;
(2) "Client B" is Project Hope, a non-profit organization attempting to start a private school to help lower the drop-out rate in the local high school;
(3) "Client C" is Marjorie Morrison who is in a conflict with her neighbor because he has started selling his home-made wine out of his house;
(4) "Client D" is Dr. Allen Field, a historian who inherits a house that he would like to restore; and
(5) "Client E" is environmentalist Josh Ward who is trying to protect his lake-front property from encroachment by neighbors.

<u>Sequence of Assignments #2</u> introduces you to five other clients:

(1) "Client F" is Richard Roth, an inventor having difficulties with a patent;
(2) "Client G" is Ana Martinez, a recent college graduate signing a contract of employment for her first post-college job;
(3) "Client H" is Christopher Smith, a sixteen year old purchasing his first car;
(4) "Client I" is Carolyn Meyer, a high school athlete attempting to retain the position she has earned on the men's soccer team at her high school; and
(5) "Client J" is Jeanne Martin, whose dispute with her landlord involves possible violations of the Fair Housing Act.

If you are using this workbook in a class, follow your professor's instructions regarding which Sequence of Assignments you will follow and which client you will represent. If you are not in a class, you are free to choose either sequence and any of the clients listed above.

All assignment sheets are printed on perforated paper so you can tear them out and turn them in to your instructor if you are working in a classroom setting. The sheets are also three-hole punched so you can keep them later as a guide you can follow when you get another legal question to research.

We have experimented with self-instruction and active learning methodology at the University of North Carolina School of Law for well over a decade. Many law students and their professors have found guided self-instruction to be an energizing and enriching way to try on a new role at a pace that works for each individual student. We hope you find the same energy and enrichment in the pages ahead as you try your hand at this new and important skill.

Chapter 2: Fundamentals of Legal Reasoning

Professional-quality legal research requires you to learn two things well: (1) what kinds of critical information lawyers think about as they answer legal questions; and (2) how to get your hands on materials that contain that critical information. As you learned from the preceding Introduction, the main body of this self-instructional workbook will guide you through the complex world of legal research sources that are available in print or hard copy and will also introduce you to a limited number of online research tools used frequently by legal professionals. The supplement to this workbook further explores online legal resources, giving you hands-on exercises to try online. Ultimately, your goal is to develop the ability to choose confidently and flexibly from among all available resources as you strive to find accurate answers to legal questions in an efficient, thorough, and cost-effective manner.

The first step in conducting research in any discipline is to understand what it is you want to find and why it might help answer the question in front of you. Legal research is no exception. Before you begin your hands-on lessons in this workbook, it is important to have an overview of the fundamentals of jurisprudence. In short, you need to know what lawyers think about as they answer legal questions. To a lawyer, what is "law"? How is it established and how does it evolve over the years? What information must decision-makers in our judicial system weigh as they try to establish or determine our legal rights and responsibilities? This chapter will help you begin to understand the answers to these questions. The hands-on assignments in the remaining sections of this workbook and in the supplement will teach you how to find and use the research resources available to lawyers and others in the legal profession as they attempt to find answers to questions rooted in the law.[6]

WHAT DO LAWYERS THINK ABOUT AS THEY ANSWER LEGAL QUESTIONS?

Law is about resolution of conflict, present or potential. People generally become involved with our legal system when they are in the midst of a conflict, or when they are trying to anticipate how to avoid a potential conflict, over their rights and responsibilities versus the rights and responsibilities of another individual, institution, or the state. More often than not, legal questions are answered and legal conflicts are settled long before the parties ever get into a courtroom.[7] Even if a conflict never gets to court, the decision-making that goes into determining how to resolve a conflict or how to avoid a potential conflict is based at least in part on an assessment of what a court of law would find the relevant legal

---

[6] For an additional introduction to principles of jurisprudence and the research process, consider also reading Chapter 1 of <u>Legal Research in a Nutshell</u> or a corresponding chapter in a research textbook listed in Appendix A.

[7] According to the 2006 <u>Judicial Facts and Figures</u> published by the federal government at www.uscourts.gov/judicialfactsfigures/2006.html, only 1.3% of all civil cases in U.S. District Courts reach trial. <u>See also generally</u> 1 <u>J. of Empirical Legal Studies</u>, Issue 3 (2004) for a collection of articles noting the decline in the number of cases that go to trial.

rights and responsibilities of the parties to be. Oliver Wendell Holmes put it this way, "The prophecies of what the courts will do in fact, and nothing more pretentious, are what I mean by the law."[8]

For a legal professional[9], then, the process of doing legal research centers on finding information that would clarify how a court of law would rule on the parties' respective rights and responsibilities in the unlikely event that the question at hand were to end up in front of a judge.[10] Thus, as you begin to learn how to do legal research, it is critical that you understand the framework judges use when weighing the merits of each party's position as they struggle to resolve a "case in controversy." (Note that in the American legal system, courts will not generally give advisory opinions concerning legal rights, but rather will only make decisions which rule on an actual conflict between the parties before them – often described in legal jargon as a requirement that there be an actual "case in controversy" between parties with a present conflict before a court will address a legal question).

A. FEDERAL COURTS AND STATE COURTS

Under our governmental structure, we have two wholly separate sets of judicial systems: a federal system that develops and enforces the laws of the United States government, and separate state systems that enforce and develop the laws of each individual state, consistent with federal law. While the federal system and each state system have individual variations, each is organized with lower courts (or, in some cases, a series of lower courts) where trials and hearings occur and moves to an appellate court (or, in some cases, a series of appellate courts) where appeals from the lower courts are heard and resolved. Both sets of judicial systems (federal and state) operate under the auspices of the federal constitution and each state judicial system also operates under that state's constitution. The chart on the next page illustrates the federal judicial system as well as a similar hierarchy in a typical state court system.

---

[8] Oliver Wendell Holmes, Path of the Law, 10 Harv. L. Rev. 457 (1897) (quoted by Richard K. Neumann, Jr. in Legal Reasoning and Legal Writing (2d ed. 1994) at p. 71). Professor Neumann's legal writing textbook is an excellent resource for further study about how to think and write about law. An impressive array of legal reasoning and writing textbooks are now in print. Check your bookstore and Appendix A of this workbook for other available titles.

[9] Individuals from many disciplines might conduct legal research for their own professional purposes. This workbook focuses primarily on the resources and processes needed for proficient research from a legal practitioner's perspective.

[10] The process of mediating or negotiating a settlement to a conflict outside of a courtroom also involves an accurate assessment of how a court would view each parties' rights and responsibilities. Other factors (such as moral, economic, or social factors) influence settlements, but an understanding of legal rights is a critical part of any negotiation or mediation process. See generally Robert F. Cochran, Jr., John M.A. DiPippa & Martha M. Peters, The Counselor-at-Law: A Collaborative Approach to Client Interviewing and Counseling (2d ed. 2006).

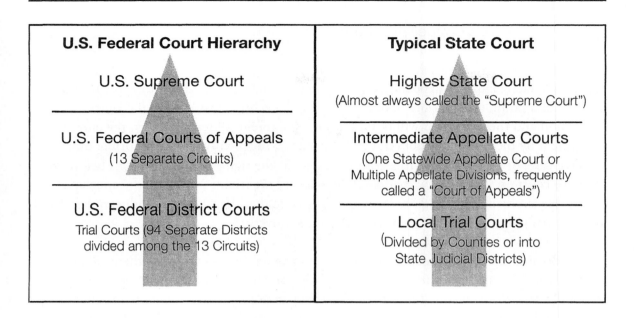

U.S. Federal Court Hierarchy	Typical State Court
U.S. Supreme Court	**Highest State Court** (Almost always called the "Supreme Court")
U.S. Federal Courts of Appeals (13 Separate Circuits)	**Intermediate Appellate Courts** (One Statewide Appellate Court or Multiple Appellate Divisions, frequently called a "Court of Appeals")
U.S. Federal District Courts Trial Courts (94 Separate Districts divided among the 13 Circuits)	**Local Trial Courts** (Divided by Counties or into State Judicial Districts)

1. The Role of Lower (Trial) Courts

Many conflicts involving individuals, institutions, or the state are resolved without involvement of the courts at all. People talk to each other, involve official or unofficial mediators such as friends or respected community leaders, or simply change their ways to avoid further conflict. When a conflict does involve the judicial system, actions are initiated when a party raises a claim in a lower court, often called a "court of first impression." Even after a claim is filed, however, it is likely that a controversy will be resolved well before the case is heard in court. Parties continue to discuss out-of-court settlements, and lawyers frequently file pre-trial motions to ask the court to dismiss or resolve the action before trial is reached.

In the event that a conflict is not mediated or settled (in a civil suit), plea-bargained (in a criminal action), or brought to resolution through pre-trial motions, the controversy must then be resolved by a trial that is held in the properly designated lower court. Two questions must be answered during the course of any trial: (1) what are the relevant _facts_ surrounding this controversy, and (2) what is the right _law_ to apply to reach a just result. The first question, what are the facts in this case, is answered by a jury (or, in some cases, by a judge sitting in place of the jury[11]). The role of the jury or "finder of fact" is to listen to testimony, weighing the credibility of the witnesses, and to view other kinds of evidence to determine what it believes really happened. The second question, what is the right law to apply, is always resolved by the judge – never by the jury. In addition to deciding what substantive law to apply, the judge also decides legal questions about how the trial should be conducted.

---

[11] When the judge is serving in place of a jury, he or she is commonly referred to as the "trier of fact" or the "finder of fact." In such a case, the judge remains responsible for making decisions of law as well as findings of fact during a trial or hearing.

2. The Role of Appellate Courts

By the end of a trial, the jury (or the judge serving as the "trier of fact") has determined factually what happened and the judge has decided what law to apply to those facts. At that point, all questions about the conflict have been answered to the court's satisfaction and the resolution will be entered as a judgment. Often, however, the entry of a judgment by the trial judge does not end the matter. Frequently, one party or the other in a civil case, or the defendant in a criminal case, has the right to raise questions before an appellate court on issues of law that developed during the trial.[12] Note that the appellate court's role is *not* to retry the case, but rather to ensure that the trial was conducted fairly and that the trial judge applied the right laws to the controversy.[13]

Because the role of an appellate court is to answer questions of law, there are never any juries at the appellate court level – only a judge or panel of judges focusing on *questions of law*. On appeal, the factual findings from a trial will not be reconsidered by the appellate judge or judges unless the factual conclusions are so clearly irrational that they present a legal question about the fundamental fairness of the trial. While the presentation of evidence and testimony at trial is a critical part of the judicial process, ultimately the resolution of a controversy in our judicial system rests on a clear and accurate understanding of the controlling substantive and procedural law.

B. THE IMPORTANCE OF JURISDICTION, STARE DECISIS, AND PRECEDENT

The term "jurisdiction" has many complex meanings in law, and you will learn more about these complexities throughout your legal career. In this workbook, we will use the term "jurisdiction" to refer to any cluster of courts that share a common body of law. Understanding jurisdiction is important because not all law is equally relevant to all legal questions. Rather, legal researchers need to find answers that would be applied in the jurisdiction that "controls" the outcome of the issue being researched.

For state statutory law, state administrative law, or state common law questions, the state court system is generally the jurisdiction with control. Where the question concerns federal law, the federal court system has control. Under some circumstances, parties may elect to raise a federal question in a state court or a state question in a federal court that is already hearing their case on a related federal matter. Regardless of which court actually entertains a

---

[12]Appellate courts are also often asked to answer questions of law that arise as a result of pre-trial motions that create a final decision – a final order or judgment – even before a trial occurs or is completed. As you continue your legal studies, you will learn more about what kinds of questions are "appealable," and when those questions can be raised.

[13]As an example of how decisions about law and decisions about facts differ, imagine you are observing a trial involving a civil suit for battery. Based on the evidence the parties present at trial, the jury might be asked to decide whether the defendant ever actually touched the plaintiff (a question of fact). The judge, and only the judge, might need to decide whether it is appropriate to instruct the jury on the defense of consent or how to define consent (both substantive legal questions). During the trial or hearing itself, the judge also has to make procedural decisions based on the law. When we hear a lawyer object to "hearsay" in a TV trial, for example, the judge's response (objection sustained or objection denied) is a legal decision only the judge can make. It is the validity of legal decisions about substantive law and procedural law that is reviewed on appeal.

claim, however, it is the law developed in the controlling jurisdiction that will be applied in that courtroom.

In addition to being mindful of jurisdiction, lawyers also consider the doctrine of stare decisis when they seek answers to a legal question. Under this doctrine, which means literally "let the decision stand,"[14] courts strive to apply law consistently. Thus, once a court has made a decision in a particular case, that court and all other courts below that court in the same jurisdiction will strive to reach similar results in similar cases in the future. This doctrine helps ensure stability in the law and stability in society. If people know what legal principles apply, then it is more likely that conflict can be avoided and people will function within their known boundaries.

Consistent with the doctrine of stare decisis, a written court opinion becomes "precedent" for all decisions applying the same law in the same or substantially same situation in the future.[15] Precedent is "binding" or "controlling" when it arises out of the same court or a court of higher standing within the same jurisdiction. Court opinions arising out of any other court (one that is below the deciding court or one from another jurisdiction – for example, from another state), can be influential and hence "persuasive" authority. But such opinions are not binding and do not establish precedent for the deciding court. Similarly, dissenting opinions (opinions written by a judge who did not vote with the majority) and even concurring opinions (opinions written by a judge who voted with the majority, but for different reasons) do not establish binding authority. Finally, it is only the direct holding of an opinion that is "binding." Mere "dicta" (interesting thoughts expressed by the court that do not directly resolve the parties' immediate conflict) carries no precedential weight.

Of course, none of this is as static as it sounds here. Much of what lawyers spend their time doing is trying to determine when a prior case controls a current situation. For purposes of learning the first steps of conducting legal research, it is enough to know that these principles exist. The next step is to learn the sources of law that are considered by judges as they strive to reach consistent results and disseminate opinions that will provide guidance for the future.

C. WEIGHT OF AUTHORITY

It is tempting for beginners trying their hand at their first legal research project to find one source to support a particular perspective, and then call it a day. Experienced researchers know that relying too quickly on only one or two authorities to determine the legal landscape is a mistake.

---

[14]See Morris L. Cohen & Kent C. Olson, Legal Research in a Nutshell 4 (9th ed. 2007).
[15]One rule of thumb that is often quoted in law school is that a case should "control" (be precedent for) later cases when the later case is on "all fours" with the first. When determining if two cases "square up," it is helpful to visualize the following cornerstones: (1) same place or type of place; (2) same parties or types of parties; (3) same question of law raised in the two cases; (4) no significant relevant changes in society brought on by a change in time or circumstances so that the purpose of the first decision would continue to be served if the old rule is applied again.

Rather, to those experienced in legal reasoning, any assessment of law is almost always subject to multiple interpretations and perspectives, and often subject to change. Thus, considering the "weight" of authority in support of any conclusions about law is a critical component of a lawyer's reasoning about that law.

Weight of authority is a subtle concept and is comprised of at least three equally important sub-parts. First, "weight" of authority is influenced by the significance of the body giving rise to a particular perspective. For example, "primary authority" (actual law itself – discussed more fully later in this chapter) carries more weight than "secondary authority" (commentary *about* the law that is not actual law itself). Similarly, authority within the jurisdiction of decision carries more weight than authority from another jurisdiction, and authority from higher courts carries more weight than authority from lower courts. Secondly, "weight" of authority is influenced by the "depth" of the authority (how far back in history has the present position been held) and how broadly (in how many jurisdictions and by how many respected players) are those opinions held? Finally, "weight" of authority is influenced by how relevant a legal document or theory may be at the present time, and by how highly regarded the source of the information is within the legal community.

Consider the following example. Imagine that you are looking into how the state of Ohio awards damages for professional malpractice. In your initial searches, you learn that damages are determined by common law principles that have evolved in the courts for over a century. Imagine you find an Ohio case that was decided in 1957 with facts remarkably similar to your own. In your efforts to assess how an Ohio court might rule on the situation you are researching, you would want to consider the weight of the authority you've found. A lawyer would ask himself or herself questions such as these: Was the Ohio case from a higher court than the court that will be deciding my case? Is the Ohio case still "good law" (in other words, are the principles followed in that case still followed in Ohio today)? Are there many other cases in Ohio that have applied these same principles in similar factual situations, or is this case simply an oddity? Given enough time, a lawyer might even ask whether other jurisdictions apply these same principles universally or if Ohio is unique in its approach. Similarly, with enough time, a lawyer might even consider checking to see if scholars and other respected authorities believe the Ohio position is a stable and wise one.

Chapter 3: The Legal Research Process

A. WHERE DO LEGAL RESEARCHERS FIND "LAW"?

Once you understand what lawyers think about as they answer legal questions, the next step is to learn how to find materials that contain the information (almost always law itself or comments about the law) needed to answer those questions. Looking at the thousands of volumes in a law library, or contemplating the seemingly endless supply of information on the web, it is easy to feel overwhelmed. One way to simplify the process is to remember that almost every resource in a law library or available online will fall into one of three categories: (1) it is primary authority (actual law itself); (2) it is secondary authority (a resource that talks about primary law); and/or (3) it is a "finding tool" (material that leads you to primary law or secondary authority).

Many resources are hybrids that combine traits from more than one of these categories. For example, most compilations of state statutes also have annotations that will help you find appellate opinions written by judges who decided a case in controversy concerning that statute. Thus, such a compilation would be a source of primary law (the statute itself) and a finding tool (containing annotations which will lead you to case law interpreting the statute). Similarly, a law review article is a secondary resource containing commentary about the law, but it is also loaded with references to relevant cases, statutes, and administrative regulations (thus being a valuable finding tool as well). As you cross the threshold from theory to practice in legal research, keep in mind the distinctions about these three categories (primary authority, secondary authority, and finding tools) explained below.

1. Primary Authority

Primary authority is law, or rules, upon which courts are authorized to make decisions. There are five sources of "primary law" (also called "primary authority") in this country. This workbook will focus on three sources of primary authority: (1) common law, (2) statutes[16], and (3) administrative regulations. Constitutional law is a fourth major source of primary authority, on both the state and federal level. The federal constitution and individual state constitutions are umbrellas under which all other primary sources of law function. Judges are responsible for applying the constitution in a variety of situations, most notably in determining the constitutionality of a given statute, administrative regulation, or government action. Research in constitutional law will not be explored separately in this workbook, although you can use many of the techniques you'll learn here to do constitutional research later. The fifth source of primary law stems from the authority of the executive branch of government. Although the executive branch is often thought of

---

[16]We use the term "statute" here in the generic sense of a rule of law promulgated by a legislative body. Laws promulgated by local elected bodies such as a Town Council or a Board of County Commissioners are conceptually similar to statutes, although the research path used to find them is different.

as setting or suggesting policy that eventually becomes law, or in its role of supervising executive agencies, the President also has authority to create law through Executive Orders and Proclamations. Consult Appendix A for a list of texts that can provide you with detailed information about constitutional research as well as how to research actions taken by the executive branch.

This workbook and its supplement will teach you how to find primary law in the form of common law, statutes and accompanying case law, and administrative regulations. To do accurate research, it is important first to understand more about each of these sources of primary law.

a. Common Law

When a situation is controlled by the common law, a judge or panel of judges is responsible for deciding the rights of the parties based on long-standing principles established in prior cases – unrelated to any legislation or even to constitutional law – in that jurisdiction. The term "common law" refers to judge-made laws that have evolved over centuries (many state common law doctrines go back to early English common law) as courts have settled cases in controversy before them. For example, a civil action for false imprisonment (interference with the right to come and go as we please) is based on common law rights in most states.

In resolving individual conflicts that are controlled by common law principles, judges are careful to follow the doctrine of *stare decisis* and principles of precedent described earlier. If you are faced with a question that may be controlled by common law, your task is to find case law explaining the common law rules and principles *within your jurisdiction* that resolved the legal question you are trying to answer in a situation similar enough to yours that the principal reasoning behind the prior decision would make the same decision sensible in your case, too. When searching for such precedent, you rarely find a case exactly on point. Rather, what you generally find is a series of related cases through which you eventually are able to synthesize a rule statement that accurately reflects the rights and responsibilities of the parties in the situation you may be bringing before the court. Common law "rules" are often not as clear cut as many beginning students would hope – and not as completely fluid as many experienced practitioners would hope. We find it helps to think of common law "rules" as principles rather than bright line edicts.[17]

Where you can't find any law at all in your jurisdiction or where you think your jurisdiction's position is illogical enough to warrant a change despite the doctrine of *stare decisis,* you can look for cases from other jurisdictions that might help your judge think about how to reach a fair result in your case. Rather than being controlling precedent that a judge

---

[17] Professor and former Dean Ken Broun of the University of North Carolina School of Law introduced us to the helpful notion of visualizing a judicial opinion as one judge's written advice to another. When reading case law, it is useful to imagine the principles stated therein as a light that can guide the next judge's decision when he or she is faced with a substantially similar situation.

must follow, such out-of-jurisdiction common law becomes persuasive authority that might influence your judge to reach a result you want (or, conversely, that the other party might use to argue that the judge should reach a result you don't want). Some secondary resources, such as learned treatises or law review articles written by noted authorities about a particular area of law, can also be persuasive to a judge faced with a "case of first impression" (one where there is no controlling law a court can follow) or with a case where justice demands that the judges consider a change in the common law. Note that the use of persuasive authority (an opinion from a jurisdiction other than the one where the question is raised, or secondary authority from a respected source) is not restricted to situations where the common law establishes the parties' rights. Use of persuasive authority is also appropriate when you are doing statutory or administrative law research on a question of statutory interpretation that has not yet been squarely addressed in the written opinions of your jurisdiction's courts, or that warrants a reversal of your jurisdiction's prior opinions.

b. Statutory Law

A statute is a law passed by the legislative branch of government (and, under our system of checks and balances, signed by the executive). Where a situation is controlled by statute, parties in conflict look to a judge who is responsible for *applying* the statute to the situation at hand and determining what the outcome of this controversy should be under the statute.

While the court's application of a statute to a present situation may seem like a straightforward task, often it is not. The breadth or reach of a statute can be unclear as courts struggle to interpret the statute's meaning in practice. Where the language of a statute is ambiguous, or if the judge is faced with a situation that the legislature may not have anticipated when the statute was passed, the judge is responsible for interpreting the statute and deciding if and how it applies.

When determining if a statute controls or when interpreting the language of a statute, the judge's task is to determine the intent of the legislative body that drafted the statute. A judge does not have the latitude to substitute his or her own value judgments for those of the legislative body. Moreover, just as with common law questions, where another judge in the same jurisdiction in a court of higher stature has already determined the ambiguous statute's meaning, the present judge must go along with that prior determination. Thus, when doing statutory research, it is important to read both the "plain language" of the statute itself and also any relevant case law that might shed light on how the statute is to be interpreted or applied.

In addition to reading case law to determine if courts have ruled on the meaning or appropriate application of a statute, legal researchers can sometimes shed light on the meaning of an ambiguous statute by uncovering the statute's legislative history.[18] Knowing

---

[18] The wisdom of using legislative history as a tool to help courts interpret legislative intent is open to debate, with some scholars and courts arguing adamantly that the legislative process is itself so obtuse that the meaning of a statute should turn only on the language as passed – not on cues derived from the legislative drafting process. See generally Roy M. Mersky & Donald J. Dunn, Fundamentals of Legal Research at 181 - 183 (8th ed. 2002) (citations omitted).

the statutory history for a piece of legislation (the history of how the law came into effect) can help a researcher understand what the legislature intended when it considered the statute and settled on its present language – information that a lawyer could use to help a judge accurately interpret or apply the statute.

Apart from the potential importance of relevant court opinions and legislative history, there are four additional things to remember when you are researching a question that you think may be controlled by a statute:

- Our system of government has created parallel statutory systems, one for each state and one for the federal government. Many statutory questions are answered exclusively by state law, some are answered exclusively by federal law, and some (for example, a lot of new environmental laws) are dealt with by state and federal law;[19]

- Even where a statute directly addresses the legal question you are exploring, there may also be common law rights or responsibilities that existed long before the statute was passed which you should also explore. One of the questions judges frequently have to answer when applying any given statute is whether the statute was intended to replace, supplement, or exist side-by-side with prior common law on the same topic;

- Statutes are frequently amended by the legislature and/or interpreted by judges, so you always have to update your research once you've found a statute to be sure what you are reading is still relevant; and

- A statute is only valid if it is constitutional – that is, only if it does not conflict with any fundamental precepts set out in the federal constitution or the applicable state constitution. If a court determines that a statute is not constitutional, the statute cannot control the situation before the court regardless of how much the legislative body wishes it could.

c. Administrative Regulations

Although we most commonly think of elected legislative bodies and the judicial branch of government as the dominant sources of law in our country, administrative agencies are responsible for promulgating huge numbers of administrative regulations with which all of us must comply. Such agencies are created by Congress in the federal government, and by state legislatures in state governments.[20] As a rule, agencies are considered part of the

---

[19]Where a state law and a federal law both attempt to address the same issue but create conflicting results, the federal law is generally considered controlling. The nuances of determining when such an overlap exists are complex and are the subject of much of the study of Constitutional Law in law schools. For now, be aware that if you explore an area of law that is addressed in a state statute and also in a federal statute, there may be questions to consider concerning whether they create parallel causes of action or whether the federal law alone controls.

[20]In some rare instances, state agencies are created through state constitutional provisions.

executive branch of government and agency heads are appointed, either by the head of the executive branch of government or by a designated legislative body.[21]

Where a situation is controlled by a regulation promulgated by an administrative agency pursuant to proper statutory authority, initial decisions concerning the applicability of the regulation to any given legal question are usually made by the agency itself or by an administrative law judge (who sits in a different type of court than the judges in our regular state or federal court systems). If the conflict is not resolved at the administrative law level, there are often avenues of appeal available through appropriate state or federal courts (but usually only after the distressed party has exhausted his or her administrative law remedies). Research in this area of law is extremely complicated, and many attorneys specialize in this field alone.

One of the questions you should sometimes explore when doing administrative law research is what kind of underlying (often called "enabling") statutory law authorized the agency to issue the regulation, because a regulation is only valid if it is consistent with legislative intent. Like statutes, regulations also have to be constitutional. In addition to being aware of a regulation's statutory roots, you should also be alert to relevant administrative law decisions interpreting and applying the relevant regulation. Also, like statutes, administrative regulations are changed frequently. Thus, once you've found the appropriate administrative regulation, you need to update your research to be sure that what you are reading is still relevant.

Finally, remember that because of our parallel legal systems (federal and state), there may be both federal and state administrative regulations which address the question before you. Because of the complexity and specialization required to do most administrative law research, this workbook will only introduce you to how to find and update a federal regulation. As you become more advanced in your legal research skills, you may want to explore other administrative law research techniques on your own.

2. Secondary Authority

The more you know about the area of law you are researching, the more efficiently and effectively you can find the answers you are seeking. Secondary sources, which contain explanations and commentaries about primary law, are an invaluable resource for legal researchers. By taking the time to use an appropriate secondary source such as a legal encyclopedia or a law journal article, you gain background knowledge of that area of law that will lead you more quickly (and with greater accuracy) to the relevant primary law.

---

[21] In addition to the traditional "executive" agencies, some agencies are considered to be "independent agencies," largely because the heads of those agencies are appointed for specific terms of office and cannot be removed on the whim of the legislative body or the head of the executive branch of government. Also, in a few states, some agency heads (e.g., the Superintendent of Schools) are elected.

In addition to educating you about the important concepts in a given area of law, secondary resources can expand your awareness of critical terms of art that you can use to develop effective searches online and in hard copy. They can also provide you with creative ideas when you need to argue for a change in the law or for a different interpretation of existing law. Additionally, secondary resources also frequently cite relevant primary law directly, leading you directly to the primary law you are seeking. Thus, for example, perusing a current book by a law professor explaining criminal law in your state and citing important cases would be an excellent use of secondary source materials. By doing so, you would be exposed to background information through the eyes of a legal expert in the field, together with citations to relevant cases and statutes in your jurisdiction, before launching headstrong into a search for primary law itself.

Finally, secondary resources can often provide you with persuasive authority when you need to argue for a change in the law or for a different interpretation of existing law. This workbook and its supplement will introduce you to a number of well-recognized secondary resources available to legal researchers, and give you the opportunity to explore how their use could be valuable to you.

3. Finding Tools

Online and print publishers of legal information have developed highly sophisticated tools over the years to help you locate primary and secondary authority with accuracy and efficiency. In order to make primary law accessible, publishers of hard copy (print) materials created systems in the last century for grouping cases by topic headings. These same systems are still in full force today, continuing to allow researchers to find primary authority that is "on point" in a systematic way.

As electronic research became available, searching was initially done in a "whole text" manner, allowing researchers to find applicable law only by searching for the presence of particular words within a case or other resource. Experienced researchers missed the conceptual edge that the print categorization systems allowed, and some online publishers are now responding by providing online "finding tools" that allow researchers to identify relevant primary and secondary authority using broader conceptual groupings as well as by initiating whole text word searches. Many of these new online "finding tools" mirror or duplicate their long-standing counterparts in hard copy and are premised on the inter-connectedness of hard copy and online research in the legal field.

In addition to using "finding tools" to locate primary and secondary authority, lawyers also routinely use these tools to determine if the research they're relying on is current. The responsibility to confirm that law is current (has not been changed or abandoned) is one of the core professional obligations undertaken by every lawyer. Failure to do so is not only unprofessional, but it can constitute malpractice.

This workbook and its supplement will introduce you to an astonishing array of finding and updating tools that are available to facilitate legal research in hard copy and online. New finding tools are introduced daily, and it is a lifelong challenge for lawyers to make the time to educate themselves about the growing resources available to help them as they search for accurate answers to legal questions.

B. HOW DO LAWYERS SEARCH FOR INFORMATION SYSTEMATICALLY?

After completing the guided exercises in this workbook and its supplement, you will know an impressive amount about legal research and may be in a position to start an independent research project of your own. To do so with confidence, you will need to decide how to approach your assignment systematically. Having a systematic plan of attack will increase your confidence and will allow you to approach the assignment in a way that ensures good results in a timely fashion.

Developing a systematic research strategy is a two-step process. First, you need to develop an initial hypothesis about what information you are seeking. You will frequently modify your initial hypothesis about what information you are seeking as your research broadens your understanding of the relevant legal issues. In legal research, answers often lead to more questions and a good researcher embraces the mercurial nature of the legal research process. Second, you need to choose what resources to use to find the information you need. As you make decisions about which resources to use, consider:

- the authoritativeness and reliability of the source (not all information is equally valuable or even equally accurate);

- the inter-connectedness of the source to other useful sources (can this source help you find additional useful information easily?);

- the accessibility of the source (is this information that you can get to fairly easily?);

- the cost of using the source (recognizing that information that is cost-free to you personally now and/or available in print in a large law school library may not be available or free when you start your first summer job and/or begin work as an attorney). Learning to use a wide variety of materials efficiently now nets economic rewards down the road.

Development of a research system that works for you takes time and a willingness to be flexible. The best legal researchers recognize over-arching principles and goals, but the exact steps they follow necessarily vary with each project they undertake. As with the development of any new skill, your initial efforts at independent legal research won't be efficient and may not even be accurate. The trick to developing a system that you can rely on consistently lies in being willing to experiment, consulting others with an open mind, double-checking your results, and learning from your mistakes.

As you develop a strategy for approaching an independent legal research project, the following ideas will help. You can also find good advice from your professors, from law librarians, and in each of the textbooks listed in Appendix A.

(1) **What is the issue you're looking into?** A clear understanding of the initial question to be researched is critically important to the choices you'll make about how to find answers. Without that, you could spend needless hours sorting through information that may be interesting, but is irrelevant to the question you are addressing. Whether you are given an assignment by someone else or are analyzing facts to determine the relevant legal questions to research for yourself, start our research with clarity about the legal issue in question. Remember also to remain flexible. Often legal research leads to a narrowing or expanding of the initial question, and an alert researcher looks for such modifications of the original task.

(2) **What jurisdiction has control?** Make a preliminary decision about which jurisdiction has law that controls the answer to your question. Is this a federal law question or does it concern state law? If state law, which state? Making preliminary decisions about jurisdiction will allow you to narrow the size of the database or identify the set of books you will use.

(3) **What primary source of law is likely to provide the answer to your question?** Although very difficult for new researchers, developing a sense of whether a legal question would be controlled by statutory law, common law, administrative regulations, and/or a constitution will come with time. Starting with the likely source (or, in many cases, sources) for controlling law is an important part of collecting accurate results efficiently.

(4) **What are your best options for where to find that primary law?** Wise researchers have learned how to find law in many places, using multiple resources. By doing so, they can make wise choices about which source to use in a wide variety of research contexts. Using the steps you will have learned in this workbook, and considering the TIPS you will have read, make some preliminary decisions about what resources you could use to locate the law you identified in paragraph (3) above. DO NOT NECESSARILY GO TO THE FIRST SOURCE YOU THINK OF. Rather, give thought to what is the most economical, efficient, and convenient resource to use to get the information you need. For practicing attorneys, using a combination of print and online sources is often the most efficient and economical approach. Thus, it is critical for you to take time now to learn about the wide variety of resources and finding tools available to lawyers and to become proficient at accessing them in hard copy and online.

(5) **Will you save time and net better results if you step back and get an overview?** It is inefficient and unwise to begin a legal research project without

an overview of the relevant area of the law. In some circumstances, you may be sufficiently experienced in a particular field to begin your research by looking first for primary authority. In most circumstances, however, you will fare significantly better by browsing a secondary authority concerning your subject. Secondary sources usually discuss and explain primary law, giving background information that will inform your research and assist you in analyzing primary law more quickly and effectively. In addition, primary law is usually cited in secondary sources, making secondary sources a rich environment for finding leads to primary authority with ease.

(6) **Finding statutory law "on point."** After reviewing secondary sources, or based on your own prior knowledge in a field, you may already have citations to primary law. If not, unless you are certain that the answer to your question is rooted in the common law, the next best step is to check for primary statutory law by searching an annotated code. As you will learn by completing the exercises in the book, an annotated code contains statutory law and also cross-references to cases, administrative regulations, and even secondary authority relevant to that law.

(7) **Finding case law "on point."** If the law you are seeking is rooted in the common law, or if you have found a statute or relevant constitutional provision, you will need to search for judicial opinions that have resolved similar conflicts in the past. If you have no citations to case law, you can begin by using the hard copy and online resources to which you will have been exposed in this workbook and its supplement.

(8) **Finding regulations "on point."** Since all administrative regulations are rooted in enabling legislation, annotated codes and case law applying enabling statutes will be rich sources of references to related administrative regulations. Additional searches can be done efficiently following the steps you will be exposed to in this workbook.

(9) **Make sure the law you've found is still current.** Law that does not accurately reflect current authority may help a researcher get a sense of the evolution of law over time, but a legal researcher assessing the current state of the law must meticulously update all primary authority before relying on it. After completing the exercises in this workbook and its supplement, you will know how to use online citators (Shepard's on LexisNexis and Keycite on Westlaw) to ensure that your research is up to date. Appendix C contains detailed instructions for updating your research using traditional hard copy methods.

(10) **Take good notes.** Proficient legal researchers take good notes in a variety of ways, depending on their personal preferences. Some researchers use notebooks with dividers to hold information about related sub-topics; others use index cards; and others keep their notes online using folders and subfolders. Researchers

who are visual learners often find using highlighters and other color-coded cues to be useful. Regardless of format, all good legal research notes should include the following:

- a clear paper trail of the research process you have followed (so you don't unnecessarily repeat steps and/or skip important steps by mistake);
- clear distinctions between your own words and exact quotations (so you don't inadvertently commit plagiarism and so you can accurately cite exact language when it is important to do so);
- paraphrased summaries and synopses of relevant authority in your own words. Liberal use of paraphrasing clarifies your thinking and is more time-efficient than mindlessly writing exact quotes or printing/duplicating large quantities of material to read later;
- clear references to the sources of authority upon which you rely, including the information you need to complete legal citation requirements following The Bluebook or the ALWD Citation Manual rules;
- your evolving thoughts about the law and modifications to your original hypotheses and research strategy so your search can grow as you learn more about the topic.

(11) **At some point, you have to stop.** Knowing when to stop is a puzzle for all researchers – but especially for beginners. Because answers to legal questions often raise a myriad of other questions, and because the specter of missing the "smoking gun" haunts all of us conducting legal research, it is very difficult to know when you can conscientiously stop. In practice, the economics of time and available resources often influence this decision. Nonetheless, professional ethics dictate that lawyers conduct research that is accurate and reliable before giving legal advice on a topic with which he or she is unfamiliar. One rule of thumb is to stop when the resources you are searching all confirm that the answer you have found is accurate. If you are finding conflicting information on the same topic, keep researching. Once you are comfortable that your answer is accurate and current, your work may be done. The final question to ask is whether the project warrants additional research beyond the obvious – does your client want and/or need you to go beyond the borders of existing law to look for arguments for a change in the law or for a different application of the law? If so, and if the economics of the situation warrant further work, you can continue your search more broadly, netting additional persuasive authority using the strategies you've been exposed to in this workbook and its supplement.

With this background information in mind, you're ready to begin the Assignment Sheets in this workbook.

Part A: Sequence of Assignments #1

START HERE *only if your professor has asked you to begin with "Sequence of Assignments 1" OR with Client A, B, C, D, or E. If you have been asked to begin with "Sequence of Assignments 2" OR with Client F, G, H, I, or J, go instead to page 167.*

This first Sequence of Assignments introduces you to legal research sources in the following order: secondary sources/common law/state statutory law/federal statutory law/administrative regulations. You can explore these resources using one of the following five client scenarios:

- **Client A:** "Client A" is Eric Arnold, a business person who has recently moved to a farming community where he is facing some unexpected legal issues. For this client, turn to page 29;

- **Client B:** "Client B" is a non-profit organization known as Project Hope. If you are working with Client B, you will advise the Board of Project Hope as its members try to open a school designed to reduce the drop-out rate in the local community. For this client, turn to page 31;

- **Client C:** "Client C" is Marjorie Morrison, an elderly woman who is experiencing a conflict with her neighbor who has started selling his home-made wine in large quantities through the region. For this client, turn to page 33;

- **Client D:** "Client D" is Dr. Allen Field, a historian who has inherited a house that he would like to restore, along with some legal questions that he didn't anticipate. For this client, turn to page 35;

- **Client E:** "Client E" is Josh Ward, an environmentalist who is trying to protect his lake-front property from encroachment by neighbors. For this client, turn to page 37.

Each of the five lessons you will complete is introduced by an "assigning memo" that tells you more about your client and asks a specific legal question related to that client's situation. As you seek an answer to the question or questions you've been asked, you will be introduced to tools and strategies available to lawyers doing similar research. The point of this workbook is to teach you how to use research materials. The questions raised in your assigning memos provide a context through which to explore these resources.

Before you begin any individual lesson, always check our website <www. LegalResearchWorkbook.com> for any corrections to the text or significant changes in the law.

MARSHALL, STORY & ASSOCIATES
ATTORNEYS AND COUNSELORS AT LAW
SUITE 101, THE JUSTICE BUILDING

⚖️

THE LITIGATION DIVISION

To: New Associate
From: Assigning Partner
Re: Eric Arnold [Client A] – File #03-2576

Welcome to the law firm of Marshall, Story & Associates. We were pleased when you accepted our offer to join the firm, and I look forward to having this opportunity to work with you on your first assignment.

Our client, Eric Arnold, is a retired executive who has recently moved here after inheriting a family farm, together with all its contents, in our state. I met with Mr. Arnold personally last week and was taken both by his desire to relax and unwind from his prior career as a successful banker, and by his commitment to his family roots. Mr. Arnold, who was the family's only surviving heir, would like to rebuild the farm to its former condition and is also interested in becoming involved with the community in which the farm is located.

Mr. Arnold has come to us with a number of legal questions, the first of which concerns some antique carving equipment that he discovered in a run-down tool shed on the edge of the farm's old apple orchard. As it happens, wood carving has been a hobby that Mr. Arnold has pursued for many years. He remembers his grandfather using carving tools like those he found, and he would like to be able to use these tools now in his own work.

Unfortunately, when he took the tools to town to have them cleaned at the local hardware store, one of the older people at the store said, "Well, I'll be. I believe I recognize those tools. I think those are James Joyner's old tools – I expect he left them in that shed when he was working for your uncle years ago and flat out forgot where he left them. His memory's been failing for years and he loses things all the time."

Concerned about starting off on the wrong foot in his new community, Mr. Arnold has asked us to do some initial research to see, in general, who would have ownership rights to these tools if Mr. Joyner had, in fact, laid them aside and forgot about them many years ago. I would appreciate your doing this research for us. Specifically, can you find out the general principles involved in determining ownership of property that has been lost, but not intentionally abandoned?

Mr. Arnold has decided not to do anything further with these tools until he hears back from us. I will be meeting with him next week and look forward to sharing the results of your research with him at that time.

▶▶ Turn to page 39 to begin your work on this assignment.

MARSHALL, STORY & ASSOCIATES
ATTORNEYS AND COUNSELORS AT LAW
SUITE 101, THE JUSTICE BUILDING

⚖

THE LITIGATION DIVISION

To: New Associate
From: Assigning Partner
Re: Project Hope [Client B] – File # 03-2575

Welcome to the law firm of Marshall, Story & Associates. We were delighted when you accepted an offer with our firm and I am pleased to have this opportunity to work with you on the present case. Our client is a non-profit corporation that operates under the name Project Hope.

This organization grew out of a grassroots effort to address a number of problems experienced by young people in our community, a topic that was recently explored in depth in an investigative report in our local paper. The series of articles highlighted the unusually high drop-out rate for students in our local public schools as well as a growing problem with drug use and crime. Organizers of Project Hope want to experiment with establishing a tuition free alternative school for students with promise in an effort to turn around the unhealthy cycle of poor education, unemployment, and poverty.

The organizers' idea is to provide a small-group learning environment supported by private funds and donations that focuses on teaching students the practical benefits of the material they learn. Having many opportunities to learn experientially is important to their vision, and participation in sports for those who are athletically talented will be a core part of their curriculum.

As the Board begins the task of assessing the kinds of facilities they will need to build, the question of whether students in a private school have a fundamental right to participate in public schools sports has arisen. The Board is also curious as to whether the local school system or Interscholastic Athletic Association could prohibit Project Hope students from participating in interscholastic public school sports.

Because the Board is only in preliminary discussions on this topic, I would like just enough background information to give them a general overview of the law in this area. Specifically, can you let us know if: (1) pupils or students have a constitutionally protected fundamental right to participate in athletics or sports, and (2) can a local school system or district, or an Interscholastic Athletic Association, prohibit non-public school students from participating on public school interscholastic teams.

I will be meeting with the Board again next week and will look forward to sharing the results of your research with them at that time.

▶▶ Turn to page 39 to begin your work on this assignment.

MARSHALL, STORY & ASSOCIATES
ATTORNEYS AND COUNSELORS AT LAW
SUITE 101, THE JUSTICE BUILDING

⚖

THE LITIGATION DIVISION

To: New Associate
From: Assigning Partner
Re: Marjorie Morrison [Client C] – File #21-2203

Welcome to the law firm of Marshall, Story & Associates. We were all delighted when you accepted an offer with our firm and I am pleased to have this opportunity to work with you on the present case. Our client is Ms. Marjorie Morrison, a retired elementary school teacher who has lived in town for all of her sixty-five years. She has come to us for help concerning a controversy that has arisen with her next-door neighbor, Mr. Charles Thompson.

Mr. Thompson and Ms. Morrison have known each other for years. In fact, Mr. Thompson, who is himself sixty years old, went to school in town with Ms. Morrison when they were children. The controversy between the two arose a few months ago when Mr. Thompson sold his hardware store and retired. Finding time hanging on his hands, Mr. Thompson spent a great deal more time around his house than he had in the past. On a number of occasions, Ms. Morrison was awakened early in the morning by his lawn-mowing and other gardening activities. In the evenings, he tended to have friends drop by, creating more traffic on their dead-end street than had been there in past years.

The final blow for Ms. Morrison, however, apparently began a few months ago when Mr. Thompson started making and storing large quantities of homemade wine in his garage. According to Ms. Morrison, Mr. Thompson had always made excellent wine that he had shared generously with family and friends during holidays. She herself enjoyed receiving the wine as a regular gift on her birthday. Since his retirement, Mr. Thompson had begun producing the wine in earnest. He had large delivery trucks bringing fruit, constructed equipment that was quite noisy (and which she feels may not be entirely safe) in his garage, and sells wine from a picnic table in his back yard.

Ms. Morrison approached Mr. Thompson a few weeks ago to ask him to cut back on his wine-making activities so that their neighborhood could regain its quiet residential character. Mr. Thompson said that he was making quite a profit on his wine and that he had no intention of cutting back on production. Moreover, he told her that he had decided to run for mayor and that she needed to get used to the idea that he would be running city hall out of his home after he had won the election.

continued on next page

Ms. Morrison, who I know personally to be fairly even-tempered, decided that she had taken all that she was willing to take in terms of changes in her lifestyle. Last week she went to town hall during the time Mr. Thompson was scheduled to announce his candidacy for mayor. Just as he began his address, Ms. Morrison stood up and told the crowd of several dozen people and reporters present that Mr. Thompson was not "fit" to run for office. She announced to all present, "Charles Thompson isn't fit to be our mayor. I'm his neighbor and I should know. He's breaking state and federal laws right and left, and he doesn't even have any political power yet. He doesn't have my vote and he shouldn't have yours."

Ms. Morrison was distressed when she came to see me today. She is remorseful about having lost her temper and publicly embarrassing her neighbor and friend, and doesn't know how to mend things between them. Perhaps even more importantly, it looks like the controversy between the two is getting worse. Ms. Morrison brought in a letter from Mr. Thompson's attorney indicating that Mr. Thompson intends to bring a slander suit against her for the statements she made at the town hall last week. While Ms. Morrison was willing to apologize to Mr. Thompson last week, the letter from the attorney has hardened her position and she says she is no longer willing to even speak to the man.

I have not had a slander case in quite some time, but my memory is that slander consists of speaking words that prejudice persons in their reputation, office, or business. I have spoken with Mr. Thompson's attorney and he tells me that his client believes that since Ms. Morrison personally educated a large segment of the town's leaders, her remarks may have had a significant impact on his ability to win the mayoral election.

I am not sure, but I believe that the law of libel and slander is slightly different when applied to a public official as opposed to a layperson. I would appreciate your doing some preliminary research in this area to see generally what constitutes slander of a public official. I'm meeting with our client again next week and will look forward to hearing about your research before that time.

▶▶ Turn to page 39 to begin your work on this assignment.

MARSHALL, STORY & ASSOCIATES
ATTORNEYS AND COUNSELORS AT LAW
SUITE 101, THE JUSTICE BUILDING

⚖

THE LITIGATION DIVISION

To: New Associate
From: Assigning Partner
Re: Allen Field [Client D] - File #21-2204

Welcome to the law firm of Marshall, Story & Associates. We were all pleased when you accepted our offer to join our firm and I am looking forward to having an opportunity to work with you on the present case.

Our client is Allen Field who recently earned his Ph.D. in history from our state university. Dr. Field's story is an interesting one and involves the preservation and development of a possible historic site here in our own town. As I understand Dr. Field's story, he researched and wrote his dissertation on the life of Geoffrey Bain, a little known statesman who was instrumental in helping draft the constitution of this state.

In conducting his research, Dr. Field became acquainted with Ms. Patricia Williams, who was Mr. Bain's last direct descendant. Ms. Williams lived at the original home site of the Bain Farm, where the first drafts of the state's constitution were written by Geoffrey Bain. He is buried in the family cemetery near the orchard that still survives on the farm. Sadly, in Ms. Williams' later years she had found it difficult to maintain the farm and the home and had allowed both to fall into almost complete disrepair.

Apparently Ms. Williams and Dr. Field hit it off well. He says she was delightful, and she had told friends how much she valued the work he was doing exploring her family history. Ms. Williams passed away last month, and in her will surprised Dr. Field by naming him heir to the Bain Farm, including the old farmhouse and the remaining ten acres of the original farm. In addition, she established a trust for the development of the property and named Dr. Field as the sole administrator of that trust, specifying that all funds were to be used for the "betterment of the property and to increase the public's awareness of the great works of Geoffrey Bain."

Dr. Field has now come to us for help in developing the property in a way that will show respect for its original owners and for Ms. Williams' wishes. He and his wife have decided to live on the property and to rehabilitate it for use as a bed and breakfast. It is their expectation that such use will draw the public's eye to the many historically significant contributions of Geoffrey Bain, will make the property economically viable, and will allow the house and grounds to become a significant part of the local community again.

continued on next page

Unfortunately, Dr. Field has run into a problem with his plan from the beginning. Although the property sits on the edge of town and is bordered on one side by an upscale residential community, on the other it is bordered by a popular restaurant/tavern. While having a successful restaurant adjacent to a bed and breakfast would seem at first to be an advantage, this one is problematic. Not only is it open very late at night and again early in the morning, with the evening crowd being especially noisy, but the restaurant's most popular meal involves roasting meat on an outdoor pit. The smoke from the open pit, which is less than a hundred feet from the edge of the Bain Farm, drifts routinely onto Dr. Field's new property and leaves a film of grit on the windows, house paint, and flowers.

Both the air pollution and the noise are in violation of local ordinances. However, the business is so profitable that the owners simply pay their fines and continue their activity. Dr. Field needs these activities to stop so that he can offer hospitable amenities to his future guests, and so that he can protect his historic property from further damage. Although it has been a while since I have handled a case with facts similar to these, it seems to me that Dr. Field may have a private cause of action under a nuisance theory which might give him some leverage in abating the noise and air pollution next to his new home.

For your first assignment, I would appreciate your doing some initial research into the general field of nuisance to refresh my memory on what conditions we would have to establish to show that a nuisance has been created. I do not expect for you to become an instant expert on the entire field of nuisance law, which can be complicated. Rather, please restrict your initial research to the following simple questions: what is a nuisance, and can noise and/or air pollution constitute a nuisance.

▶▶ Turn to page 39 to begin your work on this assignment.

MARSHALL, STORY & ASSOCIATES
ATTORNEYS AND COUNSELORS AT LAW
SUITE 101, THE JUSTICE BUILDING

⚖

THE LITIGATION DIVISION

To: New Associate
From: Assigning Partner
Re: Josh Ward [Client E] - File #21-2205

Welcome to the law firm of Marshall, Story & Associates. We were all delighted when you accepted an offer with our firm and I am pleased to have this opportunity to work with you on the present case. Our client is Josh Ward, a successful entrepreneur who recently decided to move out of the fast-paced urban setting where his business originated and begin running his business electronically from home. It is this recent relocation that has brought Mr. Ward to our firm.

When he decided to make this major change in his lifestyle, Mr. Ward looked for a setting that would be peaceful and private, and would also allow him to pursue his personal interests in the preservation of endangered plant species. He found just such a setting in a twenty-five acre tract approximately forty-five minutes south of our offices. His property is bordered on the south side by a large, state-owned lake, on the north side by a small rural road, on the west side by undeveloped private land, and on the east side by a nature preserve owned by a private conservancy. This land was particularly attractive to him because it houses a wide variety of natural plant life, including rare ferns growing in a swampy area along the far southeastern side of the property. Once he purchased the land, he commissioned a local architect to supervise the construction of an energy-efficient home on the property. Last month, he moved his business and all his personal belongings to his new residence.

Almost immediately following his move, Mr. Ward ran into problems enjoying his new home. Although he was not aware of it when he purchased the property, local residents have used his land for years to gain beachfront access to the recreational areas of the lake. Hardly a day goes by when Mr. Ward does not encounter some stranger or another on his land. On weekends, he has been startled by as many as five or ten individuals crossing his property from early morning until dusk, and is often frustrated by litter left behind and/or damage to the plants growing there. In an effort to stop this encroachment on his property, and to protect his endangered plants, Mr. Ward has posted "No Trespassing" signs along all of his property borders. The signs have been largely ignored.

While in town on an errand this week, Mr. Ward learned that a local group of citizens is looking into the possibility of joining together to hire an attorney to protect what they

continued on next page

consider to be their rights to cross his property to reach the state-owned lake where they boat, swim, and fish. It is the position of these area residents that they and their families have been crossing the land for decades. Many of these individuals who are now near retirement age have crossed the land against the express wishes of the prior owner since they were small children. It is their contention that use of the land for access to the lake has been so widespread for so many years that the public has established an easement by prescription (also known as a prescriptive easement) that entitles them to property rights across his land.

In anticipation of possible legal action, Mr. Ward has contacted us to represent him. At this point, I would like to know if the citizens have a viable cause of action based on a theory that a prescriptive easement has been established. I am particularly interested in knowing how specific a path must be followed in order to create such an easement. The facts as Mr. Ward has explained them to me are that there is no specific, clearly defined path from the rural road on the north side of his property to the lake on the south. Rather, people seem to walk in random paths across the property until they reach the lake on the south side.

It has been some time since I have looked in depth into a property law issue of this type, but my memory is that it is necessary to use the same route over and over in order to gain an easement by prescription. It would be helpful to me if you would do some general research into this question for me this week. I will be meeting again with Mr. Ward in a few days and will look forward to sharing the results of your research with him at that time.

▶▶ Begin your work on the following page.

Print Your Name:

(If you are doing this assignment as part of a class exercise, you may neatly write your answers directly on these sheets, staple all sheets together, and turn them in. If you prefer to write your answers separately using your computer, please be sure to number your answers to correspond to the appropriate questions before printing your answer sheets.)

Background Reading: To learn more about the resources and concepts introduced in this Assignment Sheet, read Chapter 2 of *Legal Research in a Nutshell* or a comparable chapter in a textbook assigned by your professor. (See Appendix A.)

Background Information: Your partner has asked you to look into a specific question on behalf of your client. Since you don't yet know a lot about the topic this question covers, secondary sources are a good place to get started. In legal research, secondary sources are a rich source of information on a variety of legal topics and also can often point you directly to primary law that may have an impact on the question before you. Re-read pages 21-22 and pages 24-25 in this workbook for more information on the importance of using secondary sources.

What You Will Learn. By the end of this assignment, you will:
- Be able to identify two leading legal research encyclopedias
- Find and update information in a legal encyclopedia
- Identify your state encyclopedia, if there is one
- Recognize the significant value of legal treatises
- Recognize the origin and purpose of Restatements
- Be alert to a number of online options for finding secondary sources

The Research Process:
A. USING LEGAL ENCYCLOPEDIAS

Introduction: Print copy legal encyclopedias are easy to use because they are akin to the general encyclopedias you have seen for years and are set out in relatively simple terms. Unlike legal periodicals (which you'll learn about later in this Assignment Sheet), they are not generally used as persuasive secondary authority (although you will still see an encyclopedia cited in a court opinion from time to time). Instead, encyclopedias are tools that introduce you to general concepts and lead you to further research. The two national encyclopedias, Corpus Juris Secundum (C.J.S.) and American Jurisprudence 2d (Am. Jur. 2d), are very similar, but it's a good idea to be able to use both. Like using the World Book Encyclopedia and The Encyclopedia Britannica, researching in both legal encyclopedias might enable you to pick up something from one that you didn't find in the other. In this assignment, you will get to try your hand at both.

1. Corpus Juris Secundum (C.J.S.) and American Jurisprudence 2d (Am. Jur. 2d)

Step 1: Although Am. Jur. 2d and C.J.S. perform pretty much the same function, you will find that they differ in some respects. Over time, you may develop a preference for one over the other, or you may find more thorough coverage of a particular subject in one or the other. Choose one of these encyclopedias to begin your research. Write the name of the encyclopedia here:_____,
then **go to the location of the encyclopedia you chose.**

ONLINE TIP: Although many resources can be found online and in hard copy, issues of cost, convenience, and scope of coverage are critical factors lawyers must consider when deciding whether to search online or to use traditional books. In addition, studies indicate that many readers browse more comfortably using actual books rather than online materials. See generally Debra Moss Curtis & Judith R. Karp, In a Case, On the Screen, Do They Remember What They've Seen? Critical Electronic Reading in the Law School Classroom, 30 Hamline L. Rev. 248 (2007). Recognizing this challenge, both Westlaw and Lexis have recently added online browsing features such as Tables of Contents, Indexes, and search tools that allow readers to move backwards and forward online. By 2008, online access to Am. Jur. and C.J.S. will be restricted to Westlaw. You can locate alternative secondary source materials on Lexis by clicking on the "Search" tab at the top of the Lexis homepage, choosing the "Search by Source" option, and then clicking on the link provided for Secondary Legal Sources. On Westlaw, you can locate additional secondary source materials on the Law School homepage by clicking on the links listed under "Secondary Source" grouping. On the main Westlaw homepage, click on the "View Westlaw Directory" hyperlink. Using secondary resources to get oriented to a new topic is as important when you are doing research online as it is when you are using hard copy materials.

Step 2: Determine which major area(s) of law your client's case falls under. Often, identification of a proper area of law where you can begin researching isn't obvious. In this case, however, you're lucky because your senior partner has already identified the legal issues that he or she would like you to investigate. As a rule in legal research you need to be flexible and creative in thinking of a variety of possible terms that will lead you to the area of the encyclopedia that will discuss what you're interested in. Look back at your partner's memo for guidance. Next, list one or two terms to begin with here:

TIP: When you are generating "search terms" in legal research, experienced teachers will wisely encourage you to keep in mind the "5 W's" that you may have learned about in a beginning journalism class (who, what, when, where, and why). In a legal context, applying these concepts helps you think about the parties or things involved (minor child, teacher, dog, etc.), the type of action or conflict (battery, robbery, trespass), when the action occurred (vacation, workday, off duty), where the action occurred (bank, school, playground) and why the action occurred (malice, self-defense, mistake, protection of property). Generating synonyms broadens the chance that you will find the law in a place where editors or publishers have also catalogued the information. It's not enough to think (although that's a good start); you have to think creatively about where the law might be stored. As you gain experience, you will become more familiar with the terms that have been used by legal publishers and practitioners over the years to categorize certain types of actions, defenses, classes of people, etc. with consistency.

Step 3: Find the multi-volume General Index located at the end of the entire set and look up the terms you listed in <u>Step 2</u> above. (Note that there are also individual Topic indexes at the end of each individual Topic). The General Index and the individual Topic Indexes contain *Topic* and *Section* numbers that will lead you to the main volume that will contain entries related to the search terms you've generated. You will find the Topics published alphabetically in the main volumes (like other print copy encyclopedias you may have used); Sections are sub-parts of the larger Topics. Spending a few extra minutes with the General Index is often a wise investment of time. The Index can help you narrow your search quickly and will also refer you to other subject areas (Topics) you hadn't even considered. In the space below, write down the references and corresponding Section numbers to at least three entries you found in the General Index that look like they might relate to your partner's question:

Please return the General Index to the shelf now so that others may use it.

Step 4: In the main set, find the text for the references you noted in <u>Step 3</u> above. Read the entries in the text. Choose one of these entries and, in the space provided, summarize the general law on the point it addresses and describe how it relates to our client's problem. If the Sections you have read do not appear to be on point, read the following "BOMB" and "TIP" and repeat Steps 1 through 3 until you find a Section that does.

BEWARE: Occasionally the sections cited in the General Index are incorrect or confusing. If the sections your search has led you to seem incorrect, consider using the individual index at the end of each Topic to find a section you want to read. See the **TIP** below for more ideas on how to find the information you want in the encyclopedia.

TIP: The General Index and the individual index for each Topic are both good resources for finding an encyclopedia Section to read. Each Section, of course, is a sub-division of a larger Topic. It is often helpful to look at the Table of Contents (called an "Analysis") that appears at the beginning of every Topic if you are having difficulty finding an entry on point. This is a good habit to get into even when you think the more narrow Section you've found is directly on point. You may find related Sections listed that would yield additional ideas for further research.

Use this space to summarize the general law on the point your Section addresses and describe how that law relates to your client's problem:

Step 5: In the space below, write the correct <u>Bluebook</u> or <u>ALWD</u> citation to the Section you have summarized (see Rule 15.8 of <u>The Bluebook</u> or Rule 26 of <u>The ALWD Manual</u> for an example of how to cite to <u>C.J.S.</u> and <u>Am. Jur. 2d</u>):

DO NOT RESHELVE YOUR ENCYCLOPEDIA VOLUME YET.

Step 6: In addition to being good sources of general background information, <u>C.J.S.</u> and <u>Am. Jur. 2d</u> entries are also a good source for locating relevant case law (court decisions) from a wide variety of jurisdictions. You will learn other ways to find case law in Assignment Sheets 2 and 3 of this Sequence of Assignments. While you still have the encyclopedia open to the section you summarized above, look at the bottom of the page for references to relevant case law. Find an entry to a case on point and write the citation exactly as it is printed there in the space below (note that the way the publisher has printed this citation may or may not be in compliance with the way <u>The Bluebook</u> or <u>The ALWD Manual</u> recommends that you cite the case if you write about it in the future. Always check your citation manual for proper citation form if you're writing an important document):

What state is that case from? (See the following **TIP**).

TIP: Written opinions reflecting the decisions that judges have reached about particular cases (usually appellate cases) are published in "reporters" in chronological order based on when the decision was handed down. These decisions are published in "official," and sometimes "unofficial," form. The "official" form is the one chosen by the proper authority to represent the actual opinion of the court, but in reality there are rarely any errors in an "unofficial" form so both versions of the case will almost always look the same. Some courts automatically publish all of their opinions. Other courts publish only select opinions. In North Carolina, for example, only about 35% of decided cases from the North Carolina Court of Appeals have opinions that are subsequently published. The North Carolina Supreme Court, on the other hand, publishes all of its written opinions. You can learn more about how lawyers access and use "unpublished" opinions by reading the "BOMB" on page 76 of Assignment Sheet 2.

continued on next page

Once a case is published, the citation to that case tells you where to find the opinion itself. For example, <u>Concerned Citizens v. Holden Beach Enters.</u>, 325 N.C. 705, 388 S.E.2d 450 (1988), is a 1988 case which you could find by looking up page 705 of volume 325 in the North Carolina Reports (the official reporter for the North Carolina Supreme Court). The parties involved in the case are the names you see underlined [usually, but not always, with the plaintiff (the party that initially filed the action) listed first]. Here, the plaintiff is a group called Concerned Citizens of Brunswick County. The defendant (the party named to defend the action filed by the plaintiff) is a business called Holden Beach Enterprises. In the citation, both parties' names have been abbreviated in accordance with <u>The Bluebook</u> rules. Not all states publish official state reporters. To find out if your state publishes one, check Table T-1 of <u>The Bluebook</u> or Appendix 1 of <u>The ALWD Manual</u>.

If your state has an official reporter, you could also find the case by looking up its "parallel cite" (the second cite listed, which is the same case printed in a different set of reporters, called "regional" reporters, where several states' cases are printed together in the same set of volumes). If you were looking for this opinion using the parallel cite, you would go to page 450 of volume 388 in West's <u>South Eastern Reporter</u> (second series) – a series of volumes that contain cases for states in the southeastern United States. Thus, if you are researching a case in a state that has its own official reporter, you could find the case either in the state reporter or in West's regional reporter. You could also find this case online through a number of fee-based and free services and websites. You will learn more about finding and reading cases in Assignment Sheet 2 of this Sequence of Assignments and in the online supplement to this workbook.

ANOTHER TIP: There are a number of major publishers in the legal field. Thomson-West is one of the oldest and largest. Many of the resources you will be learning to use contain the word "West" in their title and many of the systems that are important in legal research are found in West publications. It is common for those books and systems to be referred to using the word West, rather than Thomson-West. For example, the regional reporter referred to in the TIP above would often be referred to by lawyers as "West's <u>South Eastern Reporter</u>. The convention of using the word "West" rather than "Thomson-West" will be followed throughout this workbook.

Step 7: Law changes rapidly and you want the most recent information you can find to be sure there are no significant changes in the principles you're uncovering. To update your research in legal encyclopedias, turn to the "pocket part" at the end of the volume you are using. A "pocket part" is a supplement printed by the publisher at more frequent intervals than the main volume can be reprinted. Librarians then insert this "pocket part" either in the front or in the back of the volume the pocket part is updating so that you have access to the absolute latest information possible. In the pocket part of the volume you have been using, look up the Topic and Section you just summarized. Are there any changes to the text?:

Are there any new cases listed? If so, list at least one here:

Step 8: Turn now to the encyclopedia you have <u>not</u> been using. Write the name of that encyclopedia here: _____. In this other encyclopedia, find a Section closely related to the one you've been working on. Read that Section and put its complete cite here (be sure to check the pocket part, too):

Did you learn anything new from this entry?:

You may now reshelve all national encyclopedia volumes before moving on to the next section.

2. State Encyclopedias

Many states have their own encyclopedias that serve the same purpose as a national encyclopedia, but are focused solely on that state's law. When you are dealing with a question such as this one that will almost surely fall under the domain of your state court system, there is often no reason to begin your research with a national encyclopedia if your state has a local one. If your state does not have its own encyclopedia, you may move on to the next section now. If it does, take a few minutes to become familiar with that encyclopedia. Write a paragraph in the space below comparing your state's position on the topic you are researching with what you learned from the national encyclopedias.

B. FINDING ARTICLES IN LEGAL PERIODICALS

Introduction: The most widely regarded legal periodical articles are those found in "law reviews." A "law review" is a major academic journal. Law reviews are published by all of the leading law schools in the country. The University of North Carolina School of Law, for example, publishes The North Carolina Law Review.

There are many specialized law school journals as well. At UNC, for example, we also publish The North Carolina Journal of International Law and Commercial Regulation, the journal of The Banking Institute, The Journal of Law and Technology, and The First Amendment Law Review. As a rule, periodical articles shed new light on a subject (whereas the encyclopedias you have just used do not raise questions about existing law nor challenge cases in depth). Such articles can be used effectively by lawyers to try to persuade a court to reconsider its prior position in a particular area of law. This part of your Assignment Sheet is designed to help you find an article in a law school journal or other periodical on the subject raised by your partner's memo.

ONLINE TIP: Online research has led to the birth of new scholarly sources, beyond traditional law school journals. The Social Science Research Network (SSRN) is one such source. If your law school subscribes to SSRN, you will have access as a law student to some works in progress of many recognized scholars who post online at www.ssrn.com for scholarly comments from colleagues. Blogs are also a prevalent source of background information and scholarly comment about the law, with blogs of well-recognized experts being more credible than institutionally generated blogs or blogs of authors who are less well-established. A number of sources are available to search for available law-related blogs. Try BlawgSearch <blawgsearch.justia.com> or Google Blog Search <blogsearch.google.com>.

BEWARE: Accessing copies of journals in print format has been a mainstay of competent legal research for decades. Today many journals can also be accessed online. If you search for a journal article online using free or fee-based services and databases, be aware of possible limitations in years of coverage. You may miss important historical perspectives unintentionally.

Step 1: To complete this section of your assignment, you may use EITHER hard copy research techniques or online research techniques to locate an article on point. You should use the method that is consistent with your professor's wishes and that is supported by the materials in your law library. In the space below, indicate whether you will use an electronic (online) index or a print (hard copy) index to locate a journal article:

_____ I will be searching a print index

_____ I will be searching an online index

_____ I will be searching both an online and a print index

If you are searching a print index, or plan to search both in print and online, go immediately to Step 2 below. If you are searching online only, go immediately to Step 5 below.

Step 2: (begin here and proceed through Step 4 only if you're searching using a print index): When you are using hard copy research techniques, legal periodicals can be found by using either the Index to Legal Periodicals and Books or the Current Law Index. Often it is beneficial to search both. **Go to the location in your library where these resources are shelved.**

Step 3: Choosing one or the other of these resources, take down the latest volume that you can find on the shelf. Using any of the search topics you found profitable in Section A (Encyclopedias) above, find a reference to one interesting article and write its citation here, following the **CITATION TIP** below. (Note, if you are not able to find an article on point in the most recent volume, go back chronologically until you are successful – or try a broader or a more narrow search term.) Write the citation to your article here:

CITATION TIP: Check out Table T.13 in your <u>Bluebook</u> or Appendix 5 of <u>The ALWD Manual</u> for a complete listing of proper abbreviations for almost all widely used legal periodicals. In general, see Rule 16 of <u>The Bluebook</u> or Rule 23 of <u>The ALWD Manual</u> for directions on how to properly cite periodicals.

BEWARE: Each volume of the <u>Index to Legal Periodicals and Books</u> and of the <u>Current Law Index</u> only contains references to articles published during the time noted on the binding of that volume. Hence, to find older articles, you have to pull older volumes down (one at a time), which tends to be tedious.

Step 4: Once you have located an article using a hard copy index, you can try your hand at using an online index by following Steps 5-7 below, or you can proceed immediately to Step 8. **Before proceeding, please return all volumes of the <u>Index to Legal Periodicals and Books</u> or the <u>Current Law Index</u> so that others may use them.**

Step 5: <u>(begin here and proceed through Step 6 only if you are searching using an online index)</u>: LegalTrac is an online periodical index that is available in most academic libraries. You can search LegalTrac a number of ways (by keyword, subject, author, title, etc.) to find an article of potential interest. Begin first by finding the link to LegalTrac through your library's online catalogue.

ONLINE TIP: Your library may or may not provide access to LegalTrac. If your library does not provide access to LegalTrac, ask a librarian or search your library's online catalogue to see if an alternate online periodical index is available. Be cautious with online indexes. Many databases cover only recent articles. LegalTrac itself only indexes articles published since 1980 and for some periodicals its coverage is even more reduced. For articles published before 1980, you could use the print version of the <u>Index to Legal Periodicals and Books</u> or the <u>Current Law Index</u>. HeinOnline is another excellent tool (available by subscription) for online retrieval of law-related journal articles (and other materials as well). HeinOnline has made a point of providing full coverage for many journals, dating back often to the beginning of a journal's publication. You can check your school's online catalogue to see if HeinOnline is available to you.

Step 6: Once you are on the LegalTrac homepage, choose "search by keyword." In the space below, write down a keyword or several keywords that might yield profitable results for you. After you have entered your keyword search terms, hit "search" (not browse).

How many articles did your search yield? (The number of articles yielded will show up under the tab for the kind of journal (e.g., academic journal, magazine, book, etc.) searched.) _____

To familiarize yourself further with LegalTrac, repeat your search, choosing to search by subject instead. In what way were your results different in this search?

ONLINE TIP: Articles from law reviews and other journals (and other secondary resources such as Continuing Legal Education materials) can be found online through Lexis and Westlaw and other fee-based providers, and also through a number of free websites available on the internet. Google Scholar <scholar.google.com> is a free option for online searching of scholarly articles related to the law and other fields. As with all online searches, be aware of the limitations of the database you're accessing before relying whole-heartedly on your results. You will have the opportunity to learn more about techniques for searching secondary sources electronically in the supplement to this workbook.

Step 7: In the space below, write the name and citation to a particular article that looks like it would be useful in your research for your client:

CITATION TIP: Check out Table T.13 in your <u>Bluebook</u> or Appendix 5 of <u>The ALWD Manual</u> for a complete listing of proper abbreviations for almost all widely used legal periodicals. In general, see Rule 16 of <u>The Bluebook</u> or Rule 23 of <u>The ALWD Manual</u> for directions on how to properly cite periodical materials.

Step 8: Even in this day of widespread access to computers, it is useful to know how to find an article in print copy. Studies show that most readers vastly prefer to read a print version of a long document than an online version, and that many readers often get more out of what they read in print than what they read online. In most law libraries, periodicals are shelved alphabetically. Go to the location in your library where periodicals are shelved. If the article you want to read is in a very current journal, ask for it at the Circulation Desk.

Once you have a title and author for an article, you may locate it now in hard copy. (Alternatively, you may locate the article online, but only if online access is permitted by your professor). Ask your professor or a law librarian if you need further direction.

Once you have located the article you would like to read, skim it and summarize the author's main points in the space that follows:

Step 9: If you were a practicing attorney, in what way might this article have been useful to you as you considered the question raised by your partner about your client?

C. OTHER KINDS OF SECONDARY RESOURCES

Legal encyclopedias and legal periodicals (journal articles) are only two of the many kinds of secondary sources that are indispensable sources of information about the law. Chapter 2 of *Legal Research in a Nutshell* sets out several important additional resources. Read that chapter or a comparable chapter in one of the textbooks listed in Appendix A to learn more about the many other secondary resources available for your use.

1. Treatises and Hornbooks: Perhaps the most significant of these other secondary resources are legal treatises and hornbooks. A *legal treatise* is a definitive treatment of a particular area of law, often containing several volumes, which includes both text and references to cases and other primary resources. A *hornbook* is a similar respected scholarly work, but often printed in only one volume and often targeted to law students. Both treatises and hornbooks are generally viewed as being more scholarly and reliable treatments of a subject than is an encyclopedia. A treatise is frequently written by a recognized expert in a given field, usually a law professor, and is often cited in court opinions. A hornbook, by contrast, is generally shorter and more to the point. Like a treatise, however, it is generally written by a recognized expert in the field and is an excellent source of general scholarly information on a given topic. There are both national treatises and state treatises on many broad legal topics.

If you have time, you should look for a treatise that covers the general area of law that addresses your partner's question (for example, if your question concerns the tort of slander, look for a *treatise* on Tort Law; if your question concerns breach of contract, look for a *treatise* on Contract Law, etc.). Use the index or table of contents of the treatise you have found to identify a relevant section and see what you can learn about how the resource might be helpful to you. *If you are a law student, you will find that a treatise or hornbook can also help clarify complex areas of law that you are studying in class.*

> **TIP:** You can use your library's online catalogue to find treatises on almost any legal topic, or ask at the reference desk of your law library for recommendations about the most widely recognized treatises in the area you are researching. Additionally, faculty members who teach in a defined area of law often have specific treatises that they recommend to students. Many law libraries keep national and state treatises on reserve at their reference desks.

2. Restatements: Restatements are another important secondary source that can help you understand trends in the law. *Restatements* are collections of summaries of the common law (or, in some cases, predictions of what the common law rules may become) that have been drafted by leaders in the legal community through the American Law Institute. These "restatements" of the law are frequently relied on by judges to clarify the common law in their jurisdiction as they try to resolve a particular case in controversy, but a Restatement of the law is NOT primary law itself. There are Restatements available on a wide variety of common law topics (e.g., the Restatement on Contracts, the Restatement on Torts, etc.). If you have time, you should look through a Restatement and see how it could help you learn more about the topic your senior partner has asked you to explore. If you are a law student, you may remember having seen references to Restatements in your casebooks and perhaps even cited within cases contained in your casebooks.

ONLINE TIP: Both Westlaw and Lexis carry databases that give you access to leading hornbooks and treatises, as well as the Restatements. Check with each service to see specifically what materials are searchable.

D. TYING IT ALL TOGETHER

Now that you've had a chance to read a number of resources addressing the subject raised by your senior partner, it would be helpful to synthesize what you've learned. Please use the space provided to write a paragraph addressing your partner's question. As you write your paragraph, bear in mind that the purpose of this assignment was more to learn how to use the research materials than to find a reliable answer at this early stage of research. It is a good habit in legal writing to make sure that your reader is focused from the beginning on the exact legal question you are addressing. With that goal in mind, be sure to clearly identify the question you are answering at the beginning of your paragraph.

Congratulations! You have just completed your first assignment sheet on encyclopedias and periodicals. Based on the work you have done, we hope you have learned a little about the law covering your partner's question. More importantly, you should now have an idea of how to use some valuable secondary resources to learn about law.

Please note your actual time of completion (including background reading): _____ *hrs.*

TIP: Remember, as you work through these Assignment Sheets, if you find that you are spending a lot more time on the assignments than what has been recommended at the top of the first page of the Assignment Sheet, take a minute to think about what may be happening.

If this assignment took longer than you expected, the ideas in the following **TIME-SAVING TIP** might help you for future assignments. On the other hand, it may be that your learning style or your learning goals are such that you prefer to linger over the questions raised in this workbook. If that is the case, and you have the time to spare, do not worry about our estimated times of completion. Enjoy yourself and just recognize that the learning process will take longer than we anticipated.

TIME-SAVING TIP: If you are having difficulty completing these lessons in the time recommended, consider the following: (1) Are you sure you have a completely clear understanding of the partner's question as you're doing your research? Legal research can be very intriguing and it's easy to spend lots of time browsing (which is fun, but not necessary to learn what these lessons are designed to teach you); (2) Are you seeking perfection? Each of our questions is designed to give you lots of latitude as you explore these materials – there is rarely only one right answer to any question. Once you've found some materials that seem relevant and you've learned what you want to know in any given exercise, move on to the next step and don't worry about having the perfect answer; (3) Are you asking for help when you need it?; (4) Are you doing your research at the optimal time? It is hard to get your hands on material at peak research hours, and most students find they learn more and take less time if they do their exercises when the library is less crowded.

As with any learning task, it's important to remember that you're the student here. You are not expected to know all the answers yet. There are resources available to help you if you get stuck at any point. Most law librarians are willing to help you if you are having difficulty. In addition, the research guidelines and tips provided on our website <www.LegalResearchWorkbook.com> can point you in the right direction if you get off course. Ask your professor for the password if you are associated with a class, or contact Professor McKinney at ramckinn@email.unc.edu if you are using this workbook on your own.

MARSHALL, STORY & ASSOCIATES
ATTORNEYS AND COUNSELORS AT LAW
SUITE 101, THE JUSTICE BUILDING

⚖

THE LITIGATION DIVISION

To: New Associate
From: Assigning Partner
Re: Eric Arnold [Client A] – File #03-2576

Thank you for the research you did concerning the law controlling ownership of found property. As a result of your research, Mr. Arnold took the tools to Mr. Joyner to see if he recognized them. Mr. Joyner spontaneously said, "My goodness – look what you've found! I thought those tools were long gone. Haven't seen them in years. They were my father's. I guess, though, I've lost all rights to them now." Although Mr. Arnold was disappointed that the tools weren't, in fact, from his own family he was pleased to explain the law to Mr. Joyner and to return the tools to him.

Mr. Arnold now comes to us with a new question. He hired a local carpenter to help him restore a small barn and build a new holding bin there. When the carpenter left for the weekend, he asked Mr. Arnold if he could store his power tools in the barn until he returned on Monday. Mr. Arnold agreed. That night, a big storm came up and lightning struck the barn. The carpenter's equipment was lost in the damage that followed.

Being from the city, Mr. Arnold is concerned that he may be sued by the carpenter for the loss of the power tools. He is worried that he should have gone to extraordinary measures to protect the equipment, such as bringing it into his house for safekeeping.

I believe Mr. Arnold is holding himself to too high a standard and do not believe he is at risk for losing a lawsuit based in negligence. Would you help me confirm my initial reactions by researching our state's common law on the topic of bailments (a bailment occurs when someone holds property for someone else). Specifically, can you see what standard of care a property owner needs to practice when storing property in a bailment, like this one, that mutually benefits both parties?

▶▶ Turn to page 65 to begin your work on this assignment.

MARSHALL, STORY & ASSOCIATES
ATTORNEYS AND COUNSELORS AT LAW
SUITE 101, THE JUSTICE BUILDING

⚖

THE LITIGATION DIVISION

To: New Associate
From: Assigning Partner
Re: Project Hope [Client B] – File #03-2575

Thank you for your research on whether our potential students may have a right to participate in the local public school sports program. The Board found your work both helpful and interesting.

As the Board continues to make progress towards the opening of this new school, they have run into a potentially costly problem. Surprised by the ground swell of economic support they have received, the Board realized they will be in a position to build their own facility within two years. To that end, finding land on which to build a school has become an important priority.

Last month, the Chair of the Board, Traci Chen, was approached by Todd Baylor, head of the local realty association, who told Ms. Chen that he had a proposal that might be of interest to Project Hope. In a nutshell, he described a forty-five acre tract of land that he said was perfectly suited for a small school. The problem, he said, was that the local public school system was interested in the land and was rumored to be considering a purchase of the land – through the power of eminent domain if necessary – within the next several months. Knowing suitable land was at a premium, Ms. Chen brought the information to the Board's immediate attention and they began negotiations with Mr. Baylor.

During those negotiations, the Board emphasized the importance of having enough suitable land to develop several athletic fields for physical education, and also a construction site for the use of students who would be studying the building trades. In response, Mr. Baylor, who also operates a licensed surveying company, presented a number of drawings that he said confirmed the suitability of the site for those kinds of activities.

Satisfied that the site would work well, and feeling pressure because of Mr. Baylor's representations that the local School Board was also interested in the property, the Board gave Mr. Baylor a $10,000 cash deposit to hold the land for them for six months while they raised additional funds.

A member of the Project Hope Board of Directors who has worked as an environmental engineer has now had a chance to study the land site in detail. He has determined,

continued on next page

definitively, that the site is not only unsuitable for development of a school and any athletic facilities, but that Mr. Baylor's drawings of the site misrepresented the topography of the land. Furthermore, he has found through contacts he has with government agencies that Mr. Baylor knew full well that the land was unsuitable and, in fact, a prior Environmental Impact Statement developed for the property indicated that there were rare fossil deposits on the land that would prohibit excavation at all.

The Board has contacted Mr. Baylor directly with this information and he has refused to return their $10,000 deposit and void the contract for sale of the land. The Board has turned to us for legal advice.

While it has been some time since I have done work in this area, my instincts are that Mr. Baylor's representations may well constitute fraud under the common law principles followed in our state. I would appreciate your researching this matter for us. Specifically, please look into the common law requirements for the establishment of an action for fraud or fraudulent misrepresentation in our jurisdiction. Do not research the area of damages. For now, I would just like to know whether Mr. Baylor's action may constitute the tort of fraud.

Baylor suggests 45 acre tract of land as suitable
Baylor knew school needed construction site + athletic fields
Baylor knew land was unsuitable when he made the deal.
  - Environmental Impact Statement ⇒ rare fossils

Baylor obviously, through his profession in real estate and property surveying, he knew suitable land was at a premium. (Just like Ms. Chen did).
        - said a public school was interested and would
   use eminent domain power to get it if necessary
        - $10,000 deposit unreturned + sale not void.

Contract under false pretenses
fraud
fraudulent misrepresentation.

▶▶ Turn to page 65 to begin your work on this assignment.

MARSHALL, STORY & ASSOCIATES
ATTORNEYS AND COUNSELORS AT LAW
SUITE 101, THE JUSTICE BUILDING

⚖️

THE LITIGATION DIVISION

To: New Associate
From: Assigning Partner
Re: Marjorie Morrison [Client C] - File #21-2203

Thank you for the research you completed concerning a general overview of the law of slander as it relates to political figures. Based on that information, I am more confident than ever that Ms. Morrison may not be liable for slander or defamation at all.

I met with Ms. Morrison earlier this week and found that her statements concerning Mr. Thompson's alleged illegal activities may be true. Specifically, we talked again about Mr. Thompson's production, distribution, and transportation of wine from his home and it seems to me that he may well be violating a number of statutes and regulations. Before we look into the matter further, however, I need to know if his case against Ms. Morrison will be weakened if we can show that her allegations were true all along.

My understanding from talking with Mr. Thompson's attorney is that it is his intent to base his suit for slander on common law principles established in this state over time. Thus, while the general information we have learned concerning slander is interesting, I now need to know what the specific common law principles are in our state concerning this topic. I am particularly interested in finding out if truth is a complete defense to slander under our state's common law and would appreciate your looking into this matter at your earliest convenience.

▶▶ Turn to page 65 to begin your work on this assignment.

MARSHALL, STORY & ASSOCIATES

ATTORNEYS AND COUNSELORS AT LAW
SUITE 101, THE JUSTICE BUILDING

⚖

THE LITIGATION DIVISION

To: New Associate
From: Assigning Partner
Re: Allen Field [Client D] - File #21-2204

Thank you for the research you completed concerning a general overview of the law of nuisance and whether noise and air pollution can constitute a nuisance. Based on that information, I am more confident than ever that Dr. Field may be able to compel the restaurant next door to modify its current activities.

Before I proceed any further, however, I need to have more specific information about our own state's common law on nuisance. While it is helpful to have a general overview, our own state's specific rules are what will govern any judicial decision in Dr. Field's case. Hence, it is important that we now move forward to learn more about how our jurisdiction views nuisance.

For your next assignment, I would appreciate your looking into our state's common law to determine the general principles that are applied here to determine when a nuisance exists. Also, without putting in too much additional time, please try to determine if noise and/or air pollution can be the basis of a nuisance suit in this state.

▶▶ Turn to page 65 to begin your work on this assignment.

MARSHALL, STORY & ASSOCIATES
ATTORNEYS AND COUNSELORS AT LAW
SUITE 101, THE JUSTICE BUILDING

⚖

THE LITIGATION DIVISION

To: New Associate
From: Assigning Partner
Re: Josh Ward [Client E] - File #21-2205

Thank you for the research you completed concerning how specific a path needs to be in order to establish an easement by prescription. Based on the information you provided, we are confident that the majority of residents crossing Mr. Ward's land will have difficulty providing proof of the establishment of an easement.

Unfortunately, we have now heard that there is one elderly gentleman who claims to have followed the same path across Mr. Ward's land for at least fifty years. That gentleman has stated publicly that he intends to pursue a claim against Mr. Ward if any additional efforts are made to keep people off the property.

If this gentleman follows through on his threats to sue, his claim would be based on common law principles established in this state over time. Thus, I now need to know what the specific common law principles are in our state concerning the manner in which someone must use another's land if he or she wishes to establish an easement (or right to use the land) by prescription. I would appreciate your looking into this matter at your earliest convenience and reporting back to me with the information you find.

▶▶ Turn to page 65 to begin your work on this assignment.

Assignment Sheet 2 *in Sequence of Assignments #1* **Finding Common Law**	Estimated Time of Completion (including recommended background reading): 4.0 – 5.0 hrs.
Print Your Name:	

(If you are doing this assignment as part of a class exercise, neatly write your answers directly on these sheets, staple all sheets together, and turn them in. If you prefer to write your answers separately using a computer, please be sure to number your answers to correspond to the appropriate questions before printing your answer sheets.)

Background Reading: To learn more about the resources and concepts introduced in this Assignment Sheet, read Chapters 3 and 4 in *Legal Research in a Nutshell* or a comparable chapter in a textbook assigned by your professor. (See Appendix A.)

Background Information: The common law of your state controls the question raised by your senior partner. Re-read pages 18-19 in Chapter 3 of this workbook to learn more about the common law. To answer the question which has been raised, you will need to find judicial opinions from your state appellate courts that will show you how courts in this state have decided controversies like this one in the past. From time to time when you are doing common law research, you also need to know what courts in other states have held about similar problems. Such out-of-state cases can be helpful where there is no law on point in your state or where you want to try to persuade your court to change its view to be more like that of other states. Consequently, the exercises in this assignment will also teach you how to find what a court from another state might have decided about the common law question raised by your senior partner.

What You Will Learn. By the end of this assignment, you will:

- Know how to use an "annotated" digest ("West's Digest") to find cases
- Understand how to use West's Key Number System to find related cases by subject in all jurisdictions
- Understand how to use the American Law Reports (A.L.R.) to find common law cases and accompanying articles exploring legal issues raised in those cases
- Be able to cite and write a student "brief" of a case
- Understand the importance of updating your common law research
- Know how to use "citators" to update your common law research (make sure it's still "good law") and to find additional cases and materials on the same subject

The Research Process:
A. FINDING STATE COMMON LAW USING WEST'S STATE DIGESTS

Step 1: Since you do not know the name or citation to a case on this topic yet, one good place to start is in West's <u>Digest</u> for your individual state. The official title of the volume you will want to use would be <u>West's [your state's name] Digest</u> (e.g., <u>West's North Carolina Digest</u>). The <u>Digest</u> is usually shelved at the end of your state's "reporters," although in some large libraries it is shelved at the end of your state's *regional* reporter instead. Remember, a "reporter" is what lawyers call the books containing the published opinions of a court. Go back to the TIP on pp. 43-44 in this workbook to review more about reporters. **Go now to the location in your library where the <u>Digest</u> for your state is shelved. (See TIP below.) When you have located your state's <u>Digest</u>, write its full name (as set out on the bindings for each volume) here:**

[handwritten in left margin: West's NY Digest]

[handwritten:] ① NY Digest 4th -48- 1978 to Date -Descriptive Word Index
② West's NY Digest 4th -9A (contracts)

> **TIP:** For whatever reason, Delaware, Nevada, and Utah do not have separate West <u>Digests</u> corresponding to their reporters. If you are doing research in one of those states, you should instead use the regional digest to find cases for that state.

Step 2: West's state and national digest system is a comprehensive research tool that provides a method for locating written court opinions that have been published in an area of law in which you need to find precedent. As you learned in Chapter 2, "Fundamentals of Legal Reasoning," you would want to find precedent on a topic when you need to know how a court in your jurisdiction has treated similar cases in the past – in that way, you will know what principles a court would apply in your case to reach a just result. The West digest system, which was initiated over a century ago and remains equally vital today, gave lawyers a tool for finding chronologically published cases by *subject*.

Under the West digest system, all opinions are divided into subjects that cover the legal "Topics" raised in the case. For example you would find all cases about home schooling grouped together, and this whole cluster of cases would be located as a sub-topic under the general "Topic" heading of "Schools." The trick, then, to finding cases that would shed light on how a court might treat the question raised by your partner is to figure out the general Topic and then any sub-topics under which the West <u>Digest</u> publishers have clustered cases resolving these types of controversies in the past. (For example, in the above hypothetical, there would have been nothing illogical about starting a search for cases dealing with home

---

schooling by looking up the term "education." Eventually, though, you would have found that the West publishers have grouped the cases about home schooling under the Topic "Schools" instead.)

Finding where the West publishers have clustered your cases requires some brainstorming and guessing at first – the more research you do, the more familiar you will be with the terms Thomson-West uses to identify major legal "Topics" and sub-topics. For now, take down any volume of West's <u>Digest</u> for your state and look at the list of Topic headings (called Digest Topics) printed near the beginning of the volume. <u>In the space below, write the Topic heading that you think is most likely to cover our client's controversy</u>:

Fraud [handwritten]

Likely Topic we'd use [handwritten margin note]

(Remember: identifying the correct Topic in West's <u>Digest</u> is something of a hit and miss proposition at first. Don't get discouraged. Ask questions if your ideas aren't working). <u>If you find you want to explore more than one Topic heading, write additional Topics here</u>:

Fraudulent Misrepresentation [handwritten]
Contracts, c [handwritten]

Add'l topics [handwritten margin note]

TIP: When using print materials, you can use the <u>Descriptive Word Index</u> to find promising Topic headings and subtopic headings. The <u>Descriptive Word Index</u> for each <u>Digest</u> system is generally shelved in close proximity to the <u>Digest</u> volumes. You can use this Index to find the "buzz words" which the West editors associate with the legal concept you're exploring.

Step 3: Once you have located a potential Topic heading, your next step is to narrow your search by locating appropriate sub-topics that may yield cases that have dealt with the same legal questions raised by your client. You will find appropriate sub-topic headings by pulling the volume of West's state <u>Digest</u> that contains the Topic heading you've decided to explore. As with encyclopedias, Topic headings are arranged alphabetically in the West Digest volumes. The first page of the Topic section includes a helpful summary of the concepts covered under that general Topic heading. Skimming those summaries is often a good way to get other ideas about where to look for relevant cases. Take down the volume containing a Topic heading you chose above.

Topic; West Volume [handwritten margin note]

Scan the sub-topic headings listed in the Table of Contents (called an "Analysis") on the first page of your Topic. In the space below, write down some sub-topic headings that look interesting:

Some interesting sub-topics ↘

concealment, contracts

You will note that the sub-topic headings in the Table of Contents are preceded by a little key icon followed by a number and perhaps further followed by a number in parentheses. These numbers are called "West Key Numbers" and are a rich source of legal research information. Carefully read Chapter 4 of *Legal Research in a Nutshell* or a comparable chapter from another legal research textbook covered in Appendix A for a detailed overview of how the Key Number system works. You can also check the **"TIP"** immediately below for an introductory explanation of the system. <u>It is critical that you learn to use this system to be an efficient researcher</u>. In the space below, write down the Topic heading, key number, and corresponding sub-topic heading that appears to have potential for further investigation:

⚷ 94 (Fraud
    94(8) - suppression of Truth

Fraud

ⓣ **TIP (The Key Number System):** The West Key Number System is unique to the field of legal research and can be challenging to use at first. Because there is no parallel in non-legal research, it's hard to get your mind around it. Once you get a grasp of how the system works, however, it can be extremely useful to you.

The trick to understanding the West Key Number System is understanding how many different publications are distributed by Thomson-West, whose founder created the system. All these publications are interconnected by Key Numbers assigned by Topic so that you can move from one resource to another without having to go through indexes once you know a Key Number that is relevant to the question you're trying to answer. The Key Numbers are assigned to the West <u>Digest</u> "Topics" you are exploring in this assignment sheet. Thus, under the West Key Number System, let's say that you want to research a question about home schooling. The Topic and Key Number for that subject is "Schools 160.7."

continued on next page

Once you know that Topic name and its corresponding Key Number, you can turn to Schools 160.7 in any other state's <u>Digest</u> (which are all published by Thomson-West) and find annotations to cases addressing standards for home schools. The Key Number system is used in <u>C.J.S.</u> (originally published by West) and less extensively in <u>Am. Jur.</u> (recently acquired by West). You can also use Key Numbers when you do electronic research on Westlaw (but not on any other service provider).

ONLINE TIP: You can use the enormous power of Key Numbers in your online search as well as in hard copy. To begin from the "Welcome to Westlaw" main page or "Law School Classic" page, select the yellow-highlighted "Key Numbers" link from the top of the page. You will then find a number of options for using West Key Numbers to your advantage.

TIP (Headnotes): In addition to using Key Numbers to tie its many publications together, Thomson-West prints "headnotes" at the beginning of all cases that it publishes. Other publishers print similar "headnotes" at the beginning of cases they publish. A headnote is a short summary of a major point of law decided in a case. Each of these headnotes in any of the many Thomson-West Regional or State <u>Reporters</u> is assigned the corresponding Key Number dealing with the legal issue addressed in the headnote. Thus, if I were reading a case that raised a question about home schooling, the headnote (short explanatory paragraph) corresponding to that point would be numbered and would have the appropriate Key Number [Schools 160.7] printed next to it. These headnotes comprise the annotations that are cross-referenced in the <u>Digest</u> you are learning to use as a "finding tool." As you can see, once I find one case or even a <u>C.J.S.</u> entry on point, I'd have the "key" to finding any number of other cases on point simply by following the Key Number through other Thomson-West publications. With caution (see the BOMB immediately below), you can also use references to headnotes in the text of the opinion itself to focus your reading. In any case published by Thomson-West, references to a specific headnote (for example, Headnote 2) show up as a bracketed number in the margin of the text (for example, [2]) next to the area of the case from which the headnote arose.

BEWARE: Headnotes and Key Numbers are a great tool for legal researchers to use – in hard copy and online – to focus their search for cases that could be on point, but headnotes should *never* be used as a shortcut for actually reading a promising case. Headnotes are not part of an opinion – they are written by private editors working for the publishing companies that publish cases. Also, in general, headnote numbers are not universal among publishers. Rather, headnote numbers correspond with the subject-grouping system of each individual company.

ONLINE TIP: Headnotes can be used online as well as in print format to make your search for cases more efficient. West Key Numbers, which correspond with headnotes in cases published by Thomson-West, can be used extensively in online research on Westlaw and corresponding Thomson-West CD products. Cases found on Westlaw are hyperlinked by headnote Topic and Key Number to other cases and materials carried in the Westlaw databases. On Westlaw, use the Key Number feature to retrieve documents quickly using West Key Numbers. Lexis publications have their own headnote and Lexis has recently adopted an online legal topic grouping system (called the "LexisNexis Legal Taxonomy"). As of the time of the printing of this workbook, you could search for cases by headnotes or by subject area on Lexis by selecting "Search" on the homepage toolbar, and then using the "Search by Topic or Headnote" tab option. Note that, with a few exceptions for specific states [California, Montana, New Hampshire, New York, Ohio, Vermont, and Washington], the headnotes referenced on Lexis are increasingly less likely to be the same headnotes you'll see if you are reading a case published in a Thomson-West Reporter.

ANOTHER TIP: When you are first faced with a legal problem or question, one good way to begin is to brainstorm using the "5 Ws" covered in introductory journalism classes (Who, What, When, Where, and Why). See the TIP on page 39 of this workbook for a review of this concept. When you are able to locate appropriate terms in the <u>Descriptive Word Index</u>, the Index will indicate a Key Number for each section listed. See the Key Number TIP above to learn how to use these Key Numbers to quickly locate cases on point in many Thomson-West publications.

Step 4: Now that you have your Topic and Key Numbers, it is a simple matter to find cases that could be worth reading. Turn to the Key Number you want to explore in the section of "annotated" (summarized) cases which immediately follows the Table of Contents ("Analysis") in the state <u>Digest</u> you've been using. You will note that the cases under your Key Number are listed in reverse chronological order and by the court of decision. Thus, federal cases are listed first with the most current federal Court of Appeals cases appearing before earlier ones; federal Court of Appeals cases are followed by federal District Court cases in the same reverse chronological order. Likewise, the most recent state Supreme Court cases (if your state's supreme court is its highest court) are then listed in reverse chronological order, followed by the state's Court of Appeals cases (if your state has lower courts of appeal), in the same reverse chronological order. For this assignment, please locate an interesting case on point **that was decided in a state court before 1980** and write its name and the citation noted at the end of the annotation here (if there is no case cited earlier than 1980, skip this step):

Mallory v Watt
100 Idaho 119   594 P.2d 629

early case
late case

Next, locate an interesting case on point **that was decided in a state court sometime in the 1990's or later** and write its name and the citation noted at the end of the annotation here:

Next, turn to the "pocket part" at the back of the entire volume to see if there are any very recent cases on point. Turn to the Topic and Key Number you've been using and write the name and citation of a very recent case on point here. (Note: if there is no current case in the pocket part on the key number you've been using, look for a related Key Number and write the name and citation for that case here, together with the new topic and Key Number):

Pocket Part

90's
case

Finally, you will need to check the "Cumulative Pamphlet" for updates. The Cumulative Pamphlet is a paperback book that includes updates beyond those that have been added through the pocket parts. In the Cumulative Pamphlet, find the Topic and Key Number you've been using and note here if you saw any additional updates:

---

t TIP: When doing common law research, it is often important to read an array of cases on a particular topic to see how the common law on point has evolved over time. While newer cases affirm the current state of the law, older cases help you establish what the law used to be and help you understand the reasoning behind a rule of law. If you are arguing for a change in the law or that the current law should not be applied to your situation, knowing how the law has evolved over the years can be critical. Also, when you read cases, keep in mind that you are not just reading to find a rule statement. Rather, you are reading each case to understand what rule this court applied to a specific set of facts and *why* the court decided as it did.

We have finished using West's <u>Digest</u> for your state for now. Please reshelve all volumes so that others may use them.

Step 5: The next step in searching for case law on point is to go to the actual decision itself and read it. **<u>Never</u>** rely on the <u>Digest</u> annotations by themselves to tell you what the law in any given area might be. Like the headnotes they duplicate, the annotations are merely the summarized opinion of an individual editor; they are not part of the opinion of the court. You may not agree with what the editor thought the holding of the case was or you may find that the annotation is not an accurate representation of the nuances of the case as they relate to your client's situation.

Choose one of the cases that you cited in <u>Step 4</u> above to read. To find that case, go to either your state reporter system (if your state has its own reporter system) or go to the regional reporter for your state if there is no state reporter system. If you are in a state reporter system, make sure you are in the reporter for the court that decided your case (for example, in North Carolina the N.C. Supreme Court cases are published in the North Carolina <u>Reports</u> whereas the North Carolina Court of Appeals cases are published in the N.C. Court of Appeals <u>Reports</u>). Most law libraries have several sets of reporters (either state and/or regional) that are easily located by call number or by following your library's key and/or map to major resources.

Find the volume and page number of the case you have selected and read that case now.

TIP: As you learned in Assignment Sheet 1, the first number in a citation to a case refers to the volume number of that reporter, the letters between designate the reporter in which the case is published, the next number represents the page number in the volume where the case begins, and the date in parentheses represents the year the case was decided. Where you have a citation to a state reporter followed by a parallel citation to a regional reporter, you can find the case in either volume.

BEWARE: In some states, if you are looking for an extremely old case, you may be unable to find the case you want to read on the page where its citation indicates it should begin. That is because old cases were sometimes published in one format and, over the years, have been republished in a different format requiring repagination. For the sake of consistency, however, all citations to old cases still refer to the original, old page numbers. Where there is a mismatch of pages between the original publication and a newer edition, the publisher will put the original page numbers in parentheses alongside the text in the new publication. Thus, if you're looking for an extremely old case and find it doesn't begin on the page indicated by its citation, look along the outside margins for numbers in parentheses. These numbers are the page numbers from the original volumes and will correspond to the page numbers in the cite you have. Similarly, if you are looking at the regional reporter version of a case from a state that also has a state reporter, the regional reporter version indicates page breaks from the state reporter version in the margin of its text.

Step 6: Good legal research requires good note-taking. While you still have the case that you have read open, please do a careful "brief" of that case in the space provided on the following pages. If you are a law student, you may already know how to "brief" a case. If not, the following information might help get you started: writing a "brief" is a way to take notes about a case that will help you focus on the aspects of the case that are important to legal decision-makers. As a rule, most students of the law learn to read cases by taking notes in the following manner: (1) they put the name and citation for the case at the top of the page; (2) they next indicate the parties involved in the controversy in a way that will remind them who they were; (3) they then indicate the procedural history of the case – how did this case get to the appellate court?; (4) they synthesize the relevant facts (enough to "tell the story" of the conflict and to identify the facts that made a difference in the court's decision); (5) next, they briefly state the question before the court – where there are lots of questions, you can just list the one that's relevant to the issue you're concerned about; (6) next they state how the court ruled on that question; and (7) finally, they state briefly what the court's reasoning was.

You can look at Appendix B in this workbook for a sample brief of <u>Gideon v. Wainwright</u>, 372 U.S. 335 (1963), a well-known case in which the U. S. Supreme Court recognized the constitutional right of all accused criminals to be represented by counsel.

Review the following **READING TIP** before proceeding.

READING TIP: When you first begin to read legal cases, it is easy to become confused about how a court might use a case to help make a decision in your situation. Now would be a good time to review Chapter 2, "Fundamentals of Legal Reasoning," beginning on page 11 of this workbook.

Remember, a case must be from your jurisdiction in order to be "binding" (i.e., in order for a judge to be compelled to follow it). In addition, the case must still be "good law." To continue to be "good law," a case must make sense in modern times and it must make sense if applied to the facts in your case. A case is clearly not "good law" if it has been reversed by a later decision in a higher court within the same jurisdiction.

Finally, it is easy to become overwhelmed by all the language in a given case – what is the case really about? In order to keep yourself focused as you read a case, you need to understand the distinction between "dicta" and a "holding." The *holding* in a case is the court's resolution of the particular question before it (and it is not unusual to have more than one question, hence more than one holding). *Dictum*, on the other hand, is anything else the court expresses in the process of reaching the holding. *Dictum* may include the court's opinion of policy, of past holdings, of the parties themselves, or anything else the judge writing the opinion chooses to address. *Dictum* is important because it helps clarify the court's reasoning and can tip you off to the direction in which a court plans to move in the future. The *holding*, on the other hand, is important because it establishes bright-line precedent which the doctrine of stare decisis encourages the court to follow closely when hearing similar cases in the future.

Begin Your Brief Here:

BEWARE (Not All Opinions Are Published): In the preceding Assignment Sheet, and immediately above, you have learned how to locate cases that have been published in state or regional reporters. Remember, however, that not all written opinions of a court are published. As you have learned, some courts elect to publish only select cases (those they believe have precedential value), sending all other written opinions only to the parties involved in the underlying action. Before the onset of widespread computer use, such cases were not widely accessible and many courts adopted rules disallowing or strictly limiting their use as precedent. Today, with multiple fee-based online resources and with many courts and governments maintaining internet websites, "unpublished" cases can be located through computer word searches. Thus, it has become important for lawyers to know what the rules of court are for the jurisdiction they are researching in – will a court there allow lawyers to rely only on published opinions, or may they cite unpublished opinions as well? If they may cite unpublished opinions, what is their ethical obligation to do a thorough search for them? For an interesting article chronicling the debate over the pros and cons of allowing access to unpublished opinions, see Thomas L. Fowler, Unpublished Decisions: Should Precedent Be 'Managed' or Simply Followed? J. N.C. State Bar 16, Summer 2002, at 16.

B. OTHER WAYS TO FIND COMMON LAW

1. Finding Cases Using the American Law Reports (ALR): In the first half of this Assignment Sheet, you learned to use the West's Digest for your state to find case law clarifying the question raised by your senior partner. In Assignment Sheet 1, you learned how to use encyclopedias, periodicals, and treatises to find case law. Another good way to find cases (either at common law or where a court has applied or interpreted a statute) is through the **American Law Reports (ALR)**. If you are using a supplementary research textbook, you should go back and read the chapter covering ALR now (see Appendix A of this workbook for a list of such textbooks).

ALR is a finding tool that is very different from the West Digests you just learned to use in the first part of this Assignment Sheet, but is equally valuable and has many of the "big picture" advantages of a legal encyclopedia as well. ALR contains articles analyzing a selected case that has raised a distinct question of law. Each article discusses the legal ramifications of one case in detail, looking at how other jurisdictions have treated the question of law raised in that case. In addition to exploring a specific question of law in depth through one illustrative case, each ALR article also cites numerous cases from a variety of jurisdictions that have discussed the same or closely-related legal questions. You will learn how to use ALR by following Steps 1 through 4 below. ***Do not use ALR (lst) to complete this assignment – use a later series instead.***

Step 1: Go to the location in your library where __ALR__ is located now.

    Step 2: Using the six-volume __ALR Index__ (and the pocket parts for updating), look for a topic heading which might yield a good discussion of the issue you are trying to research. In most libraries, this Index is shelved at the end of the __ALR__ volumes themselves. (Note there is also an __ALR Quick Index__ that you can use to complete this assignment if you choose.) Again, as with the West __Digest__ system, this kind of index search takes creativity, patience, and at least some sense of serendipity. It gets easier the more experienced you are. Write the topic heading you chose here (note: if the first few topic headings you've chosen don't exist or don't have any annotated references to an __ALR__ article on point, move on until you find one that does):

Fraud + Deceit

33 ALR4d

    Step 3: Using the reference you found in Step 2 above, locate your article in the appropriate volume and __skim__ it. Note that the publishers of __ALR 2d, 3rd, and 4th__ print the main legal case being analyzed by the entry on the pages immediately __preceding__ the page the index leads you to. __ALR 5th__, on the other hand, gives you a reference to all the cases covered in a particular volume and prints them together at the end of that volume. For this assignment, you will not have time to thoroughly read the article (called an "Annotation" by the editors of __ALR__). Rather, your time will be better spent familiarizing yourself with how __ALR__ works and what it can do for you. In the space provided, please write the name and citation of the main case that is being discussed in your annotation and __briefly__ summarize the gist of the annotation here.

Mallory v. Scott (1979)

100 Idaho 117, 594 P2d 629

A real estate broker is an agent standing in a fiduciary relation to his principle +, therefore, is obligated to make full disclosure to his principal of any knowledge the broker may possess which would affect the principal's actions.

Step 4: In the annotations section of the main volume you are using **and** in the pocket parts (for updating), look for cases from your state on point. Write the name and citation for one case from your state that you found here. (If you found none, find a case from a nearby state and write its citation here instead):

> ONLINE TIP: In addition to being available in print copy, ALR is available on Westlaw and provides coverage from ALR lst through 6th as well as ALR FED first and second (exploring federal cases exclusively).

2. Finding Cases and Updating Your Research Using "Citators": A third method for finding relevant cases, and to also update your research to learn more about a case that you have found, is to use a legal "citator." A "citator" is a research tool that allows legal researchers who have found a primary source of law (in the present assignment, a case) to uncover an amazing amount of additional related information quickly.

Shepard's Citators in print form was the original and substantially exclusive legal "citator" system available to lawyers for many decades. Today, lawyers can access citators online (for a fee) using KeyCite on Westlaw or Shepard's on Lexis, or they can access much of the same information using Shepard's (now owned by LexisNexis) in a traditional print format. Updating online is an increasingly popular way to find cases and to confirm that you are relying on law that is current. Online citators are often more readily accessible than the print version and they provide the most current data available.

Regardless of which format you choose, the most important first step is to understand how a citator can help you. A citator allows you to check for all of the following once you have found a case that addresses the legal question you are researching:

- Is your case available to read in more than one reporter?
- Does your case have any "prior history"? (i.e., did this case come before a deciding court at some point *before* the opinion you are holding was decided? For example, if you are holding the state Supreme Court opinion, had this case perhaps been heard at the state Court of Appeals earlier?)
- Does your case have any "subsequent history"? (i.e., did anything happen to your case at some point *after* the opinion you are holding was decided? For example, was the opinion you are holding appealed to a higher court?)
- Have courts referred to the case you are holding when writing other opinions (i.e., was your case used as precedent in another case)? If so, which of the many

legal issues raised in your case (summarized as one or more headnotes) was addressed in the other case?

- If your case was referred to in another case, in what way did the second court make its reference? Did the second court rely favorably on your case, distinguish your case in some way, or reverse or disavow your case?

- Was your case cross-referenced elsewhere (for example, in a legal encyclopedia, in ALR, in comments to a statute, or in a journal article)?

Some of this information available in a citator is important for you to know in order to properly Bluebook the case you are holding in your hand (for example, the prior and subsequent history, and the parallel citation). Other parts of the information available in a citator helps expand your research, giving you other sources to explore as you deepen and broaden your understanding of the question you trying to answer. When you are using a citator to *expand* your research, it is important to recognize that it is an imperfect tool – many of the helpful aids (for example, those that address *how* the next opinion referred to your opinion) are based on subjective editorial decisions with which you may not agree and which may not be all-encompassing.

In this lesson, you will learn to use one or more of these tools (Shepard's online on Lexis, or KeyCite online on Westlaw) to update your common law research and to find additional cases on the common law topic your partner has asked you to research. You also have the option, at your professor's direction, of learning how to update using print materials by turning to Appendix C in the back of this workbook. Westlaw and Lexis screens change with some frequency. If you choose to search online, be sure to check the Errata section of www.LegalResearchWorkbook.com to make sure we have not modified our instructions below.

> IMPORTANT ONLINE TIP: Lawyers pay for use of KeyCite and online Shepard's features either as part of a larger contract with Westlaw or Lexis, or by arranging to charge the cost of an individual citator search to an individual credit card through a one-time fee charge available through Westlaw or Lexis. Although updating materials online provides the most recent data available, a researcher might need to check print copies in an emergency, or when there is no access to online citators, or when economics makes the use of print materials more feasible.

Step 1: In this section, you will be asked to update your research online using Westlaw, OR online using Lexis, OR in hard copy, using traditional print materials. While it's a good idea to learn how to use all three, you will not be required to do so here. In the supplement to this workbook, you'll have an opportunity to use the updating tools for both

Westlaw and Lexis, which is why we don't require you to use both here. In the space below, please indicate how you plan to search for updates for the case you have read and briefed:

_____ I have my professor's permission and a Westlaw password, and will update online using Westlaw (**go immediately to Step 2 below**)

_____ I have my professor's permission and a Lexis password, and will ` update online using Lexis (**go immediately to Step 11 below**)

_____ I will update using traditional print materials (**go immediately to Appendix C in the back of this workbook**)

Step 2: Begin here only if you plan to update online using Westlaw. Update online using Westlaw only if you have a Westlaw password and your professor's permission to use it at this point in the semester. Go to Westlaw.com and log on using the password issued to you by your school. (If you inadvertently sign-on to lawschool.westlaw.com, click on the tab that says "Westlaw Research" to get to the correct homepage.)

Step 3: For this exercise, you will be using Westlaw's online citation tool, "KeyCite", to update the case you briefed earlier in this assignment. At the top of the Westlaw Research homepage, click on the hyperlink to "KeyCite." The next screen that appears provides a dialogue box on the left side for entering the case citation that you want to update, and also an abundance of useful information about the KeyCite feature itself on the right side of the screen.

Step 4: In the box provided on that initial screen, enter either the state or regional reporter citation (volume, Reporter, opening page) for the case you briefed earlier and hit "Go."

Step 5: The results of your search will show up on the right side of the next screen. That screen will show you the full name and citation to your case. Directly under the case name, in parentheses, you will find references to any additional reporters that print your case. In the space provided here, write the references to any additional reporters found in parentheses under your case name:

Step 6: Following any parenthetical references to other reporters, you will see any "prior history" or "subsequent history" of the case, as well as other related court documents. "Prior history" means any opinions regarding your case that were handed down prior to the present decision. "Subsequent history" is a term peculiar even in the legal research world, and is a little harder to understand because we generally think of "history" as something that has gone before. In law, "subsequent history" refers to things that happen to the case *after* the present opinion came down. In the space below, note the full cite to the case you are running the KeyCite search on, and indicate whether there is any "prior" or "subsequent" history on this case:

CITATION TIP: A "parallel" citation is a citation that identifies more than one reporter where a reader could find a case. In reference to state cases, a "parallel citation" is one that identifies the state reporter in which the case is published <u>and</u> the regional reporter in which the case is published. According to the 18th edition of <u>The Bluebook</u>, parallel citations should only be used when you are writing about a case in a document that will be submitted to a court in the state in which the case originates or when the local rules of court require parallel citations. For example, if you're citing a Georgia case to a Georgia court, you should use parallel citation form. Otherwise, you should omit the parallel citation, citing only the regional reporter followed by a parenthetical reference to the state court that decided the case. Read Rule 10.3.1 in the <u>Bluebook</u> to learn more about this rule. Under <u>The ALWD Manual</u>, you never use a parallel citation unless you are submitting a document to a court that has a local rule requiring parallel citations.

Step 7: While still on this first screen, look at the top left-hand corner. You may see a small green letter "C" there, directly under the small word, "KeyCite." If you see a green letter "C," rest your cursor on that green "C" and an explanation of its meaning will appear. You will see that the presence of a green "C" means that there are "citing cases" available for this case. If you do not see a green "C," enter a different case from earlier in this assignment until you find a case that does have a green "C" on the first screen. Click on the green "C."

Step 8: The screen that appears after you have clicked on the green "C" contains a great deal of additional valuable research information about your case. The cases that show up there are cases that have *cited* your original case. In other words, the judges who wrote those opinions relied in some way, or distinguished in some way, the case you are doing a KeyCite search on. Westlaw provides green stars that illustrate an editor's decision about how thoroughly the citing case treats your original case. One green star indicates fairly light treatment; the presence of four stars indicates that your case is discussed in great depth in the citing case. In the space below, write the cite to at least one case that cited your case and indicate whether there were stars associated with that cite that would show some depth of treatment of your original case in the citing case:

Step 9: In addition to giving you a heads-up as to how thoroughly the editor thinks a citing case treated your case, the Westlaw editor may also assign "status flags" to a case that has cited your original case. The available "status flag" cues are as follows: a red flag indicates your case may have been discredited on some point by the citing case; a "yellow flag" indicates that your case may have been discussed negatively on some point by the citing case; a "blue H" indicates that your case has been cited but without specific negative findings, and the "green C" you've already discovered indicates that the case citing your case has itself been cited elsewhere. (Note: you can always remind yourself about the meaning of a "status flag" on KeyCite by resting your cursor on it and waiting until an explanatory box appears.) In the space below, give the name and citation to a citing case that has a "status" flag next to it. If there is no "status flag" next to any of the cases that have cited your case, indicate that fact here instead:

READING TIP: Do not rely on the presence or absence of "status flags" to determine which cases to read. A good legal researcher recognizes that "status flags" on KeyCite represent the decision of editors employed by Westlaw. These editors are reading cases carefully, but are nonetheless reading them out of context. While it would be wrong to ignore a flag indicating negative treatment (because it might well be an indication that your case is no longer good law), it is equally wrong to assume that the presence of a red or yellow flag is a definitive statement on the value of your case — or that the absence of a red or yellow flag confirms that the case is still good law.

> **WESTLAW HEADNOTE TIP:** Cases are complex and often resolve many legal questions in one opinion. As you have learned, these questions are often assigned headnote numbers in the West system. When you run a search using the KeyCite function to check to see if your case is good law, or to find additional related cases, you can narrow your search by looking for cases that have cited your case expressly on the headnote point that is of interest to you. The numbers introduced by a bold-face **HN** (for headnote) indicate that those particular headnotes from your case appear also in the citing case. Finally, a rich purple quotation mark next to a citing case indicates that the case quotes the case that you are running your KeyCite search on.

Step 10: We do not have time in this assignment to ask you to read another case. However, if you were going to continue your research on this case, choose one case that you might read and, in the space below, explain why you chose that case (think about the status flags and depth of treatment stars assigned to the citing case, as well as the **HEADNOTE TIP** above, when selecting what case you might read):

Step 11: <u>Begin here if you are going to update online using Lexis. Update online using Lexis only if you have a Lexis password and your professor's permission to use it at this point in the semester.</u> Go to Lexis.com and log on using the password issued to you by your school.

Step 12: Using the tabs across the top of the Lexis homepage, click on "Shepard's" to begin your updating. As of the printing of this Workbook, you would be presented with a choice of asking for a "Report" that would include "Shepard's for Validation" (showing only the *future* history of your case as well as citations for cases in which your case has been cited AND that the Lexis editors have attached an explanatory signal to) OR for a Report that would include "Shepard's for Research" (showing both the *prior* and *future* history of the case as well as all cases that have cited your case). For this exercise, choose "Shepard's for Research."

Step 13: In the space provided on the <u>Shepard's</u> page, enter *either* the state or the regional reporter citation to the case you briefed earlier in this assignment. If you are uncertain as to what "format" to insert for your reporter, click on the hyperlink to "Citation Formats" immediately to the right of the box. Finally, click "check."

Step 14: The Lexis screen that appears first shows you, in a shaded box, a succinct summary of what information is available on Lexis about your case. The first thing you will see is a statement as to whether your case has any prior history or subsequent history. Does it?

Step 15: The summary also includes visually helpful icons called "treatment letters" followed by the number of cases that fall into any of the relevant categories. Possible "treatment letters" include: a red stop sign (symbolizing actual negative treatment – such as a reversal), an orange square with the letter Q (symbolizing a questioning of your case), a yellow triangle (symbolizing possible negative treatment), a green diamond with a plus sign (symbolizing favorable treatment, such as direct reliance on your case), a blue circle with an "A" included (symbolizing discussion of your case), a blue circle with an "I" (indicating that your case is cited but no treatment letters have been assigned).

Does your case have any "treatment letters" associated with it? If so, what letter appears and how many citing cases or other sources are associated with that letter?:

Treatment letter: _____

Number of Cases indicating such treatment: _____

Step 16: Next, scroll below the shaded summary box. You will find references to the cases involved in any prior and subsequent history, followed by cases that have cited your case (in priority order, starting with the highest court in your jurisdiction and moving, then, to other jurisdictions). We do not have time in this assignment to ask you to read another case. However, if you were going to continue your research on this case, choose one case that you might read and, in the space below, explain why you chose that case (think about the treatment letters assigned to the citing case and the headnote tip below when selecting what case you might read):

LEXIS HEADNOTE TIP: Cases are complex and often resolve many legal questions in one opinion. As you have learned, these questions are often assigned headnote numbers in the West system. LexisNexis has developed a similar system and now assigns its own Lexis headnote numbers to all current cases. LexisNexis editors have also reached back and have assigned Lexis headnote numbers to all prior federal cases and a substantial number of state cases. When you run a search using the Shepard's function to check to see if your case is good law, or to find additional related cases, you can narrow your search by looking for cases that have cited your case expressly on the headnote point that is of interest to you. The numbers introduced by a bold-face **HN** (for headnote) indicate that those particular headnotes from your case appear also in the citing case. The LexisNexis headnotes referenced in citing cases show up in the shaded summary box on the first screen when you do a Full Search using Shepard's online. You can also click on the "show headnotes" feature to get a drop-down box that will highlight the content of those headnotes.

BEWARE: The presence of a "treatment letter" is a useful aid in your search. However, treatment letters are only a help – not a substitute – for reading a case yourself. You cannot assume that the editors who read the case and assigned a letter have the last word on the meaning of the case. Additionally, you cannot assume that treatment letters are attached to every relevant case – they are not. If you find a treatment letter, be grateful and use it to search further. If you do not find a treatment letter, you cannot assume definitively that there is no negative (or positive) subsequent history.

C. FINDING CASES FROM OTHER STATES

You have learned several ways to locate cases in your state. Before we move on, it is important that you also be able to find cases outside of your state. Thus, for your final task in this Assignment Sheet, we would like you to use the West Key Number system using print materials to see how the state of Georgia handles the area of common law raised by your senior partner. (Note, if your original research is in the state of Georgia, try looking up a Florida case following Steps 1 through 4 below to see how that state handles this topic.) Remember, Georgia has a whole separate state court system and can do whatever it wants in this area of the law (assuming it's consistent with federal constitutional and statutory law). The law of Georgia may or may not be the same as the law of your state on this topic. To complete this final assignment, follow Steps 1 through 4 below.

Step 1: Annotations of cases for the state of Georgia are found in the regional digest for the southeastern region. The official title of that regional digest is West's <u>South Eastern Digest 2d</u> (note the space between "South" and "Eastern" if you are using an on-line catalogue to find this title). **Go there now.**

Step 2: Using the West Topic and Key Number you uncovered earlier in this Assignment Sheet, find an annotation for a case from Georgia in West's <u>South Eastern Digest 2d</u> that you think might be worth reading. Write the name and citation for that case as it appears at the end of the annotation here:

> **t** TIP: Note that the publishers of the digest series cite the regional reporter first, followed by any state reporter (e.g., <u>West v. Slick</u>, 326 S.E.2d 601, 313 N.C. 33 (1985)). That is unusual. In your own legal writing, <u>The Bluebook</u> and <u>The ALWD Manual</u> direct you to cite the state reporter first when using a parallel cite, followed by the regional reporter. Hence, you will see the state reporter first in almost all written work about a law if there is a parallel cite (e.g., <u>West v. Slick</u>, 313 N.C. 33, 326 S.E.2d 601 (1985)). Hang in there; all this becomes easier with time and practice.

Step 3: The annotated case you just found using the <u>South Eastern Digest 2d</u> is printed in its entirety in the <u>South Eastern Reporter</u>. Using your library's cataloguing system, locate that volume now (you may find it near the <u>South Eastern Digest 2d</u> you just used). Find your case in the Reporter and skim the headnotes. Does it look to you like the common law of Georgia on this topic is the same as the common law of your state?

Step 4: If you wanted to see if this Georgia case was still good law, what resources could you use? (Hint: See Section **B(2)**, <u>Step 1</u> of this Assignment Sheet above):

Please reshelve all books now.

Summary and Writing Assignment: Take a few minutes and think about what you have learned about your state's common law principles governing the question raised by your senior partner. On a separate piece of paper, please write a <u>short</u>, *informal* memo to your senior partner answering the question raised in Memo 2 using the limited information you've uncovered to this point.

To write this short memo, follow the business heading format you've seen modeled in your partner's memos in this workbook. In legal writing, as in all writing, think about who your reading audience is. In our case, pretend your reading audience is your assigning partner and address your memo to that person. Most people who read law are busy readers, so try to write simply and with as much clarity as you can muster. It's often best to begin by repeating the question you have been asked so that you can make sure everyone is on the same wavelength. Follow your paraphrase of the question with your answer to that question, being sure to cite the authority that led you to conclude what you have (so far) about the law.

As you write your answer, try to be as logical and clear as possible – state any controlling legal principles as you understand them (followed by a citation to the material that led you to your understanding of that rule); explain what happened in your client's case as it relates to that rule; draw a conclusion. To avoid inadvertently plagiarizing, be sure to use quotation marks around language that is a direct quote. Remember: you have only done a little bit of research here – not enough to find an irrefutable response, but only enough to get some beginning ideas. Your "partner" will understand the limitations of this assignment when reading your memo. Use this writing exercise to let us know what you think at this point about your client's legal question.

Congratulations! You have now completed your Assignment Sheet on common law. Your first Assignment Sheet on secondary resources introduced you to a number of ways to find common law cases. In this Assignment Sheet, you have learned some additional ways to find case law on a given common law topic in your state. You have also learned how to cite a case properly in your state, how to update your research to make sure the case you're using is still followed in your jurisdiction, and how to find a case on the same topic in another state. **To learn more about how to do case law research electronically, read the** ONLINE TIP **on the following page.**

Please note your actual time of completion (including background reading):_____ hrs.

ONLINE TIPS for Case Law Research: Once you have completed the supplement to this workbook and have your professor's permission to use electronic resources, you can begin to explore the many fee-based and free services that can help you locate cases and update case law research online. As you think about integrating electronic resources into what you already know about finding cases in hard copy, consider the tips below:

- See Appendix A in the supplement for a list of free websites and fee-based services that you will find helpful as you expand your online skills.

- As you have learned, some courts allow lawyers to use "unpublished" cases (cases not printed in the official reporters) as precedent under restricted circumstances. Some do not. **Know the rules of court in the jurisdiction you are working in so you know if you should be looking for such cases or not.** Unpublished opinions are available to the individual lawyers who litigated the case decided (the court sends these opinions to those lawyers), and when you practice in a particular area you will learn to watch for news about such cases. For those not involved in the litigation itself, such cases can often be obtained directly from the court. You can find such cases by doing a "whole text" search online using key terms as you will learn to do in the supplement.

- Note that free internet sources for finding case law (for example, states' Supreme Court websites) generally do not include the kind of enhancements (use of headnotes, Key Numbers, <u>Shepard's</u> editorial analyses, hyperlinks, etc.) that are contained on the fee-based search engines such as LexisNexis and Westlaw. Similarly, reduced fee services generally have fewer enhancements, and sometimes no enhancements than their for-fee counterparts.

- Online databases often do not have full scope coverage. Always check your resource to see how far back cases are covered and whether coverage is comprehensive or includes only select cases.

- The importance of considering accuracy, economy, and efficiency when deciding what resources to use cannot be overemphasized. For many students, using online resources is the most convenient way to do their school-based research (and sometimes the most economical as well). It is therefore tempting to abandon hard copy research and gravitate to electronic resources. In practice, however, the choices will be more varied, and there will be a cost (often high) associated with electronic research. It is therefore critical to know how to use all available resources well so you can make wise choices as you search for law in the future.

MARSHALL, STORY & ASSOCIATES
ATTORNEYS AND COUNSELORS AT LAW
SUITE 101, THE JUSTICE BUILDING

⚖

THE LITIGATION DIVISION

To: New Associate
From: Assigning Partner
Re: Eric Arnold [Client A] – File #03-2576

I was pleased to meet again with Mr. Arnold this week.

Having now put his mind to rest about both the antique carving tools he found and the carpenter's power equipment he stored, Mr. Arnold tells me that he has stumbled across a rare opportunity that he thinks might be helpful to his new community. At a recent fund-raising event at the local volunteer fire department, Mr. Arnold donated some of his own hand-carved wooden bowls for auction. As it happens, an art dealer from New York City was present at the auction and was taken by the bowls.

The art dealer purchased one of the bowls for $200.00 and then contacted Mr. Arnold after the auction to see if he could send at least two more to the dealer's studio for the same price each. The art dealer was interested in testing the market and indicated that there might be an opportunity to sell many more of these bowls in the future.

While Mr. Arnold is not himself interested in generating that many hand-carved bowls, it has occurred to him that this might be a good fund-raising opportunity for the volunteer fire department as well as a learning opportunity for the vocational students at the local high school. His idea is that the students could learn to carve the bowls and then they could be marketed in the city with proceeds set aside for the local fire department.

The art dealer has asked Mr. Arnold to ship the two bowls to his studio directly and has said that he will pay $200 for each of them upon receipt. Mr. Arnold is comfortable with a verbal agreement covering the $400 selling price for the two bowls he will ship, but he wants to make sure that the agreement is binding even if they do not put it in writing.

Can you check our state statutes to see if Mr. Arnold needs to have a contract in writing with the art dealer in order to have a binding agreement before he ships his hand-carved bowls? I believe there is probably a statute of frauds that sets out formal requirements that must be included to make an agreement binding for the sale of goods or property such as Mr. Arnold's bowls. The Uniform Commercial Code, which addresses contracts for the sale of goods, has been incorporated in the state statutes for every state except Louisiana, so searching for our state's version of the Uniform Commercial Code would probably be a good place to begin your research.

▶▶ **Turn to page 99 to begin your work on this assignment.**

MARSHALL, STORY & ASSOCIATES
ATTORNEYS AND COUNSELORS AT LAW
SUITE 101, THE JUSTICE BUILDING

⚖️

THE LITIGATION DIVISION

To: New Associate
From: Assigning Partner
Re: Project Hope [Client B] – File #03-2575

Thank you for your research on fraud. I believe we will be able to bring this information to Mr. Baylor's attention and resolve the dispute in the Board's favor.

Turning its attention to happier topics, the Board is now in the process of writing grant proposals in search of economic support for the new school. In making their appeal to private funding sources, the Board would like to highlight the size of the population from which they might ultimately draw students as their school grows in the future.

The Board has asked us to confirm the state's compulsory attendance policy so that the Board members can determine the ages of students who are required to attend school in our state. In addition to letting us know the ages of students who must attend school, it would be helpful to know if there has been any litigation involving the state's compulsory attendance policy that the Board should be aware of.

▶▶ **Turn to page 99 to begin your work on this assignment**

MARSHALL, STORY & ASSOCIATES
ATTORNEYS AND COUNSELORS AT LAW
SUITE 101, THE JUSTICE BUILDING

⚖️

THE LITIGATION DIVISION

To: New Associate
From: Assigning Partner
Re: Marjorie Morrison [Client C] - File #21-2203

I continue to regret seeing Ms. Morrison and Mr. Thompson at such odds with one another and would like to find a way to mediate a settlement in this case. It seems to me that what Ms. Morrison wants is to have the peace and quiet of her neighborhood restored. She would also like to have the potential slander suit dropped. I think she could tolerate Mr. Thompson's political activities and gardening if he would stop running his wine business out of his home. Mr. Thompson, for his part, would like to have his reputation restored but would also like to continue his current activities.

At this point Mr. Thompson has no motivation to change his activities nor to drop his lawsuit against Ms. Morrison and his attorney tells me they are not willing to enter into any mediation conferences at this time. The attorney also indicated to me that Mr. Thompson is extremely independent-minded and has no intention of discussing his wine-making business any further. According to that attorney, Mr. Thompson thinks there is way too much government interference in individual people's lives and he has "kept the government out of his business so far, and intends to continue to do so." I take it from that remark that Mr. Thompson has not been in contact with any state or federal authorities concerning any responsibilities he might have to obtain a license or other certificate of authorization to possess, manufacture, or transport his wine.

Common sense tells me that Mr. Thompson must be breaking a number of statutes and regulations in conducting the business he is running out of his home. I think that if I could demonstrate those violations to his attorney, we might be able to increase Mr. Thompson's motivation to settle this whole matter. Moreover, if we could show that Mr. Thompson is, in fact, breaking the law by manufacturing and transporting large quantities of wine out of his home without any kind of license, it is unlikely that the remarks Ms. Morrison made at the town hall meeting would constitute slander at all.

The first place I would like to begin is with our own state's laws. Consequently, I would appreciate your taking some time at your earliest convenience to look into our state statutory law on control of liquor or alcoholic beverages to see if Mr. Thompson is in compliance with our statutory requirements for the possession, sale, manufacture, or transportation of wine. It might be helpful for you to know that the wine he is producing contains 18% alcohol, his

continued on next page

garage is completely full of crates of the wine, he has begun advertising the sale of the wine in magazines throughout the state and region, and he regularly transports the wine for sale through specialty shops and clubs. Moreover, he appears to be making a nice profit on his sales. Remember, I only need to be able to show a single violation to validate Ms. Morrison's remarks and get Mr. Thompson's attention, so you don't need to spend a lot of time looking for every violation Mr. Thompson may have made. Rather, I will be happy if you can document at least one clear violation.

▶▶ **Turn to page 99 to begin your work on this assignment.**

MARSHALL, STORY & ASSOCIATES
ATTORNEYS AND COUNSELORS AT LAW
SUITE 101, THE JUSTICE BUILDING

⚖

THE LITIGATION DIVISION

To: New Associate
From: Assigning Partner
Re: Allen Field [Client D] - File #21-2204

    I heard from Dr. Field again earlier this week and need your help answering a question which is rooted in our state statutory law. Dr. Field was recently contacted by some distant relatives of Ms. Williams who informed him that they intend to contest her will.

    Although these individuals have not yet contacted an attorney themselves, they asserted in a letter to Dr. Field that they believe that Ms. Williams' will is invalid because it only carried the signatures of two witnesses. It is their contention that at least three witnesses' signatures are required for a valid will in this state. In their letter, they offered to take a monetary settlement from Dr. Field in lieu of protesting his title to the property.

    Dr. Field has shown me a copy of the will. It contains Ms. Williams' own signature, plus the individual signatures of two adult witnesses. I would appreciate your going to our state statutory law on wills to see whether Ms. Williams' relatives are correct in their assertion that more witnesses were needed. I suspect that we will find that these relatives are not correct, but rather that the will was properly executed.

▶▶ Turn to page 99 to begin your work on this assignment.

MARSHALL, STORY & ASSOCIATES
ATTORNEYS AND COUNSELORS AT LAW
SUITE 101, THE JUSTICE BUILDING

⚖

THE LITIGATION DIVISION

To: New Associate
From: Assigning Partner
Re: Josh Ward [Client E] - File #21-2205

Mr. Ward and I met earlier this week with an attorney representing the elderly gentleman who had hoped to make a valid claim for having established an easement by prescription across Mr. Ward's land. Fortunately, based on the research that you submitted, we were able to reach an agreement with that attorney and his client that such a claim could not be established.

Unfortunately, however, Mr. Ward continues to have problems with numerous residents crossing his property without permission. Many are leaving litter along the edge of the lake and others are trampling the endangered plants he had hoped to protect. He has increased the number of "No Trespassing" signs on his property so they are impossible to miss. He would like to know if there is any further legal action he can take to enforce his property boundaries.

In response to his inquiry, I would like you to look into our state's criminal trespass statutes. If individuals crossing the land are doing so in violation of a criminal statute, Mr. Ward can seek the help of local law enforcement officers to protect his property.

I appreciate your continued attention to this case, and look forward to seeing the results of your research.

▶▶ **Turn to page 99 to begin your work on this assignment.**

Assignment Sheet 3 *in Sequence of Assignments #1* **Researching State Statutes**	Estimated Time of Completion (including recommended background reading): 2.5 – 4.0 hrs.
Print Your Name:	

(If you are doing this work as part of a class exercise, you may neatly write your answers directly on these sheets, staple all sheets together, and turn them in. If you prefer to write your answers separately using a computer, please be sure to number your answers to correspond to the appropriate questions before printing your responses.)

Background Reading: To learn more about the resources and concepts introduced in this Assignment Sheet, read Chapter 5 of *Legal Research in a Nutshell* or a comparable chapter in a textbook assigned by your professor. (See Appendix A.)

Background Information: Your senior partner has raised a question that will require you to look into your state's statutes. This assignment sheet will show you how to find the relevant legislation on point. Your research into your partner's question cannot stop once you have located the statute you need. Rather, it is important to learn how courts in your state have applied or interpreted the statute. It is equally important to learn to update your research so that you can be confident that the statute and related case law you have found are still current.

What You Will Learn. By the end of this assignment, you will:

- Know how to find and read a statute passed by the legislature of your state
- Know how to find and read a statute passed by the legislatures of other states
- Know the importance of judicial decisions applying or interpreting a statute
- Know how to find and think about judicial decisions applying or interpreting a statute
- Know how to use a citator to make sure a statute is still "good law"
- Know how to use a citator to find additional sources related to your statute

The Research Process:
A. BECOMING FAMILIAR WITH YOUR STATE'S STATUTORY SCHEME

Introduction: One of the remarkable things about this country is that, even as we have grown to develop a strong national identity and sociologists and politicians alike argue that regions are losing their individual identity (it's hard to travel any place in the country where you can't get the same fast food you could order at home), our founders' vision of a balance of power between state and national governments appears to be alive and well today. Nothing will convince you of the continuing individual identity of each of our fifty states faster than doing legal research on the state statutory level. At the state statutory level, you will be hard-pressed to find any two states that have evolved exactly the same solution to any given legal problem. Given the diversity among state statutory schemes, it is easy to panic as you begin doing legal research in this area. The best way to avoid such panic is to be patient with yourself and have faith that there is some logic to every state's statutory scheme. Your task in this lesson is to figure out what that logic is and how to apply it to find an answer to your partner's question. To answer that question, you do not need to know how to find statutes in all fifty states. Rather, you only need to find the right statute in one state for now.

Step 1: Go now to the location in your library where the state statutes relevant to your client's question are shelved.

BEWARE: Many large law libraries hold onto their old statutory volumes despite the fact that those laws have been superseded and are no longer in effect. They often store those old volumes in close proximity to the current volumes. Librarians do this because there are times when a legal researcher would want to go back and find the old version of a law rather than the new version. For example, I might want to find the old version of a law if I were reading an old case and wanted to see what the statute looked like at the time that case was decided. Similarly, I might want to look at the old version of a statute if I were researching the legislative history of a statute and wanted to read an earlier version of it.

When you are researching a question like the one your partner has asked, however, you want the current version of the law. Thus, you have to be careful not to reach for a version of the statute that is no longer in effect. One way to distinguish current from outdated statutes is to check the binding – most libraries will mark defunct statutes with a small sticker with the word "superseded" on it. Before you move to the next step, make sure you are working in a set of statutes that contains current law.

Step 2: All states organize their statutes by general subjects of law (for example, criminal laws are usually grouped together, family law or domestic statutes are usually grouped together, corporate or business statutes are usually grouped together, etc.). The majority of states combine these subject areas into volumes that are numbered consecutively. Sometimes several subject headings will be contained within one volume, but the subjects are still grouped alphabetically by the subject titles.

There are a few states that do not follow this scheme. Those states (California, New York, and Texas) divide their statutes into multiple volumes by subject and number each of these books or codes separately. For example, the New York statutes on Banking Law are contained in "Book 4" which is divided into three separate volumes, each of which is numbered "4." The next "book" contains New York's statutory laws on Benevolent Orders which contains only one volume and is labeled "5" on the binding. The next "book" contains several volumes, all of which are labeled "6", etc. Some of these states provide separate indexes (or "codes") for each book at the end of the last volume for that topical grouping.

Fortunately, the majority of states follow a simpler system, numbering their volumes from 1 to whatever number they need to cover their last volume. Look at your state's statutes now and, in the space below, note what subjects are covered in the first two volumes and what subjects are covered in the last two volumes (if you're in California, New York, or Texas, write down which books or codes come first and last):

First volumes:

Last volumes:

Step 3: It is important to understand how your state's laws are organized, and what terminology is used by the drafters as they organize the laws into logical groupings. Different states use different headings for the various components of their statutes, but most systems generally follow a scheme where there are general headings that become more refined as the relevant law becomes more specific. As an example, most states follow some variation of the following divisions:

- Volume (or "Codes" and "Books")
- Title
- Division
- Part or chapter
- Subchapter or Article
- Section
- Subsection

BEWARE: In most states, only some – not all – of the organizational divisions listed above appear. Do not expect to find all of these organizational tools used in the state in which you are conducting your search for a statute.

The best way to become familiar with your state's organizational scheme and vocabulary is to browse through several volumes to get a sense of what terms are used. You can begin by looking at the bindings to see the terms set out there (they are probably the most general terms used).

Next, take a volume off the shelf and see what you can find in the opening pages. Usually the publisher's name is listed as well as helpful hints concerning use of the volume. Sometimes the first volume in the set will contain a history of how the state's statutes have been organized for publication in the past and how they are organized now. Somewhere near the front there is also usually a Table of Contents showing the contents of that volume. That Table of Contents at the beginning of a volume usually contains the terminology that is used to describe the next layer (or layers) of organizational division.

Finally, turn randomly to a specific law listed in the Table of Contents and see if you can identify the organizational scheme (e.g., title, chapter, section) used in the state in which you're doing research. In the space below, describe the organizational terms used in order from general to specific (the following **TIP** may help):

TIP: In EVERY state, the key organizational component of the statute is the SECTION. Turn to Table T-1 (United States Jurisdictions) in The Bluebook or Appendix 1 in The ALWD Manual and find the entry for your state. You'll note the official citation form for your state's statutes there – and in every state, proper cites refer directly to appropriate sections. These same sections are the basis of references in the indexes to the statutes themselves. You will learn to use the statutory index next.

CITATION TIP: In legal citations, writers generally use a section symbol ("§") in place of the word "section," or they use "sec." as an abbreviation. See Rule 6.2 and Table T.16 in The Bluebook or Rule 6 and Appendix 3 in The ALWD Manual.

Step 4: Despite the fact that there are individual variations in how each state publishes its statutes, you have learned that all state statutory compilations have some features in common. For example, the statutes are contained in series of volumes that are followed at the end by a general index. The general index will contain subject headings and subheadings to help you find a statute on point. Some states also publish individual indexes within each volume (like <u>C.J.S.</u> and <u>Am. Jur.</u> did when you worked with them in Assignment Sheet 1). Look over the volumes in front of you for your state statute and, in the space below, write a brief description of the indexing scheme for your statutes (is there only a general index or are there individual indexes as well?):

Open the index at random and notice how the editors send you to a specific statute. Choosing any topic and statutory reference at random, write an explanation in the space below describing what you found (for example, in Maryland, most statutes are listed by subject and section, thus: EN sec. 4-601 for section 4-601 of the Environmental volume whereas Arkansas includes the title, chapter, and precise section in each section citation, thus: sec. 8-5-203 for section 203 of Chapter 5 of Title 8, Environmental Law):

ANOTHER CITATION TIP: One way to determine the section citation form used by your state is to look at the top of any given page in a statute volume. The number for the section printed on that page almost always appears at the top of that page. If you ever have to write an official citation to a statute, use Table T-1 of <u>The Bluebook</u> or Appendix 1 and 2 of <u>The ALWD Manual</u> to determine the proper citation form for statutes from each state.

TIP: At the time this workbook was printed, there were some other idiosyncrasies in a few states that might concern you if you are working in one of those states. Note that Pennsylvania publishes two complete sets of volumes mingled together. When you use the index for Pennsylvania, note carefully which

continued on next page

compilation is being referred to and be sure you are in that compilation when you look for the right law. South Carolina is a little unusual in that its index contains references both to its statutory law AND its administrative law. For this lesson, you only want to use the statutory references. Finally, the system adopted in Maryland can be somewhat confusing at first. In Maryland, part of the code (the one adopted in 1957) is bound in black and contains statutes grouped in consecutive numbers like most states. The remaining part of the code (the part adopted later) is bound in maroon and contains statutes grouped and codified by topic (like Texas, New York, and California). References to these later-adopted statutes cite the book in which the statute is published (e.g., TR § 10-101 for a statute published in the Transportation code).

B. FINDING A STATE STATUTE ON POINT

Introduction: Now that you have a basic feel for how your state's statutes are set up, you are ready to move forward to find a specific statute that will answer your partner's question concerning your state's laws.

Step 1: The General Index located at the far end of each complete set of statutes is your primary tool for finding a relevant statute. Because the Index is extremely detailed, using it can be one of the most frustrating steps in doing any statutory research. Especially when you are unfamiliar with your statutes, it is often difficult to come up with the correct term that will lead you to the statutory reference you need. Patience and creativity are virtues in this process. In the space below, write down any terms that you think might be useful places to begin looking for legislation on point (note that your senior partner may have already given you some "leads" – if so, feel free to put them here):

Step 2: Turn to the Index itself and begin exploring the terms you've developed in the brainstorming step above. Be prepared to refine or adjust your approach. Some state indexing systems are incredibly detailed. Don't get discouraged; be prepared to persevere. In the following space, write down the reference to at least one statutory section that looks like it may answer your partner's question:

BEWARE: When you are working in the Index, be aware that there are lots of divisions with subdivisions that can run for pages on end. Don't lose track of where you are. For example, if you're trying to find out if you need a license to sell alcoholic beverages, the largest division you might begin with could be Alcohol or Liquor or Alcoholic Beverages (depending on the terms used in your state). Next, you could look for a subdivision concerning "sales" (or "transportation," or "advertising," or "wine," etc.). It's easy in the process to find that you have inadvertently moved out of your original general division (e.g., "Alcohol") and into a different general division (e.g., "Alcohol Review Board"). You may never find a relevant subdivision under that second general division you inadvertently moved to because the subdivisions you're looking for only made sense when you were in the division you started in. In other words, keep alert and stay flexible as you explore the index. Also, if your first idea isn't working, try something new. For example, going straight from "Alcohol" to a subdivision of "sales" may not work in your state. You may instead need to go from "Alcohol" to "licensing" to "sales." Every state system is different, and learning to use the index calmly is a real challenge.

Step 3: Once you have a reference to a potentially useful statute, the next step is to go to the statutory volumes themselves and begin to explore the law. Go now to the shelf containing your statutes and find the volume (or book/code) containing the reference you found.

BEWARE: It is easy to confuse volume numbers with chapter numbers in many state publication schemes. As a rule, most references to a particular statute in the index will NOT refer you to a volume itself. Rather, they are references to chapters and then sections housed in consecutive order within consecutively-numbered volumes. In North Carolina, for example, if the index refers you to § 20-17, you will find that statute in VOLUME 5 of the North Carolina General Statutes. That volume contains Chapter 20 ("Motor Vehicles"), Article 2 ("Uniform Driver's License Act"), and Section 17 ("Mandatory Revocation of License by Division [of Motor Vehicles]"). You would not find a reference to Volume 5 in the General Index at all, even though you'd have to pull Volume 5 from the shelf to find § 20-17. Note also that some states do not list volume numbers on the spine of their bound statutes – rather, only the subject heading is listed.

Step 4: When you read a statute, it is important to place it in context. NEVER try to rely on a specific statutory subsection to answer a client's question until you understand how that subsection fits in the chapter (or act) as a whole. Read the statute you just located in Step 3. If the statute continues to seem on point to you, write its full cite here and the following steps will help you explore how that section fits in the chapter (or act) as a whole. (Note: if you no longer think the statute applies after you've read it, go back and repeat Steps 1 through 3 above until you find a statute that you believe addresses your partner's concerns):

TIP: Some states have more than one published version of their statutes, but all states have only one official published version (the version sanctioned by their legislative body as being the authoritative copy of that state's laws). You can find the name of the official version by checking Table T-1 in The Bluebook and Appendix 1 in The ALWD Manual. If you are writing about the law, you should always cite the "official" version if it is available to you.

ANOTHER TIP: If you find yourself in a position to write about this statute, you will need to note the year the statute was published (not the year it was enacted) at the end of the cite as indicated in Table T-1 and Rule 12 of The Bluebook, or Appendix 1 and Rule 14 of The ALWD Manual. In a state with bound versions, that publication year is found at the beginning of each volume. If you ever need to cite to a Supplement containing very recent versions of a statute (inserted at the beginning or end of each volume, or published in a separate volume of Supplements usually shelved next to the corresponding volume in the main compilation), use the date found on the front cover of the Supplement. **If you want to know when a statute was enacted or amended (rather than the publication date), check the dates listed in parentheses at the end of each statutory section.**

Step 5: Go back, now, and read any Table of Contents section you can find for the Chapter as a whole. Where did you find the Table of Contents?

TIP: Sometimes it is extremely cumbersome (and unrewarding) to try to use the General Index to locate a specific section within a complicated act. In such a case, it is sometimes easier to go straight to the Table of Contents to a specific act or chapter once you've seen enough of the Index to figure out the broader number for the act or chapter itself. If you are looking for a particular subsection, you can sometimes peruse the Table of Contents for the act as a whole to see if the legislature included a section on point. This method is often easier than trying to figure out how the editors of the statutes indexed a particular subsection in their General Index.

Step 6: Using the Table of Contents for the Act, see if there is a Definitions Section for your Chapter. If there is, skim it to make sure there are no definitions that apply to the statute you'll be relying on as you answer your partner's question. If you found a relevant definition, turn the page and summarize it in the space provided:

Step 7: Updating is important! If you find a statute in the main volume, you always need to check to make sure it has not been amended or repealed. To check on its current status, look in the Supplement at the front or back of the volume (or in the separately bound Supplement volume, depending on your state). Note also that in many states there is a paperback version of a Supplement that sets out legislation that is hot off the press. To continue updating, it is also important to check this paperback volume to make sure no very recent changes have been made to your statute. Has the statute you're relying on been amended or repealed since it appeared in the main volume of the statutory code?

ONLINE TIP: Occasionally a statute may have been amended or repealed so recently that the change does not even show up in the statutory supplement. When you are looking for the most recent statutory changes, using online legal research sources is critical. To save time as you complete this exercise, we will not ask you to check online for updates.

Step 8: In the following space, based solely on the "plain language" of the statute as you read it, write a brief synopsis of how you think this statute might help resolve your partner's question.

C. FINDING RELEVANT CASE LAW BY USING ANNOTATIONS

Step 1: In most states, you will find numerous helpful research aids at the end of each statutory section (unless the statute has been enacted so recently that not much has happened yet with it). In a very few states (for example, Montana) these helpful research aids are included in separately bound volumes of Annotations which are shelved immediately following the statutes themselves. In these research aids, the publishers often list references to relevant law review articles (see Assignment Sheet 1) directly under each statute. Sometimes you will also find a summary of the effects of amendments or comments by drafters of the legislation itself and cross-references to related statutes or administrative regulations among these research aids.

The most helpful research aid in your search for finding related case law is listed next; it is called different things in different states. In North Carolina, these annotations are called "Case Notes." In Alaska, on the other hand, they are called "Notes to Decisions." These case notes are annotated summaries and citations to court decisions where a judge had to interpret or apply the relevant statute. If there are a lot of case notes, the editor will have divided them by topical subsections. You will sometimes find a Table of Contents to the various subsections of annotations listed at the very beginning of the annotated case section of the research aids. Using the statute you are relying on to answer your partner's question, find the annotated case section of the research aids and write the name of that section here (e.g., Case Notes, Notes to Decisions, etc.):

Step 2: Skim the annotated cases summarized at the end of that statute to see if there are any cases that might help your partner answer the statutory question he or she has raised. (A case can be valuable precedent even when the parties or situation are not exactly the same as your client's – your primary concern for purposes of completing this Assignment Sheet is to find a case that sheds light on the statute you are researching.) Write the correct citation to at least one case on point here. (Remember to check the supplement for relevant cases as well.) If the statute you found does not have annotations, check around for a related statute that does and use the annotations you find there to complete the rest of this exercise so that you get the full learning experience. If you find annotations to a different statute, please note what that statute is here as well.

Please reshelve the statute volume you've been using now.

Step 3: Using your state or regional reporter, locate the case you cited immediately above.

Step 4: Read the case you have found and brief it in the space provided. Remember, you can look at Appendix B in this workbook for a sample of a case brief.

Don't forget to reshelve your reporter volume before going on to Section D below.

ONLINE TIP: There are pros and cons to doing statutory research online. On the plus side, if you know a cite to a statute to search and/or specific statutory language you can enter as search terms, it is often easy to locate the body of a statute online. On the downside, though, it is equally easy to get confused when actually reading the statute online. You have already gained an appreciation for how important it is to read a statute in context – keeping in mind the purpose of the legislation, staying alert to any available Table of Contents for the act and/or a definitions section, looking for court decisions interpreting or applying the statute. By its nature, a computer only allows you to scroll one part of a statute at a time, thus making it difficult to get oriented when reading a complex piece of legislation. Because it is critical to read a statute in its full context, many experienced researchers prefer to research statutes using hard copy materials.

ANOTHER ONLINE TIP: In addition to being able to use Westlaw, LexisNexis, and other fee-based services to research statutes electronically, researchers can also avail themselves of a number of free internet resources to find the texts of statutes. See Appendix A of the supplement to this workbook for a list of free websites providing access to statutes and other legislative material.

D. USING CITATORS TO UPDATE YOUR STATE STATUTORY RESEARCH

Step 1: In this section, you will be asked to update your research online using Westlaw, OR online using Lexis, OR in hard copy, using traditional print materials. While it's a good idea to learn how to use all three, you will not be required to do so here. In the supplement to this workbook, you'll have an opportunity to use the updating tools for both Westlaw and Lexis, which is why we don't require you to use both here. In the space below, please indicate how you plan to search for updates for the case you have read and briefed:

_____ I have my professor's permission and a Westlaw password, and will update online using Westlaw **(go immediately to Step 2 below)**

_____ I have my professor's permission and a Lexis password, and will update online using Lexis **(go immediately to Step 9 below)**

_____ I will update using traditional print materials **(go immediately to Part II of Appendix C in the back of this workbook)**

Step 2: <u>Begin here only if you plan to update online using Westlaw.</u> <u>Update online using Westlaw only if you have a Westlaw password and your professor's permission to use it at this point in the semester.</u> Go to Westlaw.com and log on using the password issued to you by your school. (If you inadvertently sign-on to lawschool.westlaw.com, click on the tab that says "Westlaw Research" to get to the correct homepage.)

Step 3: For this exercise, you will be using Westlaw's online citation tool, "KeyCite", to find additional information about the statute you located earlier in this assignment. If you used Westlaw's KeyCite function to update your case law research in the preceding Assignment Sheet, you will find the process here to be very similar. Click on the KeyCite hyperlink at the top of the homepage.

Step 4: The initial screen that appears gives you a dialogue box in which to enter the full cite to the statute you want to update. Additionally, notice that you can find an array of helpful information on the right side of the screen that will remind you exactly what sources a KeyCite search can lead you to, as well as an explanation of the meaning of KeyCite status flags. In the box provided on that screen, enter the full citation to the statute you are checking, and then hit "Go."

Step 5: Remember: online sources change frequently. Always check our website <www.LegalResearchWorkbook.com> for possible screen changes if these instructions are not consistent with what you find. As of the printing of this edition of the workbook, the results of your KeyCite search would appear first as a split screen. On the right, you will see the search results, with the full cite to your statute at the top. Pay attention to the presence of a yellow or red flag, which indicates some relevant change to or information about the statute (the yellow flag) or some possible alarming results – such as an action declaring it unconstitutional or repealing it – concerning your statute (the red flag). To the left of the screen, you will see a number of hyperlinks that will connect you with additional information about your statute. Do you see a red or a yellow flag?

_____ no red or yellow flag

_____ yes, there is a yellow ( ) or red ( ) flag

On the left side of the screen, directly next to the flag (if a flag is present), Westlaw identifies why the status flag was attached to your case. What is that flag indicating?:

Step 6: Click on the "Citing References" link on the left side of your screen. The cases that have cited your statute will appear. If you see a blue "H" to the left of a case, that status letter indicates that your statute was dealt with directly in that case. If you see a green "C" to the left of a case, that status letter indicates that the case referenced your statute, but did not directly apply nor interpret it. As with using the KeyCite feature to update case law, the presence of up to four green stars indicates depth of treatment of your statute within the case.

Step 7: Choose a citing case and write its citation below. We do not have time to ask you to read any of the cases citing your statute, but if this were a real legal issue with a real client, you would certainly need to do so. Weighing depth of treatment and considering any status letters, indicate why you might read the case you selected if you were interested in learning more about the statute you have cited.

Also, Westlaw has introduced a "ResultsPlus" tool that identifies secondary sources that might expand your research related to this statute. Finally, through its "KeyCite Alert" feature, Westlaw gives lawyers the opportunity to receive updates if new information comes online concerning a statute they are interested in.

All of these enhancements provide additional tools for the legal researchers, but none are free. Law students have unlimited access to these tools while they are in school working on school-related projects. Later, even in the summer, students are limited to the same fee-based access as other private practitioners. Learning to use these resources efficiently and with confidence now, while a student, is a wise investment of time.

Step 8: In addition to helping you determine if your case has been amended or repealed, or might be impacted by proposed legislation, and to helping you find cases that have applied or cited your statute, KeyCite can help you find additional legal references to your statute. These additional sources include secondary materials (like law review articles), court documents (like briefs filed in a case), related statutes, and even a survey of similar laws in other states. Scroll past the citing cases and list at least one other source that might be worth investigating if you had time (which you do not in this Assignment Sheet) to learn more about your statute:

Go now to the legislative history TIP on p. 117 unless you are also going to update using Lexis (Steps 9-12 below).

Step 9: Begin here if you are going to update online using Lexis. Update online using Lexis only if you have a Lexis password and your professor's permission to use it at this point in the semester. Go to Lexis.com and log on using the password issued to you by your school.

Step 10: For this exercise, you will be using Shepard's Online to update the statute you identified earlier in this assignment. If you used the Shepard's function on Lexis to update your case law research in the preceding Assignment Sheet, you will find the process here to be very similar. Using the tabs across the top of the Lexis homepage, click on "Shepard's" to begin your updating. Be sure the "Shepard's for Research" option is selected (not the Shepard's for Validation/KWIC option).

Step 11: Remember: online sources change frequently. Always check our website <www.LegalResearchWorkbook.com> for possible screen changes if these instructions are not consistent with what you find. As of the printing of this edition of the workbook, you will be presented with a box in which you should type the citation to the statute you want to update. If you are uncertain of the format to use, click on the "Citation Formats" hyperlink to the right of the box. After you have entered the citation to your statute, click the red "check" box.

Step 12: The Lexis screen that appears first shows you the history of your statute as well as cross-references to cases that have cited your statute.

> BEWARE: Before you get to the screen showing you the history of your statute and cross-references to cases citing your statute, you may see a screen that shows you subsections of your statute. **Be aware that information referenced for subsections on Lexis is NOT included cumulatively in information referenced for a larger, umbrella statute that contains that subsection. Thus, to be thorough, you would need to check references for each individual subsection if you are interested in the statute as a whole.** For purposes of completing this assignment, if you see this screen, choose the broadest statutory reference that addresses your client's legal question.

Choose a case that you might read if you had time to read a case that has cited your statute and explain below why you might read that case to learn more about your statute:

> TIP: HAVING TROUBLE YIELDING RESULTS FOR YOUR STATUTE? If your statute does not produce any citing cases, try switching to another statute related to your subject and see if it is a more richly applied statute. Alternatively, try entering N.C. Gen. Stat. 115C-391 and using that statute to complete this section on citators. That statute is related to North Carolina's corporal punishment laws and will yield good illustrative results for you. If you use N.C. Gen. Stat. 115C-391, please place a check here so your professor will be aware of your choice: _____

Step 13: Next, click on the hyperlink to the statute itself at the top of the page. When the statute appears, scroll through the language of the statute and note that you can find cross-references to secondary resources and additional cases that may cite your case. Are there any references here that you did not see on the original Shepard's screen that might be useful to you?:

Step 14: While still viewing an online version of the statute itself, look for the "Archive Directory" in the center of the screen to see if you can find an earlier version of your statute. Is there an earlier version?

Step 15: If there is legislation pending for your statute, there will be a "Legislative Alert" just above the body of the statute itself. Is there information pending about your statute?

ONLINE TIPS: Lexis has added research features to make updating and expanding statutory research online useful and efficient – and as similar as possible to using actual print copies. When you are viewing the body of the statute, you can click on the "TOC" [Table of Contents] link on the top left side of the page to see the Table of Contents for the entire statutory section in which your exact citation appears. You can also click on the "Book Browse" link at the top of the page to get to a screen that allows you to use the "previous" and "next" arrows on either side of the cite to look at the statutory sections that appear just before and just after your statute in the code. You can click on the "Archive Directory" link to find older versions of the statute as well as to be alerted to changes to the statute that may be pending. Finally, through its "Shepard's Alert" feature, Lexis gives lawyers the opportunity to receive updates if new information comes online concerning a statute they are interested in.

All of these enhancements provide additional tools for the legal researchers, but none are free. Law students have unlimited access to these tools while they are in school working on school-related projects. Later, even in the summer, students are limited to the same fee-based access as other private practitioners. Learning to use these resources efficiently and with confidence now, while you are a student, is a wise investment of time.

t LEGISLATIVE HISTORY TIP: As you know, one of the responsibilities judges have when faced with a statutory question in a case in controversy is to determine what the legislative intent was behind the statute. Determining legislative intent sometimes requires an understanding of the legislative history of a statute. You will learn more about doing legislative history research in Assignment Sheet 4 concerning federal statutes. States vary considerably in how much legislative history they preserve which can later then be uncovered and put to use to help determine the legislative intent of a statute's framers. Your individual law library will have additional information on ways of researching legislative history in your state. You might also consider reading Chapter 6 of *Legal Research in a Nutshell* or a comparable section in another textbook listed in Appendix A of this workbook for more information on this topic. Appendix B of *Legal Research in a Nutshell* contains a comprehensive list of books and pamphlets about research sources that are available for each individual state. Finally, most states now maintain a state government website. Many are rich sources of information regarding legislative history, at least as pertaining to fairly recent statutes.

t ANOTHER TIP: Any time you are faced with a situation involving state law, you should consider whether a more localized branch of government might also have the authority to pass law on the subject. Researching local charters and ordinances is an art unto itself. You can find out more about this process through your local law library, or by reading Chapter 7 of *Legal Research in a Nutshell* or a comparable chapter in another textbook listed in Appendix A of this workbook.

Congratulations! You have now completed your research in state statutory law. You have learned how to get comfortable with any state statutory system in this country as well as how to find a specific statute relating to a legal question before you. Additionally, you know how to use supplementary research aids to complete your understanding of the statute's meaning within the context of our judicial system. Finally, you now know how to use <u>Shepard's</u> to make sure your research is accurate and up-to-date.

Please note your actual time of completion (including background reading): _____*hrs.*

MARSHALL, STORY & ASSOCIATES
ATTORNEYS AND COUNSELORS AT LAW
SUITE 101, THE JUSTICE BUILDING

⚖

THE LITIGATION DIVISION

To: New Associate
From: Assigning Partner
Re: Eric Arnold [Client A] – File #03-2576

Mr. Arnold is continuing to explore his new farm and has stumbled upon an old underground storage tank in the far acreage of his property. The tank has a storage capacity of only 1,000 gallons and is presently mostly empty. I believe most storage tanks are at least 1,100 gallons, so this is an unusually small tank. It was used to store gasoline in the 1970's for the family's cars and family records indicate it was never used to fuel any farm equipment.

Mr. Arnold is an ardent environmentalist and is well aware that there is extensive federal law monitoring the storage of gas and other potentially polluting liquids, even on private property. He would like to drain and remove this tank and wants to ensure that he complies with federal law as he does so.

We would appreciate your researching federal law on the topic of underground storage tanks to see if removal of this tank is controlled by federal statutory law.

▶▶ **Turn to page 129 to begin your work on this assignment.**

MARSHALL, STORY & ASSOCIATES
ATTORNEYS AND COUNSELORS AT LAW
SUITE 101, THE JUSTICE BUILDING

⚖

THE LITIGATION DIVISION

To: New Associate
From: Assigning Partner
Re: Project Hope [Client B] – File #03-2575

Your work has been very helpful to the Board and its members continue to make significant progress towards their goal of opening a new school for our community's young people.

Many of the students the new school will serve have had documented difficulty adjusting to the behavioral and academic expectations of the more traditional public schools. The Board believes that the high drop-out rate among our community's young people is a result, at least in part, of these students' failure to "fit in" to the public school model. Preliminary research for the district, in fact, shows that a significant minority of our high school drop-outs have been diagnosed with learning disabilities or Attention Deficit Disorder (ADD) and, as a result, medication has been recommended. In addition, a number of drop-outs and potential drop-outs have been identified as intellectually gifted.

Professional teachers on the Board have highlighted the federal requirement for the school to prepare Individualized Education Programs (IEPs) for all individuals with disabilities enrolled at the school. Under the relevant federal education act, IEPs are written by a team of professionals to ensure that each pupil's needs are served.

The Board is interested in knowing at what level parents are involved in the development of, or follow-through on, a student's IEP. Specifically, they would like you to conduct research into the federal statutes pertaining to handicapped or disabled students to see if federal law requires that parents be part of the IEP team and, if so, whether a "legal guardian" can serve on the team as a parent.

▶▶ **Turn to page 129 to begin your work on this assignment.**

MARSHALL, STORY & ASSOCIATES
ATTORNEYS AND COUNSELORS AT LAW
SUITE 101, THE JUSTICE BUILDING

⚖

THE LITIGATION DIVISION

To: New Associate
From: Assigning Partner
Re: Marjorie Morrison [Client C] - File #21-2203

The information you shared concerning Mr. Thompson's state statutory problems was very interesting. I believe that Mr. Thompson may be breaking federal law as well.

Just before her final falling out with Mr. Thompson, Ms. Morrison went by his house to purchase a bottle of wine because she had finished the one he had given her as a gift on her birthday. I had her bring the bottle to the office and was surprised to note that while the bottle carried a label with the Thompson brand set out clearly, there was no statement of alcohol content anywhere on the bottle.

I know that the wines I have purchased in stores all have a label referencing alcohol content, so I am fairly sure that there must be a federal law that requires such labeling. My recollection is that making alcohol content a mandatory labeling requirement was a decision by the federal government to control unfair competition in the sale of intoxicating liquors.

For this assignment, I'd like for you to see if you can locate a federal statute that makes a statement of alcoholic content a mandatory labeling requirement.

▶▶ Turn to page 129 to begin your work for this assignment.

MARSHALL, STORY & ASSOCIATES

ATTORNEYS AND COUNSELORS AT LAW
SUITE 101, THE JUSTICE BUILDING

⚖

THE LITIGATION DIVISION

To: New Associate
From: Assigning Partner
Re: Allen Field [Client D] - File #21-2204

Thank you for the research you did last week looking into our state's statutes. I have passed your information on to Dr. Field, who has decided to respond to these relatives himself in the interest of maintaining family harmony. However, he says that if they threaten him again with further legal action, he will turn the matter over to us.

On the nuisance issue, we have successfully negotiated a settlement with the restaurant next door to the Bain Farm. They have agreed to move their parking lot and their open pit barbecue to the far side of their property, and will comply with all local noise and air pollution ordinances in the future. As a result of this agreement, Dr. Field is now ready to move forward with his plans to convert his newly-acquired home to a bed and breakfast. In order to achieve his goals of bringing Geoffrey Bain's historic contributions to the public eye, he would like to have the house and farm listed on the National Register of Historic Places. This Register is maintained by the federal government, and the procedures to follow to be listed on it are controlled by federal law.

Dr. Field has done some work with the Register in the past, and believes that a property has to be nominated for listing by the appropriate officer within each state. If he is correct about that, he may have a problem. He knows this state's historic preservation officer personally from his research into Geoffrey Bain's work, and believes that the officer does not understand the major contributions that Bain made to this state's original history. He is so certain that the state officer would not recognize Bain as a figure of historic significance, in fact, that he is concerned about proceeding at all unless he knows if there is any way he could nominate the property himself if the state officer refuses to do so.

For your next assignment, would you please find the federal law controlling historic preservation and, specifically, listings on the National Register of Historic Places. Once you have found that statute, please check to see if Dr. Field could nominate the property himself for listing if the state officer refuses to do so.

▶▶ Turn to page 129 to begin your work for this assignment.

MARSHALL, STORY & ASSOCIATES
ATTORNEYS AND COUNSELORS AT LAW
SUITE 101, THE JUSTICE BUILDING

⚖

THE LITIGATION DIVISION

To: New Associate
From: Assigning Partner
Re: Josh Ward [Client E] - File #21-2205

Although Mr. Ward has now succeeded in keeping uninvited strangers off his property, he has become aware of additional disturbing news concerning his new land. An article appeared some time ago in the local newspaper indicating that the state and federal governments intend to join forces to construct a large public access road, ending in an extensive paved parking lot, connecting the rural road on Mr. Ward's north side to the lake on the south. The road would border the east side of his property, directly adjacent to the wetlands where the rare and endangered ferns currently grow.

Mr. Ward is extremely concerned about the environmental impact of this planned government project. The water run-off from the additional asphalt alone would cause extensive damage to the delicate ecosystem he is nurturing on his land. Interestingly, many of the residents who resented Mr. Ward's initial efforts to protect his property boundaries are now in alliance with him against this project.

The government's proposal was addressed at a recent emergency town meeting attended by representatives of the federal government and several citizens' groups. The consensus among the town members was that the result of the planned project would be to increase traffic and visitors from outside the region who would be drawn to the lake for recreational use. The citizens' concerns, which parallel those of our client, are that the economic advantages to the community would not outweigh the environmental costs.

In an effort to offer a compromise alternative, Mr. Ward offered publicly to donate a wide enough strip of his land along the eastern border of his proper to allow a less intrusive footpath to the lake. His offer has been resoundingly supported by the local citizenry, but completely ignored by representatives of the federal government. In preliminary discussions, in fact, it appears that the government does not intend to mention his proposed alternative at all in the environmental impact statement that must be filed in support of the government's proposal.

On behalf of Mr. Ward and his neighbors, I would like you to look into whether the government can, in fact, submit a proper environmental impact statement without a full discussion of a legitimate alternative such as the one he has proposed.

▶▶ Begin your work on the following page.

Assignment Sheet 4 *in Sequence of Assignments #1*
Researching Federal Law

Print Your Name:

Estimated Time
of Completion
(including recommended
background reading):
3.0 – 4.0 hrs.

(If you are doing this assignment as part of a class exercise, you may neatly write your answers directly on these sheets, staple all sheets together, and turn them in. If you prefer to write your answers separately using a computer, please be sure to number your answers to correspond to the appropriate questions before printing your responses.)

Background Reading: It would be helpful to read Chapter 5 of *Legal Research in a Nutshell* or a comparable chapter in a textbook included in Appendix A to learn about statutory law in general. To learn more about finding federal cases interpreting federal statutory law, read Chapter 3 in that book or a comparable chapter from another textbook in Appendix A. To learn more about researching the legislative history of a federal statute, read Chapter 6 in the *Nutshell* or a parallel chapter from another textbook in Appendix A.

Background Information: Your senior partner has asked you to find the answer to a question involving the federal statutes. This assignment sheet is designed to teach you one of many good ways to find controlling federal law on point. There are many other good ways to find out about federal law (both case law and statutory law) and as you become more proficient in legal research you will want to develop an array of strategies of your own for doing in-depth federal research. The TIPS and ONLINE TIPS included in this chapter will be helpful as you develop more advanced research skills in the future.

What You Will Learn. By the end of this assignment, you will:

- Be able to identify and know how to find a statute in the "official" code for federal legislation
- Be able to identify and know how to use two "unofficial" publications of federal legislation that also contain useful annotations and cross-references
- Know how to use a citator to ensure that the law you have found is still current
- Know how to find the legislative history of a current law

The Research Process:
A. LOCATING A FEDERAL STATUTE

Step 1: The <u>United States Code</u> (<u>USC</u>) is the officially codified version of federal legislation. It takes years for laws passed by the federal government to come out in printed form in <u>USC</u>. Moreover, unlike the state statutory compilations you used in Assignment Sheet 3, the <u>USC</u> does not have editorial enhancements such as cross-references to relevant administrative regulations or annotations highlighting relevant cases.

For these reasons, even though you should cite to USC whenever possible in your legal writing, you should begin your search for a federal statute in either the United States Code Annotated (USCA) or the United States Code Service (USCS). USCA and USCS are compilations of federal statutes printed by private publishing companies. Laws appear much faster there and those publications include editorial enhancements to make your research easier. USCA (published by Thomson-West) has the advantage of using the West Key Number System that you learned about in Assignment Sheet 2, and also traditionally cites a large number of annotated cases in its "Notes of Decisions" section. USCS, which is published by LexisNexis, has traditionally had the advantage of citing more administrative law in its annotations. Regardless of which of these publications you choose to start with (USCA or USCS), both will do pretty much the same thing for you for many projects. However, you should be aware that each publication has variations in the cases selected for annotations and the cross-references selected for related resources, so there are times when you would be wise to look at both. You may choose either one of these publications to complete this Assignment Sheet. **Go to the location in your library where these resources are shelved now.**

CITATION TIP: Although USC is not the best place to begin your federal research, you do need to use it as the code you cite to even when you have done your actual research in USCA or USCS. You cite to USC because it is the "official" code approved by Congress to publish federal law. Where an Act has not yet been published in USC, but does appear in USCA or USCS, you can cite to one of them instead. See Rules 12.1 through 12.3 of The Bluebook or Rule 14 of The ALWD Manual for further guidance. If you ever need to cite to a very recent statute that has not yet been published in any codified form, see Chapter 5 in *Legal Research in a Nutshell* or another comparable advanced textbook. See also Rule 12.4 in the Bluebook or Rule 15 in The ALWD Manual for direction on how to do so properly.

ONLINE TIP: USCA is available exclusively online through Westlaw; USCS is available exclusively online through LexisNexis. Westlaw also offers access to the full text of statutes through its USC database without any annotations, thus allowing you to view a statute without retrieving other editorial enhancements. Appendix A of the supplement to this workbook contains a list of government sites and other fee-based and free internet sources for accessing federal statutes electronically.

Step 2: For this problem, you have not been given a cite to a specific statute or Public Law number, nor do you have a popular name for the law you are seeking. If you did, there are a number of shortcuts you could use to get into the Code to find your statute. You can read more about those shortcuts in Chapter 5 of *Legal Research in a Nutshell* or in an advanced textbook listed in Appendix A. Without such information, you'll need to start your statutory research by using the General Index to the publication you've selected (either USCA or USCS).

As with all legal research, you're going to have to be creative, flexible, and patient in finding a fruitful index term that will yield a statute worth looking into. Go back now and read the prior memos given to you by your senior partner. They may contain some useful leads for terms you can use to begin your search. In the space below, write down some terms with which you can begin:

> **TIP:** A Public Law number is the original number given to legislation when it has been passed by Congress. Appendix D in this workbook offers an overview of how laws are introduced and passed. If you had a Public Law number (assigned by Congress when it passed the law) for a statute you're trying to find, you could find the current location of the legislation in any of the Codes by using the parallel reference tables located in the "Tables" volumes of USC, USCA, or USCS. You will learn how to locate a Public Law number in the last section of this Assignment Sheet. Similarly, if you had a popular name for a statute you were looking for (such as the Taft-Hartley Act), you could find its title and section number in the Codes by using the "Acts Cited by Popular Name" table in USC or the "Popular Name" table in USCS. The "Popular Name" table in USCA is located not in the "tables" volume (as you'd expect) but rather in a separate "Popular Name" volume. Shepard's Acts and Cases by Popular Names: Federal and State will also direct you to the title and section of an Act if you know its commonly used name.

Step 3: Using the terms you identified in <u>Step 2</u> above, find the title and section number for any statute that may be able to answer the question presented to you by your senior partner. **Don't forget to check the pocket parts of both the Index and the Statutes themselves.** Sit down where you can read through the statute you've selected.

A great deal of federal legislation is too long and complicated to read thoroughly for the purposes of this Assignment Sheet. However, it is important to be familiar with the basic format which most federal legislation takes. Thus, please get oriented to the Act you've selected now by turning to the beginning of the Chapter in which it is codified and reading: (1) any index of sections (or table of contents) which may appear there; (2) the "short title" assigned to the Act, if there is one; (3) the "purpose" section of the Act, if there is one; (4) any "definitions" section for the Act, if there is one. Note that not all statutes have all of these features – their inclusion depends on how the framers chose to draft your particular Act (codified as a "Chapter"). Any time you are looking over a new statute, however, it is important to look for these features or you run the risk of reading a specific section incorrectly because you have taken it out of context. In the space below, write a short paragraph describing which of these features you found at the beginning of your Chapter.

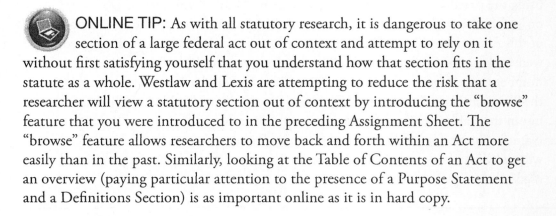

ONLINE TIP: As with all statutory research, it is dangerous to take one section of a large federal act out of context and attempt to rely on it without first satisfying yourself that you understand how that section fits in the statute as a whole. Westlaw and Lexis are attempting to reduce the risk that a researcher will view a statutory section out of context by introducing the "browse" feature that you were introduced to in the preceding Assignment Sheet. The "browse" feature allows researchers to move back and forth within an Act more easily than in the past. Similarly, looking at the Table of Contents of an Act to get an overview (paying particular attention to the presence of a Purpose Statement and a Definitions Section) is as important online as it is in hard copy.

Step 4: If you are satisfied that the statute you've selected is on point, turn to the section or sections you believe will resolve your partner's question. In the space below, write down the complete cite to the section you will be relying on. (Note: if you think more than one section applies, feel free to cite them all):

CITATION TIP: See Rule 12 of The Bluebook or Rule 14.2 of The ALWD Manual for guidance on how to properly cite a federal statute. After you have cited a statute once in a legal document, you should use a "short form" instead of the full citation to make reading (and writing) easier. See Rule 12.9 in The Bluebook and Rule 14.5 in The ALWD Manual for additional information on short citation format for statutes.

Step 5: As you have learned, in order to keep research sources current without having to republish hardback versions too frequently, publishers provide paperback supplements, called "pocket parts," which are inserted at the beginning or end of most volumes. It is critical that you get in the habit of always checking the supplement or pocket part of whatever resource you're using to make sure the law you're relying on has not been repealed or amended. Turn to the "pocket part" in the volume you're working in to make sure the statute has not been changed. Has it?:

Step 6: In the space below, write a short summary of how you believe this legislation, when read only on its "plain language", might resolve the question presented by your senior partner.

CAUTION: Do not reshelve your code volume yet; we will be using it to complete Section B below.

B. FINDING CASE LAW APPLYING OR INTERPRETING THE RELEVANT STATUTE

Introduction: As you have learned, finding a statute on point can rarely be the end of a research inquiry. Since virtually all statutes have inherent ambiguities, you need to research case law that will clarify how courts (especially in your jurisdiction) have applied or interpreted the statute in the past. Finally, you always need to update your search to make sure both the law itself and the cases applying or interpreting it are current.

Step 1: The joy of using <u>USCA</u> or <u>USCS</u> is that a great deal of your work has already been done for you by the publishers of those unofficial codes. At the end of many statutory sections, there are helpful references to other research sources (e.g., legal encyclopedias you learned about in Assignment Sheet 1, cross-references to related statutes, etc.). These source references are then followed by annotated case law references which are grouped by subject. Turn now to these "Notes of Decisions" in <u>USCA</u> or "Interpretive Notes & Decisions" in <u>USCS</u>. You'll see a listing of subjects covered at the very beginning of these annotations. Choose a subject that looks like it has potential to help you clarify details about the question raised by your senior partner. Write the name of the annotation subject area you want to look into here:

Step 2: Turn to the area of the annotated cases you selected in Step 1 and skim the annotations listed there. Note that the court of decision and the year of decision are included. REMEMBER TO CHECK THE POCKET PART FOR CURRENT CASES! Find a federal case that addresses your partner's question and write the complete cite to that case here:

Did you find this case in the main volume or in the pocket part?:

List a few other cases that you might have pinpointed to read if time had allowed:

CITATION TIP: See Rule 10 in The Bluebook, Rule 12 in The ALWD Citation Manual, and Assignment Sheet 2 for proper citation forms for cases.

At this time, please return the USCA or USCS volume you've been using to the shelf so that others may have access to it.

Step 3: Locate the first case you cited in Step 2 immediately above. Write the cite to that case and brief it in the space provided. Remember, you can turn to Appendix B to find a sample format for briefing a case. If you've selected an extremely long case (and some federal cases can be fifty pages long or more!), skim the case but carefully brief the section pertaining to the statute you're researching (remember you can use headnotes to help you pare down the reading process).

If the case you've found is cited with the letters "U.S." it is a United States Supreme Court case and will be found in the U.S. Reports (which is the official reporter for U.S. Supreme Court cases). If the case you've found is cited with the letters "L. Ed.," "L. Ed. 2d," or "S. Ct.," it is also a United States Supreme Court case and will be found in U.S. Supreme Court Reports, Lawyers' Edition, U.S. Supreme Court Reports, Lawyers' Edition 2d, or Supreme Court Reporter, respectively (each of which publishes U.S. Supreme Court cases more quickly than does the U.S. Reports). If the case you've found is cited with the letters "F.," "F.2d," or "F.3d," it is a United States Court of Appeals case and will be found in the Federal Reporter. If the case you've found is cited with the letters "F. Supp." or "F. Supp. 2d," it is a United States District Court case and can be found in the Federal Supplement. Write your brief of the relevant portion of the case you found here:

Step 4: Once you have found a good case on point, that case itself can become a rich source for finding other relevant case law on point. A case can be a good source for finding other cases if the court has closely examined a point of law you need to resolve and then cited precedent for its ruling or reasoning. In the space below, list a case cited in the case you just briefed that might be a good source for further reading (if you had time during this assignment, which you don't):

> **TIP:** If you are using <u>USCA</u> (which is published by West, and therefore uses their "Key Number System"), you could use any Topic and Key Numbers you found in the annotations to <u>USCA</u> to locate other federal and state cases on point. To use these Key Numbers to find other cases, you would turn to West's American Digest System (for federal cases) or to a state or regional Digest. Even if you used <u>USCS</u> for your research (and hence don't have any Key Numbers), you could use the <u>Descriptive Word Index</u> in any West Digest System publication to search out Key Numbers for further research.

Please return the case reporter you've been using to the proper shelf at this time before moving on to Part C below.

C. USING CITATORS TO UPDATE YOUR FEDERAL STATUTORY RESEARCH

Introduction: As you have learned in earlier Assignment Sheets, citators allow you to take a wide variety of legal research sources (such as cases or statutes) and find out a number of things about their current status fairly quickly. You can use a citator to see if a federal statute has been repealed or amended, if it has been cited (favorably or negatively) in a court case, and whether there are additional commentary or other cross-references available that could enhance your understanding of the statute.

Step 1: In this section, you will be asked to update your research online using Westlaw, <u>OR</u> online using Lexis, <u>OR</u> in hard copy, using traditional print materials. While it's a good idea to learn how to use all three, you will not be required to do so here. In the space below, please indicate how you plan to search for updates for the case you have read and briefed:

        _____ I have my professor's permission and a Westlaw password, and will update online using Westlaw **(go immediately to Step 2 below)**

        _____ I have my professor's permission and a Lexis password, and will update online using Lexis **(go immediately to Step 9 below)**

        _____ I will update using traditional print materials **(go immediately to Part III of Appendix C in the back of this workbook)**

Step 2: <u>Begin here only if you plan to update online using Westlaw. Update online using Westlaw only if you have a Westlaw password and your professor's permission to use it at this point in the semester.</u> Go to Westlaw.com and log on using the password issued to you by your school. (If you inadvertently sign-on to lawschool.westlaw.com, click on the tab that says "Westlaw Research" to get to the correct homepage.)

Step 3: For this exercise, you will be using Westlaw's online citation tool, "KeyCite", to update the statute you identified earlier in this assignment. If you used Westlaw's KeyCite function to update your case law research or your state statutory research in the preceding Assignment Sheets, you will find the process here to be familiar. Click on the hyperlink at the top of the page that says "KeyCite."

Step 4: The initial screen that appears gives you a dialogue box in which to enter the full cite to the statute you want to update. Additionally, notice that you can find an array of helpful information on the right side of the screen that will remind you exactly what sources a KeyCite search can lead you to, as well as an explanation of the meaning of West's status flags. In the dialogue box provided on the initial KeyCite screen, enter the full citation to the statute you are checking, and then hit "Go."

Step 5: Remember: online sources change frequently. Always check our website <www.LegalResearchWorkbook> for possible screen changes if these instructions are not consistent with what you find. As of the printing of this edition of the workbook, the results of your KeyCite search would appear first as a split screen. On the right, you will see the search results, with the full cite to your statute at the top. Pay attention to the presence of yellow or red flag, which indicate some relevant change to or information about the statute (the yellow flag) or some possible alarming results – such as an action declaring it unconstitutional or repealing it – concerning your statute (the red flag). To the left of the screen, you will see a number of hyperlinks that will connect you with additional information about your statute. Do you see a red or a yellow flag?

_____ no red or yellow flag

_____ yes, there is a yellow ( ) or red ( ) flag

On the left side of the screen, directly next to the flag (if a flag is present), Westlaw identifies why the status flag was attached to your case. What is that flag indicating?:

> **TIP:** <u>HAVING TROUBLE YIELDING RESULTS FOR YOUR STATUTE?</u> If your statute does not produce results that show a status flag, try switching to another statute related to your subject and see if it is a more richly applied statute. Alternatively, try entering 29 USC 2611 and using that statute for the remainder of this section on use of citators. That statute is part of the federal Family and Medical Leave Act and will yield good illustrative results for you. If you use 29 USC 2611, please place a check here so your professor will be aware of your choice: _____

Step 6: Click on the "Citing References" link on the left side of your screen. The cases that have cited your statute will appear. If you see a blue "H" to the left of a case, that status letter indicates that your statute was dealt with directly in that case. If you see a green "C" to the left of a case, that status letter indicates that the case referenced your statute, but did not directly apply nor interpret it. As with using the KeyCite feature to update case law, the presence of up to four green stars indicates depth of treatment of your statute within the case.

Step 7: Choose a citing case and write its citation below. We do not have time to ask you to read any of the cases citing your statute, but if this were a real legal issue with a real client, you would certainly need to do so. Weighing depth of treatment and considering any status letters, indicate why you might read the case you selected if you were interested in learning more about the statute you have cited.

ONLINE TIPS: As you learned in the preceding lesson on state statutes, Westlaw has added many research features to make updating and expanding research for statutes online useful and efficient – and as similar as possible to using actual print copies. Scroll down the left side of the screen and note that you can view the Table of Contents for your statute (which would help you get an overview of the statutory scheme), you can see earlier versions of the statute, and you can see a quick overview of the types of citing resources available to aid your understanding of this area of the law. If you click on the link to the statute itself, you can even "browse" sections located in proximity to the section you've searched by clicking on the "previous section"/"next section" at the top of the screen.

Also, Westlaw has introduced a "ResultsPlus" tool that identifies secondary sources that might expand your research related to this statute. Also, through its "KeyCite Alert" feature, Westlaw gives lawyers the opportunity to receive updates if new information comes online concerning a statute they are interested in. Finally, Westlaw has introduced a "Graphical Statutes" feature that gives you a quick visual overview of a statute's history and pending legislation along with quick hyperlink connections to that information.

All of these enhancements provide additional tools for the legal researchers and have gone a long way towards making online statutory research useful, but none are free. Law students have unlimited access to these tools while they are in school working on school-related projects. Later, even in the summer, students are limited to the same fee-based access of other private practitioners. Learning to use these resources efficiently and with confidence now, while a student, is a wise investment of time.

Step 8: In addition to helping you determine if your case has been amended or repealed, or might be impacted by proposed legislation, and to helping you find cases that have applied or cited your statute, KeyCite can help you find additional legal references to your statute. These additional sources include secondary materials (like law review articles), court documents (like briefs filed in a case), related statutes, and even a survey of similar laws in states. Scroll past the citing cases and list at least one other source that might be worth investigating if you had time (which you do not in this Assignment Sheet) to learn more about your statute:

Step 9: <u>Begin here if you are going to update online using Lexis. Update online using Lexis only if you have a Lexis password and your professor's permission to use it at this point in the semester.</u> Go to Lexis.com and log on using the password issued to you by your school.

Step 10: For this exercise, you will be using Shepard's Online to update the statute you identified earlier in this assignment. If you used the Shepard's function on Lexis to update your case law research in the preceding Assignment Sheet, you will find the process here to be very similar. Using the tabs across the top of the Lexis homepage, click on "Shepard's" to begin your updating. Be sure the "Shepard's for Research" option is selected (not the Shepard's for Validation/KWIC option).

Step 11: Remember: online sources change frequently. Always check our website <www.LegalResearchWorkbook> for possible screen changes if these instructions are not consistent with what you find. As of the printing of this edition of the workbook, you will be presented with a box in which you should type the citation to the statute you want to update. If you are uncertain of the format to use, click on the "Citation Formats" hyperlink to the right of the box. After you have entered the citation to your statute, click the red "check" box.

Step 12: The Lexis screen that appears first shows you the history of your statute as well as cross-references to cases that have cited your statute.

BEWARE: Before you get to the screen showing you the history of your statute and cross-references to cases citing your statute, you may see a screen that shows you subsections of your statute. **Be aware that information referenced for subsections on Lexis is NOT included cumulatively in information referenced for a larger, umbrella statute in which the subsection is included. Thus, to be thorough, you would need to check references for each individual subsection if you are interested in the statute as a whole.** For purposes of completing this assignment, if you see this screen, choose the broadest statutory reference that addresses your client's question.

Choose a case that you might read if you had time to read a case that has cited your statute and explain below why you might read that case to learn more about your statute:

Step 13: Next, click on the hyperlink to the statute itself at the top of the page. When the statute appears, scroll through the language of the statute and note that you can find cross-references to secondary resources and additional cases that may cite your case. Are there any references here that you did not see on the original Shepard's screen that might be useful to you?:

Step 14: While still viewing an online version of the statute itself, look for the "Archive Directory" in the center of the screen to see if you can find an earlier version of your statute. Is there an earlier version?

Step 15: If there is legislation pending for your statute, there will be a "Legislative Alert" just above the body of the statute itself. Is there information pending about your statute?

ONLINE TIPS: Lexis has added research features to make updating and expanding statutory research online useful and efficient – and as similar as possible to using actual print copies. When you are viewing the body of the statute, you can click on the "TOC" [Table of Contents] link on the top left side of the page to see the Table of Contents for the entire statutory section in which your exact citation appears. You can also click on the "Book Browse" link at the top of the page to get to a screen that allows you to use the "previous" and "next" arrows on either side of the cite to look at the statutory sections that appear just before and just after your statute in the code. You can click on the "Archive Directory" link to find older versions of the statute as well as to be alerted to changes to the statute that may be pending. Finally, through its "Shepard's Alert" feature, Lexis gives lawyers the opportunity to receive updates if new information comes online concerning a statute they are interested in.

D. RESEARCHING FEDERAL LEGISLATIVE HISTORY

Introduction: Like all legal research, researching legislative history requires patience and a clear sense of purpose. In the study and practice of law, many lawyers and law students do not need to research legislative history routinely. However, lawyers might need to know the history of a statute for a variety of reasons ranging from lobbying and political activism to presenting a court with a plausible interpretation of an ambiguous term in a statute. There are also times when a lawyer might want to look at the original version of an act that has since been amended (for example, when relying on a case interpreting an earlier version of an act). Even while in law school, a student might need to research legislative history as part of an advanced seminar assignment, to write a law review article, or to compete as a member of a moot court team.

It is beyond the scope of this workbook to exhaust all of the available means of unraveling a statute's history. Rather, we will explore a few tips to get you started. To learn more, read Chapter 6 in the *Nutshell* or a chapter on legislative history in another textbook listed in Appendix A.

TIP: Legislative intent is the light that guides judges as they interpret and apply statutes. The consideration of legislative history is viewed by some courts as a valuable means of discerning the legislative intent of those who passed a statute. Other jurists, however, believe that looking to legislative history as a means

continued on next page

of interpreting statutes can be misleading – believing that legislation changes markedly from introduction to passage, and that the history of individuals' thoughts, or even a committee's report prepared in that process, does not necessarily reflect the intent of the legislature that ultimately passed the bill. See Roy M. Mersky and Donald J. Dunn, Fundamentals of Legal Research (8th ed. 2002) for an interesting discussion of these conflicting views.

ONLINE TIP: Westlaw and LexisNexis have numerous tools to help streamline the process of tracing a statute's history. Coverage, however, is not comprehensive. The U.S. Government and most states maintain free websites that provide some access to documents that can help you track a bill's history. See Appendix A in the online supplement to this workbook for a list of electronic resources to explore with your professor's permission as you become more proficient in legal research.

Step 1: Turn to Appendix D ("How Statutes Come Into Being") in this workbook and read that Appendix now. By understanding the legislative process, you can begin to visualize the types of documents that would be generated (and accessible through research) during the different stages from introduction to passage of a bill. It is those documents that provide the history of a piece of legislation.

Step 2: Much federal legislative history research turns on knowing the bill number and/or the Public Law number assigned to the legislation. The Public Law number can be found in either USCA or USCS. Choosing one of those resources now, turn to the statute you used to complete Section A of this Assignment Sheet above. Look at the information contained in parentheses at the very end of the statute (just before any cross-references or annotated cases). If there is a Public Law number for the statute you have researched, please write it here: _____. Public Laws are amended frequently, resulting in citations to multiple Public Law ("P.L.") numbers at the end of a statute. If you find this to be the case, write the first "P.L." number from the list. The first number references the original piece of legislation. Also, Public Law numbers were not routinely assigned before 1957. If your statute does not have a Public Law number at all, write the Chapter number here instead:

Step 3: In addition to listing the Public Law or Chapter number, USCA and USCS also list a cite to United States Statutes at Large in the parenthetical information immediately following the text of a statute. <u>United States Statutes at Large</u> contains all bills passed by Congress in chronological order by date of passage. Amendments are also entered by date of their passage (so you can't find all parts of an act in one place using <u>United States Statutes at Large</u> – what you can find, instead, is the original form of a bill or amendment filed at the time and in the form it was passed). In contrast, bills are codified in <u>USC</u>, <u>USCA</u>, and <u>USCS</u> by *subject*, not chronologically. Look again at the parenthetical information at the end of the text of your statute. Where in <u>United States Statutes at Large</u> would you find this statute as it was originally passed? (Write the cite):

Step 4: Parenthetical information in <u>USCA</u> and <u>USCS</u> also includes references to amendments. If your statute has been amended, what are the dates of those amendments?:

Step 5: Go to <u>United States Statutes at Large</u> in your library and look up the cite from Step 3 above. Find the first page of the Act. In most cases, the statute you used for Step 3 will be a very small section of a much larger Act of Congress. Be sure that you turn all the way to the beginning of the Act in its entirety – many Acts can be hundreds of pages long. TIP: At the top of the page on which your statute is published, you will see its accompanying Public Law ("P.L.") number. One way to know you're at the beginning of an Act is to keep flipping backwards until you see the Public Law number change (because no two Acts have been assigned the same P.L. number). Write the bill number here:

> **TIP:** Bills introduced in the house carry the letters "H.R." in front of the bill number; bills introduced in the Senate are introduced by the letter "S". The vast majority of Public Laws will be introduced as a bill in one of these chambers and will carry one of these designations to indicate their origin.

> **TIP:** Since 1975, <u>Statutes at Large</u> has included a summary of the legislative history of each law at the end of the text of the law. If you're doing legislative history research for a statute passed since that date (and you're curious), turn to the end of the text now and see if you can locate that summary.

TIP: Almost all research into legislative history can be done using the Public Law number or the bill number. Use United States Code Congressional and Administrative News (USCCAN) – published by West and cross-referenced in the historical notes of USCA – to find a variety of useful information ranging from tables tracing the status of a bill to Presidential messages proposing legislation. Of perhaps most significance are the collections of committee reports – often relied on by courts interpreting legislative intent – prepared when the bill was introduced in the House or Senate. Other kinds of documents that might be interesting to you when you conduct legislative history research in the future are records of floor debates (debates on the floor of the Senate or Congress) and public hearings that may have been held after the bill was introduced.

TIME-SAVING TIP: Often, legislative histories of major acts have been compiled already. If you can find a history that has already been published, you can save a lot of research time. References that can help you locate such compilations can be found in Sources of Compiled Legislative Histories by Nancy P. Johnson, which is carried in most large law libraries. Check your library's online catalogue for other titles that might help you find compiled legislative histories or ask a law librarian for additional resources.

ONLINE TIP: Lexis, Westlaw, and other fee-based services listed in Appendix A of the supplement to this workbook have all developed means for conducting legislative history research. Electronic resources are often the best way to search for the status of recently passed or recently proposed federal legislation. When conducting legislative history research online, always check for scope of coverage. Appendix A of the supplement to this workbook also lists free websites that provide useful access to legislative history documents. Most notably, THOMAS (http://thomas.loc.gov) (maintained by the Library of Congress) and GPO Access (http://www.gpoaccess.gov) (maintained by the Government Printing Office) are each a rich source of information about federal statutes and their historical development.

You have now learned at least a few of the many ways that you can conduct research into federal questions. You can use <u>USCA</u> and <u>USCS</u> to find a federal law on point, you know one way to find cases interpreting or applying that law, you know how to update your research to make sure it's current, and you know how to begin doing research into the legislative history of a statute.

Please note your actual time of completion (including background reading): _____ *hrs.*

MARSHALL, STORY & ASSOCIATES
ATTORNEYS AND COUNSELORS AT LAW
SUITE 101, THE JUSTICE BUILDING

⚖

THE LITIGATION DIVISION

To: New Attorney
From: Assigning Partner
Re: Eric Arnold [Client A] – File #03-2576

Thank you for the research you found concerning federal statutory law and underground storage tanks.

Because of his strong environmental commitment, Mr. Arnold wants to follow all procedures recommended by the government when he shuts down his family's storage tank even if he is not legally obligated to do so. He has asked us for help in determining if there are any federal regulations that would give him some guidance.

As your final assignment for this case, we would appreciate it if you would check the federal administrative regulations promulgated by the Environmental Protection Agency to see if there are regulations offering specific instructions for how to close a tank permanently.

▶▶ Turn to page 157 to begin your work for this assignment.

MARSHALL, STORY & ASSOCIATES
ATTORNEYS AND COUNSELORS AT LAW
SUITE 101, THE JUSTICE BUILDING

⚖️

THE LITIGATION DIVISION

To: New Associate
From: Assigning Partner
Re: Project Hope [Client B] – File #03-2575

Project Hope is successfully off the ground. While waiting to raise funds to open a private school, the organizers have obtained a grant that is funding a pilot project within the existing local high school program. The pilot project has begun with ten high school students, each of whom was carefully chosen for his or her untapped potential and drive to achieve.

Among these first ten students is Robert Wallace, who dropped out of school last year at fifteen years old despite unusually high competency test scores and a gift for singing. Robert is also diagnosed with Attention Deficit Disorder (ADD), a diagnosis that came about in early elementary school when teachers reported that Robert was difficult to control in class and could not concentrate.

Project Hope hired a private consultant to re-test Robert before preparing an IEP for him. After testing Robert, the consultant has stated unequivocally that Robert does not presently show symptoms of ADD and should not receive medication at school. Robert is pleased with the results of these tests and says that he left the public schools at least in part because he had to take medication there under his IEP.

The school team has drafted Robert's IEP based on the consultant's assessment that he is gifted, but that he does not have Attention Deficit Disorder. The problem now is that Robert's parents do not agree with the consultant's assessment and they want his IEP to contain accommodations, including mandated medication, for ADD. The parents are requesting a second assessment or evaluation at public expense.

The Board has asked us to research the extent to which the parents can compel an independent evaluation of Robert, and whether it is likely that the test would have to be paid for out of public funds. I am sure that the Office of Elementary and Secondary Education with the U.S. Department of Education has created regulations that would be pertinent. For your last assignment for this project, would you please look into the federal administrative regulations promulgated under the Individuals with Disabilities Education Act to resolve these questions.

▶▶ Turn to page 157 to begin your work for this assignment.

MARSHALL, STORY & ASSOCIATES
ATTORNEYS AND COUNSELORS AT LAW
SUITE 101, THE JUSTICE BUILDING

⚖

THE LITIGATION DIVISION

To: New Associate
From: Assigning Partner
Re: Marjorie Morrison [Client C} - File #21-2203

The research you have done to date has been most helpful and I thought the information you found concerning the requirement that there be an alcohol-content label was particularly interesting.

To my surprise, when I spoke with Mr. Thompson's attorney this morning, he told me that Mr. Thompson does attach an alcohol-content label to all of his bottles of wine. Apparently the label, which also carries the requisite health warnings for intoxicating liquors, is attached by a ribbon that is tied around the neck of the bottle. The attorney said that since Mr. Thompson occasionally sells his wine from a display table in his backyard, the wind will sometimes blow the warning tag off a bottle. The attorney believes this must be what happened to the bottle Ms. Morrison purchased.

For your final assignment on Ms. Morrison's behalf, I would like for you to check the federal administrative regulations passed by the Bureau of Alcohol, Tobacco, and Firearms within the Department of the Treasury to see if it is sufficient to have the health warning label, which also contains the alcohol content information in Mr. Thompson's case, tied to the neck of a bottle of wine rather than permanently affixed to it.

▶▶ **Turn to page 157 to begin your work for this assignment.**

MARSHALL, STORY & ASSOCIATES
ATTORNEYS AND COUNSELORS AT LAW
SUITE 101, THE JUSTICE BUILDING

⚖

THE LITIGATION DIVISION

To: New Associate
From: Assigning Partner
Re: Allen Field [Client D] - File #21-2204

Dr. Field was encouraged by the research you did into the federal statute controlling historic preservation. Meanwhile, he has continued his dialogue with the state historic preservation officer who has offered to compromise on his earlier refusal to nominate the property by recognizing the house itself as being of historic worth because of it's unique architectural features. However, he is steadfastly refusing to recognize the grounds around the house, including the family cemetery where Geoffrey Bain is buried, as being of historic significance.

While Dr. Field was encouraged that the officer has agreed to nominate the house for listing on the National Register of Historic Places, he is frustrated at the officer's continuing refusal to list the farm and to recognize Geoffrey Bain as a historic figure of significance to the state. The entire thesis of his dissertation was that Geoffrey Bain's work has gone unnoticed and unappreciated in this state since his death, and he would like to correct that wrong.

For your final assignment, our client has asked us to look at the federal administrative regulations promulgated by the Department of the Interior to implement the National Historic Preservation Act. I am interesting in learning if a specific procedure has been established for appealing the state's decision if, in fact, the state officer declines to nominate both the house and surrounding grounds for listing on the National Register of Historic Places. If you find such a procedure, please do not feel like you have to gather all the details about it at this time. Rather, just for a start, please see if you can determine who would make the final decision on appeal.

▶▶ **Turn to page 157 to begin your work for this assignment.**

MARSHALL, STORY & ASSOCIATES
ATTORNEYS AND COUNSELORS AT LAW
SUITE 101, THE JUSTICE BUILDING

⚖

THE LITIGATION DIVISION

To: New Associate
From: Assigning Partner
Re: Josh Ward [Client E] - File #21-2205

I have spent some time doing research on my own into the National Environmental Policy Act, which mandates the filing of an environmental impact statement whenever a government project will have a significant impact on the human environment. The information you have contributed concerning requirements to address alternatives to the proposed project is interesting new information. Unfortunately, from other work I have done in this area, it is clear that the Environmental Policy Act does not create boundaries on many environmentally intrusive projects beyond a duty on the government to present a full report of its planned activity.

It is my understanding, however, that the Federal Highway Administration has promulgated regulations creating a higher threshold on government actions in wetlands involving the expenditure of Federal-aid Highway Funds. Much of Mr. Ward's property, and certainly the majority of the land in the southeastern portion adjacent to the proposed government road, is in a flood plain and would qualify as national wetlands. I would appreciate your looking into the administrative regulations drafted by the Federal Highway Administration to see exactly what the government would have to establish in order to be able to continue with this proposed project.

▶▶ **Begin your work on the following page.**

Assignment Sheet 5 *in Sequence of Assignments #1*
Researching Administrative (Government Agency) Law

Estimated Time
of Completion
(including recommended
background reading):
1.5 – 3.0 hrs.

Print Your Name:

(If you are doing this assignment as part of a class exercise, you may neatly write your answers directly on these sheets, staple all sheets together, and turn them in. If you prefer to write your answers separately using a computer, please be sure to number your answers to correspond to the appropriate questions before printing your responses).

Background Reading: To learn more about the resources and concepts introduced in this Assignment Sheet, read Chapter 7 of *Legal Research in a Nutshell* or a comparable chapter in a textbook listed in Appendix A of this workbook.

Background Information: We are all familiar with administrative agencies and routinely interact with them (e.g., the state Division of Motor Vehicles has rules about how to get your driver's license; the Food and Drug Administration has rules about what kinds of chemicals our produce can be sprayed with; the Federal Aviation Administration has rules that determine how close an airplane can fly to your home).

Because government agencies are not part of an elected body (they're not legislative) and are not part of our court systems, we sometimes fail to recognize that the rules they promulgate and their decisions about those rules are very much a part of our legal system. Knowing how to find both administrative regulations and administrative decisions interpreting and applying those regulations is a critical legal research skill. Here, your partner has asked you to find the answer to a specific regulatory question. By the time you finish this lesson, you will have an answer.

What You Will Learn. By the end of this assignment you will:

- Know how to find out the roles and functions of various federal agencies
- Be able to use the Code of Federal Regulations (CFR) to find a controlling federal administrative regulation
- Understand how to use the List of CFR Sections Affected (LSA) and the Federal Register to make sure a federal regulation is still current
- Understand how decisions of administrative law courts influence the application of administrative regulations
- Be introduced to resources to help you research state administrative regulations

The Research Process:
A. GETTING THE BIG PICTURE

It is often valuable to get the big picture when doing administrative law research in order to identify what agencies may be drafting regulations that impact your client's situation. Your partner's memo has indicated that the question raised is controlled by a specific federal agency. The U.S. Government Manual has long been a useful tool for getting an overview of the roles and functions (and current status) of individual federal agencies. Go now to http://www.gpoaccess.gov/gmanual/index.html to locate the online version of this manual. Alternatively, if your law library has a print version of the manul, you may use that instead. In the space below, briefly describe this agency's mission (feel free to quote the Manual, but be sure to use quotation marks if you do):

> **TIP:** Almost all federal agencies now maintain their own websites that include helpful information about the agency. In practice, when you know the agency that you believe is promulgating relevant regulations, you can go directly to that agency's website to learn more about its function and its regulations.

B. FINDING THE CONTROLLING REGULATION

Step 1: The place to begin your administrative law research is with the Code of Federal Regulations (CFR). The CFR, the official publication of federal rules and regulations, is the logical place to begin any regulatory research because the regulations are grouped there by subject. Just as the federal statutes you explored in Assignment Sheet 4 are grouped by Title and Section number in the United States Code, federal regulations are grouped by Title and Section number in the CFR. (Unfortunately, there is no correlation between the Title and Section numbers of federal statutes and their counterparts in the regulations.) **Go now to the location in your library where the CFR is shelved.**

Step 2: Find the "Index and Finding Aids" volume of the CFR at the far end of all the titles. The "Index and Finding Aids" volume is the index provided by the publishers of

CFR to help you find the regulation you're looking for. If someone else has that volume out, as an alternative you can use a more detailed index provided by private publishers: the Index to the Code of Federal Regulations. This alternative index is almost always shelved immediately after the CFR. In any event, find one of these tools now (**make sure you're using a current index**) and use either the subject index or the agency index (since you already know the agency's name) to look for a regulation that is likely to answer the question or to contain a more detailed section that would answer the question. Write the Title, Chapter, and Part number of any regulations with potential here:

> **TIP:** Note that the most refined entry in the index is to "Part" numbers. When you get to the actual regulation, you will note that these "Parts" are further broken down into related "Sections." To find an answer to most legal questions, you will need to find a specific Section.

PLEASE PUT THE INDEX YOU USED BACK ON THE SHELF NOW FOR OTHERS TO USE.

Step 3: Find the volume in CFR that contains the Chapter, Title, and Part number you identified in Step 2 above. Go to the Table of Contents at the beginning of the Title and see if there are specific Section references that look even more promising. There is no easy way to skim for such relevant Sections. Just keep an open mind and look for what might be promising. List at least one relevant Section in the space provided:

Step 4: Turning to the text of the regulations, skim each promising Section entry (there may only be one) until you find the answer to your partner's question. In the space provided, please summarize what you think the outcome of your client's situation will be under the regulation and why.

Step 5: In the space below, write the proper citation for the regulation you have relied on (see Rule 14 of the <u>Bluebook</u> or Rule 19 of <u>The ALWD Manual</u>):

TIP: All administrative regulations are promulgated under the authority of some specific "enabling legislation." If you have the citation to a statute, you can often find cross-references to administrative regulations that have been drafted under its authority by checking for cross references in print copy or online versions of annotated codes such as <u>U.S.C.S.</u> or <u>U.S.C.A.</u> For purposes of this Assignment Sheet, we would like you to use the <u>CFR</u> to locate a regulation so that you become familiar with that resource.

ONLINE TIP: Searching for administrative regulations online is often a good choice, especially if you know narrow terms that would lend themselves well to a specific word search. Westlaw and Lexis both have databases covering the <u>Code of Federal Regulations (CFR)</u>, and the text of regulations is also available free through GPO Access (http://www.gpoaccess.gov/index.html), which is maintained by the Government Printing Office. See Appendix A in the supplement to this workbook for additional fee-based and free resources that may help you locate (and update) administrative regulations. Westlaw and Lexis, as well as the GPO Access site, allow you to update regulations online.

C. MAKING SURE YOUR REGULATION IS STILL CURRENT

Step 1: Administrative regulations are constantly changing, so it is critical that you always check to make sure a regulation is current before you rely on it to answer a client's question. Begin your updating by checking the date on the front of the <u>CFR</u> volume where you found the regulation. You need to start your updating from this date. Write that date in the space below:

PLEASE PUT THE <u>CFR</u> VOLUME YOU HAVE BEEN USING BACK ON THE SHELF NOW.

Step 2: Go to the <u>List of CFR Sections Affected</u> (<u>LSA</u>) (usually shelved immediately after the <u>CFR</u>). Take down the volume with the most current date; check the page just inside the front cover. Write down the dates listed for changes in your title:

The <u>LSA</u> volume you just took down (the one with the most current date) will allow you to update your regulation through the last date listed on the inside front cover. Look inside the volume to see if the regulation you are working with has been mentioned/changed/amended. The references you see are to pages in the <u>Federal Register</u> (a pamphlet-type publication). Has your regulation been changed in any way? If so, write below the page number in the <u>Federal Register</u> where you would find the text of the change:

> **BEWARE:** Note that <u>LSA</u> uses both the Title AND the Section number when listing changes to a federal regulation that have become final, but only lists <u>proposed</u> changes by Part number (presumably because a "Part" is a more general subdivision and many proposed changes are not yet refined enough to be arranged by Section number). Hence, when updating federal regulations, you need to stay alert to Part numbers even if you have a specific Section number you are researching.

PLEASE PUT THE <u>LSA</u> VOLUME YOU'VE BEEN USING BACK ON THE SHELF NOW.

Step 3: In Step 2 above, you noted any page references to the <u>Federal Register</u> that would contain changes to your regulation up to the date covered in the latest issue of the <u>LSA</u>. Now you need to make sure that no additional changes have occurred to the regulation since that date. To do so, **go to the location in your library where the Federal Register is shelved now.**

Look in the *most current issue* of every month not covered by the <u>LSA</u> (e.g., if you're doing research in September, and if the latest <u>LSA</u> update is through July 31st, you would check the <u>Federal Register</u> for the most current issue in August and also the most current issue available for September. Using this example, the last August issue would have entries for all of August, and the most current September issue would have relevant entries for September up to the date of the latest issue available. Thus, your research would be comprehensive up to that last date).

Select the issues you need and turn to the back where you will find a list of "CFR Parts Affected" in the Reader's Aids section. Look for your Title and Part number in each of the issues you have pulled. If you found any changes, list the <u>Federal Register</u> pages where you would find one of those changes here:

BEWARE: When doing administrative law research (as with statutory research), it is critical to know if a court has made a significant ruling on the regulation's meaning, application, or constitutionality. You can find this information in hard copy by using <u>Shepard's Code of Federal Regulations Citations</u> to shepardize the Title, Section, and/or Part number in the usual manner, or online through a variety of sources. <u>Shepard's Code of Federal Regulations Citations</u> can also lead you to law review articles and entries in <u>ALR</u> (<u>American Law Report</u>) that cite your regulation.

Step 4: If you found that your regulation has been altered since it was published in the <u>CFR</u>, go to the <u>Federal Register</u> pages you listed in Steps 2 and 3 above and see if the changes apply to your client's concerns. (The spines of volumes in the <u>Federal Register</u> do not list the page numbers covered within them. You have to open a volume to see if the pages you are looking for are contained within it). If the changes apply to your client's situation, use the space below and on the following page to write how you think they will affect your answer to your client's question:

TIP: From time to time, you may want to look up an old regulation to see what was in force at an earlier time. For example, if you are reading an old court case that refers to your regulation, you'd want to make sure the judges had been looking at a version of the regulation that was substantially similar to the current one when they made their ruling. Otherwise, the ruling might no longer be applicable. To check on an earlier version of a regulation, you could use the prior edition of <u>CFR</u>, which is often kept on the shelves in large law libraries even though the regulations have been revised. If you are working where there are no prior editions of the <u>CFR</u> available, you could find the original language of the regulation by looking at the beginning of the current regulation where the date and cite to the regulation's original entry in the <u>Federal Register</u> are given. Use that information to go back and read the original language printed in the relevant issue of the <u>Federal Register</u>.

Step 5: In the space provided here, please write a short paragraph answering the question raised in your partner's most recent memo.

D. LOOKING TO THE FUTURE

1. Completing Administrative Law Research

As with statutes, you can't study administrative regulations in a vacuum. Before you rely on the plain language of an administrative regulation, you may need to check for significant administrative law decisions and/or cases on point. Finding administrative law decisions (the quasi-judicial actions taken by agencies when they hear appeals about the meaning or application of their regulations) is beyond the scope of this assignment. In the years ahead, stay alert to the need to learn more about this kind of research. If you find yourself in a position where you need to find agency decisions about a regulation, consider any of the following options:

- Use a "looseleaf service" (which you can learn more about by reading Chapter 9 of the *Nutshell* or a comparable section in a textbook listed in Appendix A)
- Use Shepard's United States Administrative Citations in print form
- Use the Shepard's tool on Lexis
- Use the KeyCite tool on Westlaw
- Use an agency's website to check for listings of that agency's decisions

In addition to being aware of an agency's decisions about its regulations, you also need to consider how the regulation relates to its enabling statute and to the Constitution.

An "enabling" statute is legislation that authorizes a specific government agency to promulgate regulations to forward the intent of the legislation passed. Administrative regulations are only valid if they are constitutional and within the scope of their enabling legislation. Hence, in-depth administrative law research requires careful attention to the boundaries set in the enabling statute, to administrative law decisions applying or interpreting the regulation, and also to federal and state court cases interpreting and applying the regulation and its enabling statute.

2. Conducting State Administrative Law Research

Each state organizes its own state administrative regulations using a system of the state's choosing. However, the principles of federal administrative law research generalize to any state or local agency. The actual process of conducting that research varies widely from state to state and from local government unit to local government unit. For example, the North Carolina Administrative Code has twenty-eight titles, which includes one for each of the major departments in the North Carolina executive branch of government. The titles are divided into chapters, subchapters, and sections as appropriate. If you are interested in doing additional administrative law research in your state, check with your law librarian. If you have the time, you might consider looking to see if your state has any regulations arising from the state statute you uncovered in Assignment Sheet 3.

TIP: States commonly maintain websites that provide easy access to information about the state's government, including legislation and administration regulations. Many state homepages can be found at <www.state.[insert U.S. Postal Service state initials here].us>. If you spend a short time searching a state government's website, you can often find a link to its administrative regulations and, with some luck, information about its administrative law process, links to the text of regulations, and information about pending regulations. Also, Appendix B of *Legal Research in a Nutshell* contains a comprehensive list of books and pamphlets to help you conduct research in individual states and there are many privately published books that explain the research process within a specific state. If you are interested in finding resources to help you conduct research specific to your state, ask your law librarian for assistance.

CONGRATULATIONS! You have completed your last Assignment Sheet for Part A, Sequence of Assignments #1, and have now been introduced to the basics of administrative law research. You know how to find a federal regulation in the <u>Code of Federal Regulations</u> and how to update your research to make sure it is current.

Please note your actual time of completion (including background reading): _____ hrs.

Part B: Sequence of Assignments #2

START HERE *only if your professor has asked you to begin with "Sequence of Assignments 2" OR with Client F, G, H, I, or J. If you have been asked to begin with "Sequence of Assignments 1" OR with Client A, B, C, D, or E, go instead to page 27.*

This second Sequence of Assignments introduces you to legal research sources in the following order: state statutes/federal statutes/administrative regulations/common law/ secondary sources. You can explore these resources using one of the following five client scenarios:

- **Client F:** "Client F" is Richard Roth, a Ph.D. candidate studying computer science after having recently completed a tour of duty with the military. He is interested in marketing an invention. For this client, turn to page 169;

- **Client G:** "Client G" is Ana Martinez, a recent college graduate, who is experiencing contract difficulties in her first job. For this client, turn to page 171;

- **Client H:** "Client H" is Christopher Smith, a young man who may have been fraudulently deceived when buying his first car. For this client, turn to page 173;

- **Client I:** "Client I" is Carolyn Meyer, a talented high school soccer player who is trying to retain the position she earned on the men's soccer team. For this client, turn to page 175;

- **Client J:** "Client J" is Jeanne Martin, a college student in a dispute with her landlord involving The Fair Housing Act. For this client, turn to page 177.

Each of the five lessons you will complete is introduced by an "assigning memo" that tells you more about your client and asks a specific legal question related to that client's situation. As you seek an answer to the question or questions you've been asked, you will be introduced to tools and strategies available to lawyers doing similar research. The point of this workbook is to teach you how to use research materials. The questions raised in your assigning memos provide a context through which to explore these materials.

Before you begin any individual lesson, always check our website <wwwLegal ResearchWorkbook.com> for any corrections to the text or significant changes in the law.

MARSHALL, STORY & ASSOCIATES
ATTORNEYS AND COUNSELORS AT LAW
SUITE 101, THE JUSTICE BUILDING

⚖️

THE LITIGATION DIVISION

To: New Associate
From: Assigning Partner
Re: Richard Roth [Client F] – File #03-2578

Welcome to the law firm of Marshall, Story & Associates. We were delighted when you accepted our offer to join the firm and I look forward to working with you on your first assignment.

Our client is Richard Roth, a former Army officer who recently finished his tour of active duty. Richard is an unusually creative and intelligent individual, and served six years as a Signal Corps officer before deciding to leave the service. He has now enrolled at our state university in a doctoral program in computer science.

While serving in the military, he pursued his interest in computers as a hobby, and became interested in playing computer games. He and his best friend from college, Christine, maintained contact throughout his tour of duty.

One of the interests Richard and Christine shared was a curiosity about computer games. Christine was encouraging when she learned that Richard was not only starting to program some games himself, but had also invented a new kind of external controller that was better than any existing mouse or joy stick.

They talked many times by phone – using Richard's private line that was separate from his roommate's line – about his invention, and she shared his enthusiasm for the fact that his invention made playing most interactive games more fun. Richard and Christine believed that his invention was highly marketable and, with her encouragement, he told no one but Christine about his invention and kept it in a locked safe in his room when he was not working on it. Only Richard and Christine knew the combination to the safe.

Richard has come to us because he is now ready to market his invention and has run into a number of major difficulties in the process. We would appreciate your unraveling the legal questions involved.

To begin, when Richard applied for a patent for his invention, he found that the officer who shared his off-base housing during his last year of active duty somehow learned about Richard's invention and has applied for a patent for the invention himself.

continued on next page

I do not want to look into the federal patent questions at this time. Rather, I would like you to begin your research in our own state law. From work I have done in the past, I am certain that if Richard's invention is a trade secret, then it is protected by state law from being misappropriated by the roommate. While there are other laws that might protect Richard's invention as well, right now I am interested in learning more about our state's Trade Secrets Act.

Specifically, I would appreciate your finding out if Richard's invention of a unique new external controller or mouse would constitute a trade secret. I look forward to seeing the results of your work.

▶▶ **Turn to page 179 to begin your work for this assignment.**

MARSHALL, STORY & ASSOCIATES
ATTORNEYS AND COUNSELORS AT LAW
SUITE 101, THE JUSTICE BUILDING

⚖

THE LITIGATION DIVISION

To: New Associate
From: Assigning Partner
Re: Ana Martinez [Client G] – File #03-2577

Welcome to the law firm of Marshall, Story & Associates. We were pleased when you accepted an offer to join our firm and I look forward to having the opportunity to work on this first assignment with you.

Our client is Ana Martinez. Ana graduated recently with highest honors from our state university. She majored in biochemistry and earned a minor in exercise physiology. Her parents are long-standing business clients of our firm, and we have agreed to represent her on this case at no cost.

Upon graduation, Ana was uncertain what to do next. She had been in school for sixteen straight years, so she did not want to attend graduate school immediately. Moreover, she was not certain what she would want to study even if she did continue in school.

As luck would have it, she learned through family friends about a business opportunity that she thought might be exactly what she was looking for. An acquaintance of one of her roommates was starting a small, homeopathic pharmaceutical business based largely on the internet and needed recent graduates to cover new sales markets for the company.

With an interest in the sciences and in health, Ana thought this would be a good opportunity. She met with the company founder, who introduced himself as Dr. Thomas Townsend, and was pleased with what he had to say. The sole patented drug that she would be marketing was a youth-enhancing hormone designed to help reduce the impact of aging. Dr. Townsend, who said he was a physician, had invented the drug himself.

Ana and Dr. Townsend entered a six-month employment contract that entitled her to minimum wage reimbursement for her time plus potentially large commissions. As part of the agreement, she was obligated to purchase $1,000 worth of the hormone in advance, and $500 worth for each subsequent month that the contract was in effect (for a total of $3,500 investment committed to by Ana).

When Ana began to develop her market, she started by meeting with some of her exercise physiology professors on campus. One of the professors raised concerns about the wisdom of her agreement, noting that Dr. Townsend was not affiliated with an academic

continued on next page

research institution and had presented no documentation about the safety of the drug. With the professor's help, Ana researched Dr. Townsend's background and found that he was not, in fact, a medical doctor but rather had a Ph.D. in business management from a small school in another state. When she approached Dr. Townsend about this fact, he said, "I am a natural healer and have personally seen the benefit that this drug has on my patients."

Ana is now concerned about her relationship with Dr. Townsend and comes to us with several questions. To begin to help her unravel her predicament, can you research our state statutes to confirm that a person is required to be licensed before practicing medicine here?

▶▶ **Turn to page 179 to begin your work for this assignment.**

MARSHALL, STORY & ASSOCIATES
ATTORNEYS AND COUNSELORS AT LAW
SUITE 101, THE JUSTICE BUILDING

⚖

THE LITIGATION DIVISION

To: New Associate
From: Assigning Partner
Re: Christopher Smith [Client H] – File #21-2206

Welcome to the law firm of Marshall, Story & Associates. We were all pleased when you accepted our offer to join our firm and I am looking forward to having an opportunity to work with you on the present case.

Our clients are Christopher Smith and his parents. The Smiths have been my neighbors for years and I have had the privilege of watching Christopher grow up since they moved into the neighborhood ten years ago. Christopher just turned sixteen years old. He has been mowing lawns and doing odd jobs in the neighborhood since he was twelve, and had amassed what was to him a sizable savings account. His dream was to buy a car of his own to drive to and from school. Last month, Christopher was with some friends downtown when they ran into the older sister of an acquaintance he knew from school. The older sister, Susan Adams, is a graduate student at a university in our neighboring state who had come back to town for summer break.

During the course of their conversation downtown, it came out that Susan was planning to sell her car. The car is a bright red 1982 Nissan 'Z' that appears to be meticulously restored to mint condition. Needless to say, it was the car of Christopher's dreams. Christopher only had $5,000 to spend on a car and was hesitant to put that much into an older model car like this 'Z'. Susan assured him, however, that the car had hardly been driven and had, in fact, been stored here in town throughout Susan's college career. As proof of what she called the car's "mint condition," Susan showed Christopher that there were only 25,000 miles on the odometer. Christopher said he was interested in the car, but wanted to talk with his parents about it and also have the car seen by a mechanic. Susan said she was returning to her university that night and that if Christopher wanted the car, he'd have to buy it then.

One thing led to another, and Christopher and Susan struck a deal that day. Christopher withdrew all but $100.00 from his savings account and had a cashier's check issued in Susan's name. In exchange, Susan signed over the title of her car and handed Christopher the keys right there. The next day, Susan was indeed gone. Christopher took the car to a mechanic who said that even a cursory glance from someone who knew engines would reveal that the car probably had well in excess of 100,000 miles on it. Moreover, the suspension was damaged and there had been extensive body work done on the car. In summary, the mechanic felt the car had been in a major wreck and was probably not worth over $1,000.

continued on next page

Needless to say, the Smiths are extremely upset for Christopher. While there are some lessons that need to be learned the hard way, this seems like an extraordinarily expensive one. They called me last week to see what legal recourse Christopher might have. During that initial conference, the Smiths said that they have learned that Susan Adams is not the incidental car seller she led Christopher to believe she was. Rather, she has made a business of sorts out of selling cars over the past three or four years. Apparently she purchases older cars in our neighboring state and then brings them here to sell to local students at a profit. Christopher's 'Z' is at least the sixth or seventh car she has sold here in town.

For your first assignment, I would like you to explore whether Ms. Adams has violated our state statutes by failing to properly report the correct odometer reading on this car when she sold it to Christopher. If her failure to accurately report the correct odometer reading is a state statutory violation, I think it should be an easy matter to bring the violation to her attention so that she will return Christopher's money and void their contract.

▶▶ **Turn to page 179 to begin your work for this assignment.**

MARSHALL, STORY & ASSOCIATES
ATTORNEYS AND COUNSELORS AT LAW
SUITE 101, THE JUSTICE BUILDING

⚖

THE LITIGATION DIVISION

To: New Associate
From: Assigning Partner
Re: Carolyn Meyer [Client I] - File #21-2207

Welcome to the law firm of Marshall, Story & Associates. We were all pleased when you accepted our offer to join our firm and I am looking forward to having an opportunity to work with you on the present case.

Our client is Carolyn Meyer, a seventeen year old girl who has recently moved to our town from another state. In the state where she previously lived, soccer is a popular sport enjoyed by both men and women, boys and girls. At the new high school in which Carolyn is now enrolled, however, soccer is only offered as a men's sport although there are other sports open to women.

The absence of a women's soccer team has presented a problem for Carolyn, who is an extremely competent athlete with the potential to earn an athletic scholarship to play soccer at the college level if she maintains her skills through high school. Prior to her family's move to our state, college coaches had already expressed an interest in her potential. Thus, Carolyn is anxious to decide how to maintain her skills as well as her scholarship opportunities despite the fact that there is no women's team in the area on which she can play. She has approached our firm to explore the legality of a number of options she is considering.

Carolyn's first idea is that, since she is a senior, perhaps she does not have to attend school at all but rather can elect to leave high school before graduating. She would like to leave school now and work voluntarily within the community to help facilitate the development of a girl's soccer program while maintaining her own skills by traveling to a nearby town to practice soccer with a women's team there. She plans to earn her high school diploma through a local community college program that would allow her to enter college with her peers. Her parents are supportive of this plan and have encouraged her to explore her options while assuring her that they would continue to allow her to live at home even if she is not enrolled in a formal educational program. The family contacted the local school board concerning Carolyn's idea, and was told that the school board would not approve a request for her to leave school.

For your first assignment, I would appreciate your looking into our state's compulsory education laws to determine if Carolyn could withdraw from school without violating our relevant state statutes. I will look forward to finding out what you have learned when you have completed this assignment.

▶▶ **Turn to page 179 to begin your work for this assignment.**

MARSHALL, STORY & ASSOCIATES
ATTORNEYS AND COUNSELORS AT LAW
SUITE 101, THE JUSTICE BUILDING

⚖️

THE LITIGATION DIVISION

To: New Associate
From: Assigning Partner
Re: Jeanne Martin [Client J] – File #21-2208

Welcome to the law firm of Marshall, Story & Associates. We were all pleased when you accepted our offer to join our firm and I am looking forward to having an opportunity to work with you on this case.

Our client is Jeanne Martin, a college senior attending school in a near-by town. Since her sophomore year, she has lived in a garage apartment on a large estate on the outskirts of town. Ms. Martin has come to us for help concerning a conflict with her landlady. Up until very recently, Ms. Martin and her landlady have gotten along extremely well. In fact, both women share a common interest in dogs and, with her landlady's encouragement, Ms. Martin purchased a pure-bred golden retriever puppy from a litter born to the landlady's show quality retriever.

Unfortunately, the relationship between these former friends deteriorated when Ms. Martin told her landlady that she would be leaving her apartment upon graduation in a few months. The landlady apparently became upset because she realized that Ms. Martin would be taking her puppy with her, and the landlady was not yet ready to part with the dog. In any event, the landlady has not been maintaining the condition of the apartment since Ms. Martin gave her notice. Most recently, the hot water heater has broken and there is no hot water for washing dishes, taking showers, or doing laundry.

When Ms. Martin brought the problem to her landlady's attention, her landlady told her that she would just have to "make do" with lukewarm water until she vacated the apartment. The landlady has taken the position that she does not intend to repair the hot water heater, despite the fact that she acknowledges that failure to do so is a violation of local building ordinances and makes the apartment uninhabitable.

Ms. Martin has come to us to see what her legal rights are concerning her apartment. For your first assignment, I would appreciate you looking into our state's landlord-tenant laws to see what remedies are available to Ms. Martin. I am meeting with her again in about a week, and will look forward to sharing the results of your research with her at that time.

▶▶ Begin your work on the following page.

Assignment Sheet 1 *in Sequence of Assignments #2* **Research State Statutes**	Estimated Time of Completion (including recommended background reading): 2.5 – 4.0 hrs.
Print Your Name:	

(If you are doing this work as part of a class exercise, you may neatly write your answers directly on these sheets, staple all sheets together, and turn them in. If you prefer to write your answers separately using a computer, please be sure to number your answers to correspond to the appropriate questions before printing your responses.)

Background Reading: To learn more about the resources and concepts introduced in this Assignment Sheet, read Chapter 5 of *Legal Research in a Nutshell* or a comparable chapter in a textbook assigned by your professor. (See Appendix A.)

Background Information: Your senior partner has raised a question that will require you to look into your state's statutes. This assignment sheet will show you how to find the relevant legislation on point. Your research into your partner's question cannot stop once you have located the statute you need. Rather, it is important to learn how courts in your state have applied or interpreted the statute. It is equally important to learn to update your research so that you can be confident that the statute and related case law you have found are still current.

What You Will Learn. By the end of this assignment, you will:

- Know how to find and read a statute passed by the legislature of your state
- Know how to find and read a statute passed by the legislatures of other states
- Know how to find and think about judicial decisions applying or interpreting a statute
- Know how to use a citator to make sure a statute is still "good law"
- Know how to use a citator to find additional sources related to your statute

The Research Process:

A. BECOMING FAMILIAR WITH YOUR STATE'S STATUTORY SCHEME

Introduction: One of the remarkable things about this country is that, even as we have grown to develop a strong national identity and sociologists and politicians alike argue that regions are losing their individual identity (it's hard to travel any place in the country where you can't get the same fast food you could order at home), our founders' vision of a balance of power between state and national governments appears to be alive and well today. Nothing will convince you of the continuing individual identity of each of our fifty states faster than doing legal research on the state statutory level. At the state statutory level, you will be hard-pressed to find any two states that have evolved exactly the same solution to any given legal problem. Given the diversity among state statutory schemes, it is easy to panic as you begin doing legal research in this area. The best way to avoid such panic is to be patient with yourself and have faith that there is some logic to every state's statutory scheme. Your task in this lesson is to figure out what that logic is and how to apply it to find an answer to your partner's question. To answer that question, you do not need to know how to find statutes in all fifty states. Rather, you only need to find the right statute in one state for now.

Step 1: Go now to the location in your library where the state statutes relevant to your client's question are shelved.

BEWARE: Many large law libraries hold onto their old statutory volumes despite the fact that those laws have been superseded and are no longer in effect. They often store those old volumes in close proximity to the current volumes. Librarians do this because there are times when a legal researcher would want to go back and find the old version of a law rather than the new version. For example, I might want to find the old version of a law if I were reading an old case and wanted to see what the statute looked like at the time that case was decided. Similarly, I might want to look at the old version of a statute if I were researching the legislative history of a statute and wanted to read an earlier version of it.

When you are researching a question like the one your partner has asked, however, you want the current version of the law. Thus, you have to be careful not to reach for a version of the statute that is no longer in effect. One way to distinguish current from outdated statutes is to check the binding – most libraries will mark defunct statutes with a small sticker with the word "superseded" on it. Before you move to the next step, make sure you are working in a set of statutes that contains current law.

Step 2: All states organize their statutes by general subjects of law (for example, criminal laws are usually grouped together, family law or domestic statutes are usually grouped together, corporate or business statutes are usually grouped together, etc.). The majority of states combine these subject areas into volumes that are numbered consecutively. Sometimes several subject headings will be contained within one volume, but the subjects are still grouped alphabetically by the subject titles.

There are a few states that do not follow this scheme. Those states (California, New York, and Texas) divide their statutes into multiple volumes by subject and number each of these books or codes separately. For example, the New York statutes on Banking Law are contained in "Book 4" which is divided into three separate volumes, each of which is numbered "4." The next "book" contains New York's statutory laws on Benevolent Orders which contains only one volume and is labeled "5" on the binding. The next "book" contains several volumes, all of which are labeled "6", etc. Some of these states provide separate indexes (or "codes") for each book at the end of the last volume for that topical grouping.

Fortunately, the majority of states follow a simpler system, numbering their volumes from 1 to whatever number they need to cover their last volume. Look at your state's statutes now and, in the space below, note what subjects are covered in the first two volumes and what subjects are covered in the last two volumes (if you're in California, New York, or Texas, write down which books or codes come first and last).

First volumes:

Last volumes:

Step 3: It is important to understand how your state's laws are organized, and what terminology is used by the drafters as they organize the laws into logical groupings. Different states use different headings for the various components of their statutes, but most systems generally follow a scheme where there are general headings that become more refined as the relevant law becomes more specific. As an example, most states follow some variation of the following divisions:

- Volume (or "Codes" and "Books")
- Title
- Division
- Part or chapter
- Subchapter or Article
- Section
- Subsection

BEWARE: In most states, only some – not all – of the organizational divisions listed above appear. Do not expect to find all of these organizational tools used in the state in which you are conducting your search for a statute.

The best way to become familiar with your state's organizational scheme and vocabulary is to browse through several volumes to get a sense of what terms are used. You can begin by looking at the bindings to see the terms set out there (they are probably the most general terms used).

Next, take a volume off the shelf and see what you can find in the opening pages. Usually the publisher's name is listed as well as helpful hints concerning use of the volume. Sometimes the first volume in the set will contain a history of how the state's statutes have been organized for publication in the past and how they are organized now. Somewhere near the front there is also usually a Table of Contents showing the contents of that volume. That Table of Contents at the beginning of a volume usually contains the terminology that is used to describe the next layer (or layers) of organizational division.

Finally, turn randomly to a specific law listed in the Table of Contents and see if you can identify the organizational scheme (e.g., title, chapter, section) used in the state in which you're doing research. In the space below, describe the organizational terms used in order from general to specific (the following **TIP** may help):

TIP: In EVERY state, the key organizational component of the statute is the SECTION. Turn to Table T-1 (United States Jurisdictions) in The Bluebook or Appendix 1 in The ALWD Manual and find the entry for your state. You'll note the official citation form for your state's statutes there – and in every state, proper cites refer directly to appropriate sections. These same sections are the basis of references in the indexes to the statutes themselves. You will learn to use the statutory index next.

CITATION TIP: In legal citations, writers generally use a section symbol ("§") in place of the word "section," or they use "sec." as an abbreviation. See Rule 6.2 and Table T.16 in The Bluebook or Rule 6 and Appendix 3 in The ALWD Manual.

Step 4: Despite the fact that there are individual variations in how each state publishes its statutes, you have learned that all state statutory compilations have some features in common. For example, the statutes are contained in series of volumes that are followed at the end by a general index. The general index will contain subject headings and subheadings to help you find a statute on point. Some states also publish individual indexes within each volume. Look over the volumes in front of you for your state statute and, in the space below, write a brief description of the indexing scheme for your statutes (is there only a general index or are there individual indexes as well?):

Open the index at random and notice how the editors send you to a specific statute. Choosing any topic and statutory reference at random, write an explanation in the space below describing what you found (for example, in Maryland, most statutes are listed by subject and section, thus: EN sec. 4-601 for section 4-601 of the Environmental volume whereas Arkansas includes the title, chapter, and precise section in each section citation, thus: sec. 8-5-203 for section 203 of Chapter 5 of Title 8, Environmental Law):

ANOTHER CITATION TIP: One way to determine the section citation form used by your state is to look at the top of any given page in a statute volume. The number for the section printed on that page almost always appears at the top of that page. If you ever have to write an official citation to a statute, use Table T-1 of The Bluebook or Appendix 1 and 2 of The ALWD Manual to determine the proper citation form for statutes from each state.

TIP: At the time this workbook was printed, there were some other idiosyncrasies in a few states that might concern you if you are working in one of those states. Note that Pennsylvania publishes two complete sets of volumes mingled together. When you use the index for Pennsylvania, note carefully which compilation is being referred to and be sure you are in that compilation when you

continued on next page

look for the right law. South Carolina is a little unusual in that its index contains references both to its statutory law AND its administrative law. For this lesson, you only want to use the statutory references. Finally, the system adopted in Maryland can be somewhat confusing at first. In Maryland, part of the code (the one adopted in 1957) is bound in black and contains statutes grouped in consecutive numbers like most states. The remaining part of the code (the part adopted later) is bound in maroon and contains statutes grouped and codified by topic (like Texas, New York, and California). References to these later-adopted statutes cite the book in which the statute is published (e.g., TR § 10-101 for a statute published in the Transportation code).

B. FINDING A STATE STATUTE ON POINT

Introduction: Now that you have a basic feel for how your state's statutes are set up, you are ready to move forward to find a specific statute that will answer your partner's question concerning your state's laws.

Step 1: The General Index located at the far end of each complete set of statutes is your primary tool for finding a relevant statute. Because the Index is extremely detailed, using it can be one of the most frustrating steps in doing any statutory research. Especially when you are unfamiliar with your statutes, it is often difficult to come up with the correct term that will lead you to the statutory reference you need. See the TIP immediately below for one systematic approach to generating search terms. Patience and creativity are virtues in this process. In the space below, write down any terms that you think might be useful places to begin looking for legislation on point (note that your senior partner may have already given you some "leads" – if so, feel free to put them here):

TIP: When you are generating "search terms" in legal research, experienced teachers will wisely encourage you to keep in mind the "5 W's" that you may have learned about in a beginning journalism class (who, what, when, where, and why). In a legal context, applying these concepts helps you think about the parties or things involved (minor child, teacher, dog, etc.), the type of action or conflict (battery, robbery, lie), when the action occurred (vacation, workday, off duty), where the action occurred (bank, school, playground) and why the action occurred (malice, self-defense, mistake, protection of property). Generating synonyms broadens the chance that you will find the law in a place where editors or publishers have also catalogued the information. It's not enough to think (although that's a good start); you have to think creatively about where the law might be stored. As you gain experience, you will become more familiar with the terms that have been used over the years to categorize certain types of actions, certain defenses, classes of people, etc.

Step 2: Turn to the Index itself and begin exploring the terms you've developed in the brainstorming step above. Be prepared to refine or adjust your approach. Some state indexing systems are incredibly detailed. Don't get discouraged; be prepared to persevere. In the following space, write down the reference to at least one statutory section that looks like it may answer your partner's question:

BEWARE: When you are working in the Index, be aware that there are lots of divisions with subdivisions that can run for pages on end. Don't lose track of where you are. For example, if you're trying to find out if you need a license to sell alcoholic beverages, the largest division you might begin with could be Alcohol or Liquor or Alcoholic Beverages (depending on the terms used in your state). Next, you could look for a subdivision concerning "sales" (or "transportation," or "advertising," or "wine," etc.). It's easy in the process to find that you have inadvertently moved out of your original general division (e.g., "Alcohol") and into a different general division (e.g., "Alcohol Review Board"). You may never find a relevant subdivision under that second general division you inadvertently moved to because the subdivisions you're looking for only made sense when you were in the division you started in. In other words, keep alert and stay flexible as you explore the index. Also, if your first idea isn't working, try something new. For example, going straight from "Alcohol" to a subdivision of "sales" may not work in your state. You may instead need to go from "Alcohol" to "licensing" to "sales." Every state system is different, and learning to use the index calmly is a real challenge.

Step 3: Once you have a reference to a potentially useful statute, the next step is to go to the statutory volumes themselves and begin to explore the law. Go now to the shelf containing your statutes and find the volume (or book/code) containing the reference you found.

BEWARE: It is easy to confuse volume numbers with chapter numbers in many state publication schemes. As a rule, most references to a particular statute in the index will NOT refer you to a volume itself. Rather, they are references to chapters and then sections housed in consecutive order within consecutively-numbered volumes. In North Carolina, for example, if the index refers you to § 20-17, you will find that statute in VOLUME 5 of the North Carolina General Statutes. That volume contains Chapter 20 ("Motor Vehicles"), Article 2 ("Uniform Driver's License Act"), and Section 17 ("Mandatory Revocation of License by Division [of Motor Vehicles]"). You would not find a reference to Volume 5 in the General Index at all, even though you'd have to pull Volume 5 from the shelf to find § 20-17. Note also that some states do not list volume numbers on the spine of their bound statutes – rather, only the subject heading is listed.

Step 4: When you read a statute, it is important to place it in context. NEVER try to rely on a specific statutory subsection to answer a client's question until you understand how that subsection fits in the chapter (or act) as a whole. Read the statute you just located in Step 3. If the statute continues to seem on point to you, write its full cite here and the following steps will help you explore how that section fits in the chapter (or act) as a whole. (Note: if you no longer think the statute applies after you've read it, go back and repeat Steps 1 through 3 above until you find a statute that you believe addresses your partner's concerns):

TIP: Some states have more than one published version of their statutes, but all states have only one official published version (the version sanctioned by their legislative body as being the authoritative copy of that state's laws). You can find the name of the official version by checking Table T-1 in The Bluebook and Appendix 1 in The ALWD Manual. If you are writing about the law, you should always cite the "official" version if it is available to you.

ANOTHER TIP: If you find yourself in a position to write about this statute, you will need to note the year the statute was published (not the year it was enacted) at the end of the cite as indicated in Table T-1 and Rule 12 of The Bluebook, or Appendix 1 and Rule 14 of The ALWD Manual. In a state with bound versions, that publication year is found at the beginning of each volume. If you ever need to cite to a Supplement containing very recent versions of a statute (inserted at the beginning or end of each volume, or published in a separate volume of Supplements usually shelved next to the corresponding volume in the main compilation), use the date found on the front cover of the Supplement. If you want to know when a statute was enacted or amended (rather than the publication date), check the dates listed in parentheses at the end of each statutory section.

Step 5: Go back, now, and read any Table of Contents section you can find for the Chapter as a whole. Where did you find the Table of Contents?

 TIP: Sometimes it is extremely cumbersome (and unrewarding) to try to use the General Index to locate a specific section within a complicated act. In such a case, it is sometimes easier to go straight to the Table of Contents to a specific act or chapter once you've seen enough of the Index to figure out the broader number for the act or chapter itself. If you are looking for a particular subsection, you can sometimes peruse the Table of Contents for the act as a whole to see if the legislature included a section on point. This method is often easier than trying to figure out how the editors of the statutes indexed a particular subsection in their General Index.

Step 6: Using the Table of Contents for the Act, see if there is a Definitions Section for your Chapter. If there is, skim it to make sure there are no definitions that apply to the statute you'll be relying on as you answer your partner's question. If you found a relevant definition, summarize it in the space provided:

Step 7: Updating is important! If you find a statute in the main volume, you always need to check to make sure it has not been amended or repealed. To check on its current status in many states, look in the "pocket part" supplement at the front or back of the volume (or in the separately bound Supplement volume, depending on your state). A "pocket part" is a supplement printed by the publisher at more frequent intervals than the main volume is printed. Librarians insert this "pocket part" either in the front or the back of the volume the pocket part is updating so that you have access to the absolute latest information. Note also that in many states there is a free-standing paperback version of a Supplement that sets out legislation that is hot off the press. To continue updating, it is also important to check this paperback volume to make sure no very recent changes have been made to your statute. Has the statute you're relying on been amended or repealed since it appeared in the main volume of the statutory code?

ONLINE TIP: Occasionally a statute may have been amended or repealed so recently that the change does not even show up in the statutory supplement. The most dependable way to look for very recent statutory changes is to use online legal research sources. To save time as you complete this exercise, we will not ask you to check online for udates.

Step 8: In the following space, based solely on the "plain language" of the statute as you read it, write a brief synopsis of how you think this statute might help resolve your partner's question.

C. FINDING RELEVANT CASE LAW BY USING ANNOTATIONS

Step 1: In most states, you will find numerous helpful research aids at the end of each statutory section (unless the statute has been enacted so recently that not much has happened yet with it). In a very few states (for example, Montana) these helpful research aids are included in separately bound volumes of Annotations which are shelved immediately following the statutes themselves. In these research aids, the publishers often list references to relevant law review articles (which will be introduced in Assignment Sheet 5) directly under each statute. Sometimes you will also find a summary of the effects of amendments or comments by drafters of the legislation itself and cross-references to related statutes or administrative regulations among these research aids.

The most helpful research aid in your search for finding related case law is listed next; it is called different things in different states. In North Carolina, these annotations are called "Case Notes." In Alaska, on the other hand, they are called "Notes to Decisions." These case notes are annotated summaries and citations to court decisions where a judge had to interpret or apply the relevant statute. If there are a lot of case notes, the editor will have divided them by topical subsections. You will sometimes find a Table of Contents to the various subsections of annotations listed at the very beginning of the annotated case section of the research aids. Using the statute you are relying on to answer your partner's question, find the annotated case section of the research aids and write the name of that section here (e.g., Case Notes, Notes to Decisions, etc.):

Step 2: Skim the annotated cases summarized at the end of that statute to see if there are any cases that might help your partner answer the statutory question he or she has raised. (A case can be valuable precedent even when the parties or situation are not exactly the same as your client's – your primary concern for purposes of completing this Assignment Sheet is to find a case that sheds light on the statute you are researching.) Following the format in the annotation itself (without worrying about proper legal citation form at this point), write the citation to at least one case on point here. Remember to check the supplement for relevant cases as well. If the statute you found does not have annotations, check around for a related statute that does and use the annotations you find there to complete the rest of this exercise so that you get the full learning experience. If you find annotations to a different statute, please note what that statute is here as well.

Please reshelve the statute volume you've been using now.

Step 3: Using your state or regional reporter, locate the case you cited immediately above. (See the TIP below for instructions on how to locate a case once you have a citation.)

TIP: Written opinions reflecting the decisions that judges have reached about particular cases (usually appellate cases) are published in "reporters" in chronological order based on when the decision was handed down. These decisions are published in "official," and sometimes "unofficial," form. The official" form is the one authorized by the proper authority to represent the actual opinion of the court, but in reality "official" and "unofficial" versions of a case will almost always look the same.

continued on next page

Some courts automatically "publish" all of their opinions. Other courts publish only select opinions. In North Carolina, for example, only about 35% of decided cases from the North Carolina Court of Appeals have opinions that are subsequently published. You will learn a little more about how lawyers access and use "unpublished" opinions in Assignment Sheet 4.

Once a case is published, the citation to that case tells you where to go to find the opinion itself. For example, <u>Concerned Citizens v. Holden Beach Enters.</u>, 325 N.C. 705, 388 S.E.2d 450 (1988) is a 1988 case which you could find by looking up page 705 of volume 325 in the North Carolina Reports (the official reporter for the North Carolina Supreme Court). The parties involved in the case are the names you see underlined (usually, but not always, with the plaintiff listed first – here, a group called Concerned Citizens of Brunswick County versus a business called Holden Beach Enterprises – the names have been abbreviated in accordance with <u>The Bluebook</u> rules). To find out the name of your state's official reporter where your state's cases are published (and not all states have their own official reporter), check Table T-1 of <u>The Bluebook</u> or Appendix 1 of <u>The ALWD Manual</u>.

You could also find the case by going to the regional reporter cited in the "parallel cite" if you are working in a state with both a state and regional reporting system. If you were looking for this opinion in the parallel cite, you would go to page 450 of volume 388 in West's <u>South Eastern Digest</u> (second series) – a series of volumes that contain cases for states in the southeastern region of the United States.

ANOTHER TIP: There are a number of major publishers in the legal field. Thomson-West is one of the oldest and largest. Many of the resources you will be learning to use contain the word "West" in their title and many of the systems that are important in legal research are found in West publications. It is common for those books and systems to be referred to using the word West, rather than Thomson-West. For example, the regional reporter referred to in the **TIP** above would often be referred to by lawyers as "West's <u>South Eastern Reporter</u>. The convention of using the word "West" rather than "Thomson-West" will be followed throughout this workbook.

Step 4: Read the case you have found and brief it in the space provided. Writing a "brief" of a case is a way to take notes about the case that will help you focus on the aspects of the case that are important to legal decision-makers. If you are a law student, you may already know how to "brief" a case. Most students of the law learn to read cases by taking notes in the following (or a very similar) manner: (1) they put the name and citation for the case at the top of the page; (2) they next indicate the parties involved in the controversy in a way that will remind them later who the parties are; (3) they then indicate the procedural history of the case – how did this case get to the appellate court?; (4) they then summarize the facts that were relevant to the court's decision; (5) next, they briefly state the question before the court – where there are lots of questions, you can just list the one that's relevant to the issue you're concerned about for purposes of your research assignment; (6) next they state how the court ruled on that question; and (7) finally, they state briefly what the court's reasoning was (why did the court rule as it did?). Look at Appendix B in this workbook for a sample brief of <u>Gideon v. Wainwright</u>, 372 U.S. 335 (1963), a well-known case in which the U.S. Supreme Court recognized the constitutional right of all accused criminals to be represented by counsel.

Review the READING TIP below before proceeding.

READING TIP: When you first begin to read legal cases, it is easy to become confused about how a court might use a case to help make a decision in your situation. Now would be a good time to review "Fundamentals of Legal Reasoning" beginning on page 11 of this workbook.

Remember, a case must be from your jurisdiction in order to be "binding" (i.e., in order for a judge to be compelled to follow it). Also, the case must still be "good law" – it can't have been overturned or substantially disavowed. In addition, the case must make sense in modern times and it must make sense if applied to the facts in your case. Also, a court only has to "follow" its own prior decisions and the decisions of a higher court in its jurisdiction. Thus, a state supreme court doesn't ever have to "follow" a decision from its own lower court of appeals. Similarly, opinions of courts from other jurisdictions are interesting in an advisory sort of way to judges in your jurisdiction – they are considered "persuasive" authority.

Finally, it is easy to become overwhelmed by all the language in a given case – what is the case really about? In order to keep yourself focused as you read a case, you need to understand the distinction between "dicta" and a "holding." The holding in a case is the court's resolution of the particular question before it (and it is not unusual to have more than one question, hence more than one holding). Dictum, on the other hand, is anything else the court expresses in the process of reaching the holding. Dictum may include the court's opinion of policy, of past holdings, of the parties themselves, or anything else the judge writing the opinion chooses to address. Dictum is important because it helps clarify the court's reasoning and can tip you off to the direction in which a court plans to move in the future. The holding, on the other hand, is important because it establishes bright-line precedent which the doctrine of stare decisis encourages the court to follow closely when hearing similar cases in the future.

Write your case brief here:

Don't forget to reshelve your reporter volume before going on to Section D on the next page.

ONLINE TIP: There are pros and cons to doing statutory research online. On the plus side, if you know a citation to a statute to search and/or specific statutory language you can enter as search terms, it is often easy to locate the body of a statute online. On the downside, though, it is equally easy to get confused when actually reading the statute online. You have already gained an appreciation for how important it is to read a statute in context – keeping in mind the purpose of the legislation, staying alert to any available Table of Contents for the act and/or a definitions section, looking for court decisions interpreting or applying the statute. By its nature, a computer only allows you to read one section of material at a time, thus making it difficult to get oriented when reading a complex piece of legislation. Because it is critical to read any subsection of a statute in its full context, many experienced researchers prefer to research statutes using hard copy materials. As you will learn as you continue to work through this workbook and its supplement, the major online research services (Westlaw and Lexis) are adding editorial enhancements such as browsing features in an effort to close the gap between reading statutes online and reading statutes in print.

ANOTHER ONLINE TIP: In addition to being able to use Westlaw, LexisNexis, and other fee-based services to research statutes electronically, researchers can also avail themselves of a number of free internet resources to find the texts of statutes. See Appendix A of the supplement to this workbook for a list of free websites providing access to statutes and other legislative material.

D. USING CITATORS TO UPDATE YOUR STATE STATUTORY RESEARCH

Step 1: A "citator" is a research tool that allows legal researchers who found a primary source of law (in the present assignment, a statute) to uncover an amazing amount of additional related information quickly.

Shepard's Citators in print form was the original and substantially exclusive legal "citator" system available to lawyers for many decades. Today, lawyers can access citators online (for a fee) using KeyCite on Westlaw or Shepard's on Lexis, or they can access much of the same information using Shepard's (now owned by LexisNexis) in a traditional print format. Updating online is an increasingly popular way to find cases and to confirm that you are relying on law that is current. Online citators are often more readily accessible than the print version and they provide the most current data available.

In this section, we will show you how to use a citator to update your statutory research online using Westlaw, OR online using Lexis, OR in hard copy, using traditional print materials. While it's a good idea to learn how to use all three, you will not be required to do so here. In the supplement to this workbook, you'll have an opportunity to use the updating tools for both Westlaw and Lexis, which is why we don't require you to use both here. In the space below, please indicate how you plan to search for updates for the statute you have read and briefed:

_____ I have my professor's permission and a Westlaw password, and will update online using Westlaw (**go immediately to Step 2 below**)

_____ I have my professor's permission and a Lexis password, and will update online using Lexis (**go immediately to Step 9 below**)

_____ I will update using traditional print materials (**go immediately to Appendix C in the back of this workbook**)

Step 2: Begin here only if you plan to update online using Westlaw. Update online using Westlaw only if you have a Westlaw password and your professor's permission to use it at this point in the semester. Go to Westlaw.com and log on using the password issued to you by your school. (If you inadvertently sign-on to lawschool.westlaw.com, click on the tab that says "Westlaw Research" to get to the correct homepage.)

Step 3: For this exercise, you will be using Westlaw's online citation tool, "KeyCite", to find additional information about the statute you located earlier in this assignment. Click on the KeyCite hyperlink at the top of the homepage.

Step 4: The initial screen that appears gives you a dialogue box in which to enter the full cite to the statute you want to update. Additionally, notice that you can find an array of helpful information on the right side of the screen that will remind you exactly what sources a KeyCite search can lead you to, as well as an explanation of the meaning of KeyCite "status flags." In the box provided on that screen, enter the full citation to the statute you are checking, and then hit "Go."

Step 5: Remember: online sources change frequently. Always check our website <www.LegalResearchWorkbook.com> for possible screen changes if these instructions are not consistent with what you find. As of the printing of this edition of the workbook, the results of your KeyCite search would appear first as a split screen. On the right, you will see the search results, with the full cite to your statute at the top. Pay attention to the presence of yellow or red flag, which indicates some relevant change to or information about the statute (the yellow flag) or some possible alarming results – such as an action declaring it unconstitutional or repealing it – concerning your statute (the red flag). To the left of the screen, you will see a number of hyperlinks that will connect you with additional information about your statute. Do you see a red or a yellow flag?

_____ no red or yellow flag

_____ yes, there is a yellow (   ) or red (   ) flag

On the left side of the screen, directly next to the flag (if a flag is present), Westlaw identifies why the status flag was attached to your case. What is that flag indicating?:

> **TIP: HAVING TROUBLE YIELDING RESULTS FOR YOUR STATUTE?** If your statute does not produce results that show a status flag, try switching to another statute related to your subject and see if it is a more richly applied statute. Alternatively, try entering N.C. Gen. Stat. 115C-391 and using that statute to complete this section on citators. That statute is related to North Carolina's corporal punishment laws and will yield good illustrative results for you. If you use N.C. Gen. Stat. 115C-391, please place a check here so your professor will be aware of your choice: _____

Step 6: Click on the "Citing References" link on the left side of your screen. Cases that have cited your statute will appear. Reading such cases would give you additional information about how your statute has been interpreted or applied. If you see a blue "H" to the left of a case, that status letter indicates that your statute was dealt with directly in that case. If you see a green "C" to the left of a case, that status letter indicates that the case referenced your statute, but did not directly apply nor interpret it. In addition to status flags and letters, Westlaw provides green stars that illustrate an editor's decision about how thoroughly the citing case treats your original case. One green star indicates fairly light treatment; the presence of four stars indicates that the case discussed your statute in depth.

Step 7: Choose a citing case and write its citation below. We do not have time to ask you to read any of the cases citing your statute, but if this were a real legal issue with a real client, you would certainly need to do so. Weighing depth of treatment stars and considering any status letters, indicate why you might read the case you selected if you were interested in learning more about the statute you have cited.

ONLINE TIPS: Westlaw has added many research features to make updating and expanding research online useful and efficient – and as similar as possible to using actual print copies. Scroll down the left side of the screen and note that you can view the Table of Contents for your statute (which would help you get an overview of the statutory scheme), you can see earlier versions of the statute, and you can see a quick overview of the types of citing resources available to aid your understanding of this area of the law. If you click on the link to the statute itself, you can even "browse" sections located in proximity to the section you've searched by clicking on the "previous section"/"next section" at the top of the screen.

Also, Westlaw has introduced a "ResultsPlus" tool that identifies secondary sources that might expand your research related to this statute. Finally, through its "KeyCite Alert" feature, Westlaw gives lawyers the opportunity to receive updates if new information comes online concerning a statute they are interested in.

All of these enhancements provide additional tools for the legal researchers, but none are free. Law students have unlimited access to these tools while they are in school working on school-related projects – but their schools have paid for that privilege. As graduates or even as summer associates, students are limited to the same fee-based access as other private practitioners. Learning to use these resources efficiently and with confidence now, while you are a student, is a wise investment of time.

Step 8: In addition to helping you determine if your case has been amended or repealed, or might be impacted by proposed legislation, and to helping you find cases that have applied or cited your statute, KeyCite can help you find additional legal references to your statute. These additional sources include secondary materials (like law review articles), court documents (like briefs filed in a case), related statutes, and even a survey of similar laws in other states. Scroll past the citing cases and list at least one other source that might be worth investigating if you had time (which you do not in this Assignment Sheet) to learn more about your statute:

Go now to the LEGISLATIVE HISTORY TIP on p. 200 unless you are also going to update using Lexis (Steps 9-15 below).

Step 9: <u>Begin here if you are going to update online using Lexis. Update online using Lexis only if you have a Lexis password and your professor's permission to use it at this point in the semester.</u> Go to Lexis.com and log on using the password issued to you by your school.

Step 10: For this exercise, you will be using Shepard's Online to update the statute you identified earlier in this assignment. Using the tabs across the top of the Lexis homepage, click on "Shepard's" to begin your updating. Be sure the "Shepard's for Research" option is selected (not the Shepard's for Validation/KWIC option).

Step 11: Remember: online sources change frequently. Always check our website <www.LegalResearchWorkbook.com> for possible screen changes if these instructions are not consistent with what you find. As of the printing of this edition of the workbook, you will be presented with a box in which you should type the citation to the statute you want to update. If you are uncertain of the format to use, click on the "Citation Formats" hyperlink to the right of the box. After you have entered the citation to your statute, click the red "check" box.

Step 12: The Lexis screen that appears first shows you the history of your statute as well as cross-references to cases that have cited your statute.

BEWARE: Before you get to the screen showing you the history of your statute and cross-references to cases citing your statute, you may see a screen that shows you subsections of your statute. **Be aware that information referenced for subsections on Lexis is NOT included cumulatively in information referenced for a larger, umbrella statute that contains that subsection. Thus, to be thorough, you would need to check references for each individual subsection if you are interested in the statute as a whole.** For purposes of completing this assignment, if you see this screen, choose the broadest statutory reference that addresses your client's legal question.

Choose a case that you might read if you had time to read a case that has cited your statute and explain below why you might read that case to learn more about your statute:

Step 13: Next, click on the hyperlink to the statute itself at the top of the page. When the statute appears, scroll through the language of the statute and note that you can find cross-references to secondary resources and additional cases that may cite your case. Are there any references here that you did not see on the original Shepard's screen that might be useful to you?:

Step 14: While still viewing an online version of the statute itself, look for the "Archive Directory" in the center of the screen to see if you can find an earlier version of your statute. Is there an earlier version?

Step 15: If there is legislation pending for your statute, there will be a "Legislative Alert" just above the body of the statute itself. Is there information pending about your statute?

the page to get to a screen that allows you to use the "previous" and "next" arrows on either side of the cite to look at the statutory sections that appear just before and just after your statute in the code. You can click on the "Archive Directory" link to find older versions of the statute as well as to be alerted to changes to the statute that may be pending. Finally, through its "Shepard's Alert" feature, Lexis gives lawyers the opportunity to receive updates if new information comes online concerning a statute they are interested in.

All of these enhancements provide additional tools for the legal researchers, but none are free. Law students have unlimited access to these tools while they are in school working on school-related projects – but their schools have paid for this privilege. As graduates, or even as summer associates, students are limited to the same fee-based access as other private practitioners. Learning to use these resources efficiently and with confidence now, while you are a student, is a wise investment of time.

LEGISLATIVE HISTORY TIP: As you know, one of the responsibilities judges have when faced with a statutory question in a case in controversy is to determine what the legislative intent was behind the statute. Determining legislative intent sometimes requires an understanding of the legislative history of a statute. You will learn more about doing legislative history research in Assignment Sheet 4 concerning federal statutes. States vary considerably in how much legislative history they preserve which can later then be uncovered and put to use to help determine the legislative intent of a statute's framers. Your individual law library will have additional information on ways of researching legislative history in your state. You might also consider reading Chapter 6 of *Legal Research in a Nutshell* or a comparable section in another textbook listed in Appendix A of this workbook for more information on this topic. Appendix B of Legal Research in a Nutshell contains a comprehensive list of books and pamphlets about research sources that are available for each individual state. Finally, most states now maintain a state government website. Many are rich sources of information regarding legislative history, at least as pertaining to fairly recent statutes.

ANOTHER TIP: Any time you are faced with a situation involving state law, you should consider whether a more localized branch of government might also have the authority to pass law on the subject. Researching local charters and ordinances is an art unto itself. You can find out more about this process through your local law library, or by reading Chapter 7 of *Legal Research in a Nutshell* or a comparable chapter in another textbook listed in Appendix A of this workbook.

Congratulations! You have now completed your research in state statutory law. You have learned how to get comfortable with any state statutory system in this country as well as how to find a specific statute relating to a legal question before you. Additionally, you know how to use supplementary research aids to complete your understanding of the statute's meaning within the context of our judicial system. Finally, you now know how to use Shepard's to make sure your research is accurate and up-to-date.

Please note your actual time of completion (including background reading): _____*hrs.*

TIP: If you find that you are spending a lot more time on the assignments than what has been recommended at the top of the first page of the Assignment Sheet, take a minute to think about what may be happening.

If this assignment took longer than you expected, the ideas in the following TIP might help you as you work through future assignments. On the other hand, it may be that your learning style or your learning goals are such that you prefer to linger over the questions raised in this workbook. If that is the case, and you have the time to spare, do not worry about our estimated times of completion. Enjoy yourself and just recognize that the learning process will take longer than we anticipated.

TIME-SAVING TIP: If you are having difficulty completing these lessons in the time recommended, consider the following: (1) Are you sure you have a completely clear understanding of the partner's question as you're doing your research? Legal research can be very intriguing and it's easy to spend lots of time browsing (which is fun, but not necessary to learn what these lessons are designed to teach you); (2) Are you seeking perfection? Each of our questions is designed to give you lots of latitude as you explore these materials – there is rarely only one right answer to any question. Once you've found some materials that seem relevant and you've learned what you want to know in any given exercise, move on to the next step and don't worry about having the perfect answer; (3) Are you asking for help when you need it?; (4) Are you doing your research at the optimal time? It is hard to get your hands on material at peak research hours, and most students find they learn more and take less time if they do their exercises when the library is less crowded.

As with any learning task, it's important to remember that you're the student here. You are not expected to know all the answers yet. There are resources available to help you if you get stuck at any point. Most law librarians are willing to help you if you are having difficulty. In addition, the research guidelines and tips provided on our website www.LegalResearchWorkbook.com can point you in the right direction if you get off course. Ask your professor if you may have access to the password to the Guidelines section of that website if you are associated with a class, or contact the author at ramckinn@email.unc.edu if you are using this workbook on your own.

MARSHALL, STORY & ASSOCIATES
ATTORNEYS AND COUNSELORS AT LAW
SUITE 101, THE JUSTICE BUILDING

⚖

THE LITIGATION DIVISION

To: New Associate
From: Assigning Partner
Re: Richard Roth [Client F] – File #03-2578

Thank you for the research you conducted concerning our state's Trade Secrets Act and the protection it affords.

Curious about how the roommate would have known about his invention in the first place, Richard has now learned that his roommate had all telephone conversations in their apartment taped without Richard's knowledge or approval. Among the conversations that were taped were the conversations with Richard's friend, Christine, about the external controller he was developing. The roommate recorded the conversations and learned about the invention, the safe, and the safe's combination from those tapes.

The roommate's actions do not stop there. In addition to using the tapes to learn about Richard's invention, the roommate also took portions of these conversations out of context and created a tape that made it sound as if Richard had invented the computer games on government time using government material – which was not true.

Over a year ago, the roommate sent a copy of this tape to Richard's former commanding officer. Richard just found out about the tapes this week.

As we continue to unravel Richard's situation, I would appreciate your doing some research into our federal wiretapping statutes. I believe that, under the federal law, a private citizen like Richard can bring a lawsuit for civil damages when his conversations have been illegally taped. I am concerned, however, that too much time may have gone by since the tapes were made and that Richard may have lost his right to bring suit since the tapes were made over a year ago. I would appreciate your looking into the federal wiretapping statutes to see how much time Richard has to take legal action if he decides to file a suit for civil damages against his former roommate.

▶▶ Turn to page 213 to begin your work for this assignment.

MARSHALL, STORY & ASSOCIATES

ATTORNEYS AND COUNSELORS AT LAW
SUITE 101, THE JUSTICE BUILDING

⚖

THE LITIGATION DIVISION

To: New Associate
From: Assigning Partner
Re: Ana Martinez [Client G] – File #03-2577

Thank you for your help confirming our state laws concerning the licensing of physicians.

Armed with her new found concerns about the drug Dr. Townsend is marketing, Ana contacted him this week to ask him to send her more information about the drug's safety and effectiveness. Dr. Townsend responded that no such information was available because the drug was so new. He stated further that the federal agencies responsible for approving new drugs are prohibited from giving any information to the public on those drugs. He refused to discuss the matter further with her.

Dr. Townsend's response does not sound correct, but I am not familiar with the federal law in this area. For your next assignment, could you research federal statutory law to see if the Food and Drug Administration is authorized to provide the public with information on a new drug's safety and effectiveness?

▶▶ Turn to page 213 to begin your work for this assignment.

MARSHALL, STORY & ASSOCIATES
ATTORNEYS AND COUNSELORS AT LAW
SUITE 101, THE JUSTICE BUILDING

⚖

THE LITIGATION DIVISION

To: New Associate
From: Assigning Partner
Re: Christopher Smith [Client H] - File #21-2206

Thank you for the research you did last week looking into our state statutes concerning the reporting of odometer readings in the sale of a motor vehicle. I have continued to think about ways we can help Christopher regain his losses in this case and would now like you to look into some federal law on Christopher's behalf.

I am almost certain that there is a federal requirement, quite apart from any state requirement, that anyone selling a used car must sign a statement revealing the true odometer or mileage reading. I would like you to find that statute for me and check to see if it would give Christopher some additional protection here. It may be that we will have difficulty bringing a suit against Ms. Adams in our own state courts, but we might be able to bring an action in federal court if we find there has been a violation of federal law. The index to the federal statutes is somewhat peculiar. I expect you can begin to locate this statute by starting with search terms such as Sales or Sales/Motor Vehicles.

Thank you for taking the time to look into this matter for me. I will look forward to having you share the results of your work.

▶▶ Turn to page 213 to begin your work for this assignment.

MARSHALL, STORY & ASSOCIATES
ATTORNEYS AND COUNSELORS AT LAW
SUITE 101, THE JUSTICE BUILDING

⚖

THE LITIGATION DIVISION

To: New Associate
From: Assigning Partner
Re: Carolyn Meyer [Client I] - File #21-2207

Thank you for the research you did last week looking into our state statutes concerning whether Carolyn can legally withdraw from school in her senior year.

As it turns out, Carolyn has made a number of friends at her new school and would like to remain there. In addition, Carolyn and her parents have been advised by several college coaches that she would be wise to remain in school but that she should consider simply joining the men's soccer team for the season. Unfortunately, although the men's soccer coach has said that he thinks her presence would be a benefit to the team, the school administration does not want to start a precedent of allowing women to play on men's teams, or vice versa. Hence, the school principal has told Carolyn and her family that she may not join the men's team. Carolyn and her family have asked us for help in determining the legality of the school's decision.

Quite apart from the constitutional questions that the school's decision raises, I am almost certain that there is federal legislation that addresses whether Carolyn has the right to play on the men's team. I would like you to find the controlling federal statutes on this point for me so that we can advise Carolyn and her parents about whether her school, which is a public educational institution, has violated federal statutory law by excluding Carolyn from the soccer team because of her gender.

Thank you for taking the time to look into this matter for me. The Meyers will be meeting with me again next week, and I will look forward to sharing your research with them at that time.

▶▶ Turn to page 213 to begin your work for this assignment.

MARSHALL, STORY & ASSOCIATES
ATTORNEYS AND COUNSELORS AT LAW
SUITE 101, THE JUSTICE BUILDING

⚖

THE LITIGATION DIVISION

To: New Associate
From: Assigning Partner
Re: Jeanne Martin [Client J] – File #21-2208

Thank you for the information you found concerning Ms. Martin's legal options in resolving her conflict with her landlady. She made the decision to move to a different apartment for her final months in school, and began looking in earnest for a new apartment last week. Happily, she has settled her personal conflict with her former landlady, who has even agreed to keep her golden retriever for her while she looks for her new place.

While searching for her new apartment, she has run into an unusual situation and has asked for additional legal advice from us. Apartments are apparently difficult to find mid-semester, and Ms. Martin was pleased when she heard through friends that there was an opening in a complex near campus that would also allow her to keep her pet retriever. The large, newly designed loft apartment was managed by John Jordan, a licensed realtor who has had a reputation around campus for years of only renting to female students. Rumor has it that he prefers renting to women because he finds that they are "more mature" residents and take better care of the property than do undergraduate men. Although concerned about the discriminatory overtones of such a policy, Ms. Martin decided to go look at the apartment anyway because she had such few housing options available this time of year.

She was disappointed to find that the apartment was not to her liking, but was excited because it looked like it would be perfect for her twin brother, Paul, who was moving to the area to start a graduate program. Ms. Martin told Mr. Jordan that she was not interested in the property, but asked if she could send her twin by to look at it. Mr. Jordan said that would be fine. Ms. Martin then emailed her brother, Paul, who immediately contacted Mr. Jordan by phone to set up a time to see the apartment. Mr. Jordan told him over the phone that he had no property available. Paul contacted his sister with this information, and she called Mr. Jordan herself. To her, he confirmed that the apartment was still on the market.

Recalling the earlier rumors of discriminatory renting practices on Mr. Jordan's behalf, Ms. Martin has become frustrated over the possibility that her brother will lose his opportunity to rent a suitable apartment based on Mr. Jordan's prejudices. She has contacted us to see if the practice of renting to women but not men is a possible violation of federal law. On instinct alone, I tend to think that she is right. Setting constitutional issues aside for now, I would appreciate your looking into the federal statutory law to see if Mr. Jordan is in possible violation of federal legislation against discriminatory practices in property rentals.

▶▶ Your work begins on the following page.

Assignment Sheet 2 *in Sequence of Assignments #2*
Researching Federal Law

Print Your Name:

<table>
<tr><td>Estimated Time
of Completion
(including recommended
background reading):
3.0 – 4.0 hrs.</td></tr>
</table>

(If you are doing this assignment as part of a class exercise, you may neatly write your answers directly on these sheets, staple all sheets together, and turn them in. If you prefer to write your answers separately using a computer, please be sure to number your answers to correspond to the appropriate questions before printing your responses.)

Background Reading: It would be helpful to read Chapter 5 of *Legal Research in a Nutshell* or a comparable chapter in a textbook included in Appendix A to learn about statutory law in general. To learn more about finding federal cases interpreting federal statutory law, read Chapter 3 in that book or a comparable chapter from another textbook in Appendix A. To learn more about researching the legislative history of a federal statute, read Chapter 6 in the Nutshell or a parallel chapter from another textbook in Appendix A.

Background Information: Your senior partner has asked you to find the answer to a question involving the federal statutes. This assignment sheet is designed to teach you one of many good ways to find controlling federal law on point. There are many other good ways to find out about federal law (both case law and statutory law) and as you become more proficient in legal research you will want to develop an array of strategies of your own for doing in-depth federal research. The TIPS and ONLINE TIPS included in this chapter will be helpful as you develop more advanced research skills in the future.

What You Will Learn. By the end of this assignment, you will:

- Be able to identify and know how to find a statute in the "official" code for federal legislation
- Be able to identify and know how to use two "unofficial" publications of federal legislation that also contain useful annotations and cross-references
- Know how to use a citator to ensure that the law you have found is still current
- Know how to find the legislative history of a current law

The Research Process:
A. LOCATING A FEDERAL STATUTE

Step 1: The <u>United States Code</u> (<u>USC</u>) is the officially codified version of federal legislation. It takes years for laws passed by the federal government to come out in printed form in <u>USC</u>. Moreover, unlike the state statutory compilations you used in Assignment Sheet 1, the <u>USC</u> does not have editorial enhancements such as cross-references to relevant administrative regulations or annotations highlighting relevant cases.

For these reasons, even though you should cite to <u>USC</u> whenever possible in your legal writing, you should begin your search for a federal statute in <u>either</u> the <u>United States Code Annotated</u> (<u>USCA</u>) or the <u>United States Code Service</u> (<u>USCS</u>). <u>USCA</u> and <u>USCS</u> are compilations of federal statutes printed by private publishing companies. Laws appear much faster there and those publications include editorial enhancements to make your research easier. <u>USCA</u> (published by Thomson-West) has the advantage of using the West Key Number System that you will learn about in Assignment Sheet 4, and also traditionally cites a large number of annotated cases in its "Notes of Decisions" section. <u>USCS</u>, which is published by LexisNexis, has traditionally had the advantage of citing more administrative law in its annotations. Regardless of which of these publications you choose to start with (<u>USCA</u> or <u>USCS</u>), both will do pretty much the same thing for you for many projects. However, you should be aware that each publication has variations in the cases selected for annotations and the cross-references selected for related resources, so there are times when you would be wise to look at both. You may choose either one of these publications to complete this Assignment Sheet. **Go to the location in your library where these resources are shelved now.**

CITATION TIP: Although <u>USC</u> is not the best place to begin your federal research, you do need to use it as the code you cite to even when you have done your actual research in <u>USCA</u> or <u>USCS</u>. You cite to <u>USC</u> because it is the "official" code approved by Congress to publish federal law. Where an Act has not yet been published in <u>USC</u>, but does appear in <u>USCA</u> or <u>USCS</u>, you can cite to one of them instead. See Rules 12.1 through 12.3 of <u>The Bluebook</u> or Rule 14 of <u>The ALWD Manual</u> for further guidance. If you ever need to cite to a very recent statute that has not yet been published in any codified form, see Chapter 5 in *Legal Research in a Nutshell* or another comparable advanced textbook. See also Rule 12.4 in the <u>Bluebook</u> or Rule 15 in <u>The ALWD Manual</u> for direction on how to do so properly.

ONLINE TIP: <u>USCA</u> is available exclusively online through Westlaw; <u>USCS</u> is available exclusively online through LexisNexis. Westlaw also offers access to the full text of statutes through its <u>USC</u> database without any annotations, thus allowing you to view a statute without being distracted by other editorial enhancements. Appendix A of the supplement to this workbook contains a list of government sites and other fee-based and free internet sources for accessing federal statutes electronically.

Step 2: For this problem, you have not been given a cite to a specific statute or Public Law number, nor do you have a popular name for the law you are seeking. If you did, there are a number of shortcuts you could use to get into the Code to find your statute. You can read more about those shortcuts in Chapter 5 of *Legal Research in a Nutshell* or in an advanced textbook listed in Appendix A. Without such information, you'll need to start your statutory research by using the General Index to the publication you've selected (either USCA or USCS).

As with all legal research, you're going to have to be creative, flexible, and patient in finding a fruitful index term that will yield a statute worth looking into. Go back now and read both memos given to you by your senior partner. They may contain some useful leads for terms you can use to begin your search. In the space below, write down some terms with which you can begin:

> **TIP:** A Public Law number is the original number given to legislation when it has been passed by Congress. Appendix D in this workbook offers an overview of how laws are introduced and passed. If you had a Public Law number (assigned by Congress when it passed the law) for a statute you're trying to find, you could find the current location of the legislation in any of the Codes by using the parallel reference tables located in the "Tables" volumes of USC, USCA, or USCS. You will learn how to locate a Public Law number in the last section of this Assignment Sheet. Similarly, if you had a popular name for a statute you were looking for (such as the Taft-Hartley Act), you could find its title and section number in the Codes by using the "Acts Cited by Popular Name" table in USC or the "Popular Name" table in USCS. The "Popular Name" table in USCA is located not in the "tables" volume (as you'd expect) but rather in a separate "Popular Name" volume. Shepard's Acts and Cases by Popular Names: Federal and State will also direct you to the title and section of an Act if you know its commonly used name.

Step 3: Using the terms you identified in <u>Step 2</u> above, find the title and section number for any statute that may be able to answer the question presented to you by your senior partner. **Don't forget to check the pocket parts of both the Index and the Statutes themselves.** Sit down where you can read through the statute you've selected.

A great deal of federal legislation is too long and complicated to read thoroughly for the purposes of this Assignment Sheet. However, it is important to be familiar with the basic format which most federal legislation takes. Thus, please get oriented to the Act you've selected now by turning to the beginning of the Chapter in which it is codified and reading: (1) any index of sections (or table of contents) which may appear there; (2) the "short title" assigned to the Act, if there is one; (3) the "purpose" section of the Act, if there is one; (4) any "definitions" section for the Act, if there is one.

Not all statutes have all of these features – their inclusion depends on how the framers chose to draft your particular Act (codified as a "Chapter"). Any time you are looking over a new statute, however, it is important to look for these features or you run the risk of reading a specific section incorrectly because you have taken it out of context. In the space below, write a short paragraph describing which of these features you found at the beginning of your Chapter.

ONLINE TIP: As with all statutory research, it is dangerous to take one section of a large federal act out of context and attempt to rely on it without first satisfying yourself that you understand how that section fits in the statute as a whole. As you learned in the preceding Assignment Sheet, Westlaw and Lexis are attempting to reduce the risk that a researcher will view a statutory section out of context by introducing the "browse" feature that you were introduced to in the preceding Assignment Sheet. The "browse" feature allows researchers to move back and forth within an Act more easily than in the past. Similarly, looking at the Table of Contents of an Act to get an overview (paying particular attention to the presence of a Purpose Statement and a Definitions Section) is as important online as it is in hard copy.

Step 4: If you are satisfied that the statute you've selected is on point, turn to the section or sections you believe will resolve your partner's question. In the space below, write down the complete cite to the section you will be relying on. (Note: if you think more than one section applies, feel free to cite them all):

CITATION TIP: See Rule 12 of The Bluebook or Rule 14.2 of The ALWD Manual for guidance on how to properly cite a federal statute. After you have cited a statute once in a legal document, you should use a "short form" instead of the full citation to make reading (and writing) easier. See Rule 12.9 in The Bluebook and Rule 14.5 in The ALWD Manual for additional information on short citation format for statutes.

Step 5: As you have learned, in order to keep research sources current without having to republish hardback versions too frequently, publishers provide paperback supplements, called "pocket parts," which are inserted at the beginning or end of most volumes. It is critical that you get in the habit of always checking the supplement or pocket part of whatever resource you're using to make sure the law you're relying on has not been repealed or amended. Turn to the "pocket part" in the volume you're working in to make sure the statute has not been changed. Has it?:

Step 6: In the space below, write a short summary of how you believe this legislation, when read only on its "plain language", might resolve the question presented by your senior partner.

CAUTION: Do not reshelve your code volume yet; we will be using it to complete Section B below.

B. FINDING CASE LAW APPLYING OR INTERPRETING THE RELEVANT STATUTE

Introduction: As you have learned, finding a statute on point can rarely be the end of a research inquiry. Since virtually all statutes have inherent ambiguities, you need to research case law that will clarify how courts (especially in your jurisdiction) have applied or interpreted the statute in the past. Finally, you always need to update your search to make sure both the law itself and the cases applying or interpreting it are current.

Step 1: The joy of using <u>USCA</u> or <u>USCS</u> is that a great deal of your work has already been done for you by the publishers of those unofficial codes. At the end of many statutory sections, there are helpful references to other research sources (e.g., legal encyclopedias you learned about in Assignment Sheet 1, cross-references to related statutes, etc.). These source references are then followed by annotated case law references which are grouped by subject. Turn now to these "Notes of Decisions" in <u>USCA</u> or "Interpretive Notes & Decisions" in <u>USCS</u>. You'll see a listing of subjects covered at the very beginning of these annotations. Choose a subject that looks like it has potential to help you clarify details about the question raised by your senior partner. Write the name of the annotation subject area you want to look into here:

Step 2: Turn to the area of the annotated cases you selected in Step 1 and skim the annotations listed there. Note that the court of decision and the year of decision are included. REMEMBER TO CHECK THE POCKET PART FOR CURRENT CASES! Find a federal case that addresses your partner's question and write the complete cite to that case here:

Did you find this case in the main volume or in the pocket part?:

List a few other cases that you might have pinpointed to read if time had allowed:

 CITATION TIP: See Rule 10 in The Bluebook, Rule 12 in The ALWD Citation Manual, and Assignment Sheet 2 for proper citation forms for cases.

At this time, please return the <u>USCA</u> or <u>USCS</u> volume you've been using to the shelf so that others may have access to it.

Step 3: Locate the first case you cited in <u>Step 2</u> immediately above. Write the cite to that case and brief it in the space provided. Remember, you can turn to Appendix B to find a sample format for briefing a case. If you've selected an extremely long case (and some federal cases can be fifty pages long or more!), skim the case but carefully brief the section pertaining to the statute you're researching.

If the case you've found is cited with the letters "U.S." it is a United States Supreme Court case and will be found in the <u>U.S. Reports</u> (which is the official reporter for U.S. Supreme Court cases). If the case you've found is cited with the letters "L. Ed.," "L. Ed. 2d," or "S. Ct.," it is also a United States Supreme Court case and will be found in <u>U.S. Supreme Court Reports, Lawyers' Edition</u>, <u>U.S. Supreme Court Reports, Lawyers' Edition 2d</u>, or <u>Supreme Court Reporter</u>, respectively (each of which publishes U.S. Supreme Court cases more quickly than does the <u>U.S. Reports</u>). If the case you've found is cited with the letters "F.," "F.2d," or "F.3d," it is a United States Court of Appeals case and will be found in the <u>Federal Reporter</u>. If the case you've found is cited with the letters "F. Supp." or "F. Supp. 2d" it is a United States District Court case and can be found in the <u>Federal Supplement</u>.

Write your brief of the relevant portion of the case you found here:

Step 4: Once you have found a good case on point, that case itself can become a rich source for finding other relevant case law on point. A case can be a good source for finding other cases if the court has closely examined a point of law you need to resolve and then cited precedent for its ruling or reasoning. In the space below, list a case cited in the case you just briefed that might be a good source for further reading (if you had time during this assignment, which you don't):

TIP: You will find out about the "Key Number System" developed by Thomson-West Publishing Company in Assignment Sheet 4. If you are using <u>USCA</u> (which is published by West, and therefore uses their "Key Number System"), you could use the West Key Number System to easily find other federal and state cases on point in any other Thomson-West publication.

Please return the case reporter you've been using to the proper shelf at this time before moving on to Part C below.

C. USING CITATORS TO UPDATE YOUR FEDERAL STATUTORY RESEARCH

Introduction: As you learned in the preceding Assignment Sheet, a citator is a legal research tool that allows you to take a wide variety of legal research sources (such as cases or statutes) and find out a number of things about their current status fairly quickly. As with state statutory research, you can use a citator to see if a federal statute has been repealed or amended, if it has been cited (favorably or negatively) in a court case, and whether there are additional commentary or other cross-references available that could enhance your understanding of the statute.

Step 1: In this section, you will be asked to update your research online using Westlaw, <u>OR</u> online using Lexis, <u>OR</u> in hard copy, using traditional print materials. While it's a good idea to learn how to use all three, you will not be required to do so here. With your professor's permission, consider using a resource to update your federal statutory research that you did not use in the preceding Assignment Sheet. In the space below, please indicate how you plan to search for updates for the case you have read and briefed:

_____ I have my professor's permission and a Westlaw password, and will update online using Westlaw **(go immediately to Step 2 below)**

_____ I have my professor's permission and a Lexis password, and will update online using Lexis **(go immediately to Step 9 below)**

_____ I will update using traditional print materials **(go immediately to Appendix C in the back of this workbook)**

Step 2: <u>Begin here only if you plan to update online using Westlaw. Update online using Westlaw only if you have a Westlaw password and your professor's permission to use it at this point in the semester.</u> If you used Westlaw to update your state statutory research, you will find the process familiar here. Go to Westlaw.com and log on using the password issued to you by your school. (If you inadvertently sign-on to lawschool.westlaw.com, click on the tab that says "Westlaw Research" to get to the correct homepage.)

Step 3: For this exercise, you will be using Westlaw's online citation tool, "KeyCite", to update the statute you identified earlier in this assignment. Click on the hyperlink at the top of the page that says "KeyCite."

Step 4: The initial screen that appears gives you a dialogue box in which to enter the full cite to the statute you want to update. Additionally, notice that you can find an array of helpful information on the right side of the screen that will remind you exactly what sources a KeyCite search can lead you to, as well as an explanation of the meaning of West's status flags. In the dialogue box provided on the initial KeyCite screen, enter the full citation to the statute you are checking, and then hit "Go."

Step 5: Remember: online sources change frequently. Always check our website <www.LegalResearchWorkbook> for possible screen changes if these instructions are not consistent with what you find. As of the printing of this edition of the workbook, the results of your KeyCite search would appear first as a split screen. On the right, you will see the search results, with the full cite to your statute at the top. Pay attention to the presence of a yellow or red flag, which indicate some relevant change to or information about the statute (the yellow flag) or some possible alarming results – such as an action declaring it unconstitutional or repealing it – concerning your statute (the red flag). To the left of the screen, you will see a number of hyperlinks that will connect you with additional information about your statute. Do you see a red or a yellow flag?

_____ no red or yellow flag

_____ yes, there is a yellow (   ) or red (   ) flag

On the left side of the screen, directly next to the flag (if a flag is present), Westlaw identifies why the status flag was attached to your case. What is that flag indicating?:

TIP: HAVING TROUBLE YIELDING RESULTS FOR YOUR STATUTE? If your statute does not produce results that show a status flag, try switching to another statute related to your subject and see if it is a more richly applied statute. Alternatively, try entering 29 USC 2611 and using that statute for the remainder of this section on use of citators. That statute is part of the federal Family and Medical Leave Act and will yield good illustrative results for you. If you use 29 USC 2611, please place a check here so your professor will be aware of your choice: _____

Step 6: Click on the "Citing References" link on the left side of your screen. The cases that have cited your statute will appear. If you see a blue "H" to the left of a case, that status letter indicates that your statute was dealt with directly in that case. If you see a green "C" to the left of a case, that status letter indicates that the case referenced your statute, but did not directly apply nor interpret it. As with using the KeyCite feature to update case law, the presence of up to four green stars indicates depth of treatment of your statute within the case.

Step 7: Choose a citing case and write its citation below. We do not have time to ask you to read any of the cases citing your statute, but if this were a real legal issue with a real client, you would certainly need to do so. Weighing depth of treatment and considering any status letters, indicate why you might read the case you selected if you were interested in learning more about the statute you have cited.

ONLINE TIPS: As you learned in the preceding lesson on state statutes, Westlaw has added many research features to make updating and expanding research for statutes online useful and efficient – and as similar as possible to using actual print copies. Scroll down the left side of the screen and note that you can view the Table of Contents for your statute (which would help you get an overview of the statutory scheme), you can see earlier versions of the statute, and you can see a quick overview of the types of citing resources available to aid your understanding of this area of the law. If you click on the link to the statute itself, you can even "browse" sections located in proximity to the section you've searched by clicking on the "previous section"/"next section" at the top of the screen.

Also, Westlaw has introduced a "ResultsPlus" tool that identifies secondary sources that might expand your research related to this statute. Also, through its "KeyCite Alert" feature, Westlaw gives lawyers the opportunity to receive updates if new information comes online concerning a statute they are interested in. Finally, Westlaw has introduced a "Graphical Statutes" feature that gives you a quick visual overview of a statute's history and pending legislation along with quick hyperlink connections to that information.

All of these enhancements provide additional tools for the legal researchers and have gone a long way towards making online statutory research useful, but none are free. Law students have unlimited access to these tools while they are in school working on school-related projects. Later, even in the summer, students are limited to the same fee-based access of other private practitioners. Learning to use these resources efficiently and with confidence now, while a student, is a wise investment of time.

Step 8: In addition to helping you determine if your case has been amended or repealed, or might be impacted by proposed legislation, and to helping you find cases that have applied or cited your statute, KeyCite can help you find additional legal references to your statute. These additional sources include secondary materials (like law review articles), court documents (like briefs filed in a case), related statutes, and even a survey of similar laws in states. Scroll past the citing cases and list at least one other source that might be worth investigating if you had time (which you do not in this Assignment Sheet) to learn more about your statute:

Go now to Section D on p. 226 unless you also want to update using Lexis (Steps 9-15 below).

Step 9: <u>Begin here if you are going to update online using Lexis. Update online using Lexis only if you have a Lexis password and your professor's permission to use it at this point in the semester.</u> If you used Lexis to update your state statutory research, you will find the process familiar here. Go to Lexis.com and log on using the password issued to you by your school.

Step 10: For this exercise, you will be using Shepard's Online to update the statute you identified earlier in this assignment. Using the tabs across the top of the Lexis homepage, click on "Shepard's" to begin your updating. Be sure the "Shepard's for Research" option is selected (not the Shepard's for Validation/KWIC option).

Step 11: Remember: online sources change frequently. Always check our website <www.LegalResearchWorkbook> for possible screen changes if these instructions are not consistent with what you find. As of the printing of this edition of the workbook, you will be presented with a box in which you should type the citation to the statute you want to update. If you are uncertain of the format to use, click on the "Citation Formats" hyperlink to the right of the box. After you have entered the citation to your statute, click the red "check" box.

Step 12: The Lexis screen that appears first shows you the history of your statute as well as cross-references to cases that have cited your statute.

BEWARE: Before you get to the screen showing you the history of your statute and cross-references to cases citing your statute, you may see a screen that shows you subsections of your statute. **Be aware that information referenced for subsections on Lexis is NOT included cumulatively in information referenced for a larger, umbrella statute in which the subsection is included. Thus, to be thorough, you would need to check references for each individual subsection if you are interested in the statute as a whole.** For purposes of completing this assignment, if you see this screen, choose the broadest statutory reference that addresses your client's question.

Choose a case that you might read if you had time to read a case that has cited your statute and explain below why you might read that case to learn more about your statute:

> TIP: HAVING TROUBLE YIELDING RESULTS FOR YOUR STATUTE? If your statute does not produce any citing cases, try switching to another statute related to your subject and see if it is a more richly applied statute. Alternatively, try entering 29 USC 2611 and using that statute for the remainder of section on citators. That statute is part of the federal Family and Medical Leave Act and will yield good illustrative results for you. If you switch to 29 USC 2611, please place a check here so your professor will be aware of your choice: _____

Step 13: Next, click on the hyperlink to the statute itself at the top of the page. When the statute appears, scroll through the language of the statute and note that you can find cross-references to secondary resources and additional cases that may cite your case. Are there any references here that you did not see on the original Shepard's screen that might be useful to you?:

Step 14: While still viewing an online version of the statute itself, look for the "Archive Directory" in the center of the screen to see if you can find an earlier version of your statute. Is there an earlier version?

Step 15: If there is legislation pending for your statute, there will be a "Legislative Alert" just above the body of the statute itself. Is there information pending about your statute?

> ONLINE TIPS: Lexis has added research features to make updating and expanding statutory research online useful and efficient – and as similar as possible to using actual print copies. When you are viewing the body of the statute, you can click on the "TOC" [Table of Contents] link on the top left side of the page to see the Table of Contents for the entire statutory section in which your exact citation appears. You can also click on the "Book Browse" link at the top of the page to get to a screen that allows you to use the "previous" and "next" arrows on either side of the cite to look at the statutory sections that appear just before and just after your statute in the code. You can click on the "Archive Directory" link to find older versions of the statute as well as to be alerted to changes to the statute that may be pending. Finally, through its "Shepard's Alert" feature, Lexis gives lawyers the opportunity to receive updates if new information comes online concerning a statute they are interested in.

D. RESEARCHING FEDERAL LEGISLATIVE HISTORY

Introduction: Like all legal research, researching legislative history requires patience and a clear sense of purpose. In the study and practice of law, many lawyers and law students do not need to research legislative history routinely. However, lawyers might need to know the history of a statute for a variety of reasons ranging from lobbying and political activism to presenting a court with a plausible interpretation of an ambiguous term in a statute. There are also times when a lawyer might want to look at the original version of an act that has since been amended (for example, when relying on a case interpreting an earlier version of an act). Even while in law school, a student might need to research legislative history as part of an advanced seminar assignment, to write a law review article, or to compete as a member of a moot court team.

It is beyond the scope of this workbook to exhaust all of the available means of unraveling a statute's history. Rather, we will explore a few tips to get you started. To learn more, read Chapter 6 in the *Nutshell* or a chapter on legislative history in another textbook listed in Appendix A.

TIP: Legislative intent is the light that guides judges as they interpret and apply statutes. The consideration of legislative history is viewed by some courts as a valuable means of discerning the legislative intent of those who passed a statute. Other jurists, however, believe that looking to legislative history as a means of interpreting statutes can be misleading – believing that legislation changes markedly from introduction to passage, and that the history of individuals' thoughts, or even a committee's report prepared in that process, does not necessarily reflect the intent of the legislature that ultimately passed the bill. See Roy M. Mersky and Donald J. Dunn, <u>Fundamentals of Legal Research</u> (8th ed. 2002) for an interesting discussion of these conflicting views.

ONLINE TIP: Westlaw and LexisNexis have numerous tools to help streamline the process of tracing a statute's history. Coverage, however, is not comprehensive. The U.S. Government and most states maintain free websites that provide some access to documents that can help you track a bill's history. See Appendix A in the online supplement to this workbook for a list of electronic resources to explore with your professor's permission as you become more proficient in legal research.

Step 1: Turn to Appendix D ("How Statutes Come Into Being") in this workbook and read that Appendix now. By understanding the legislative process, you can begin to visualize the types of documents that would be generated (and accessible through research) during the different stages from introduction to passage of a bill. It is those documents that provide the history of a piece of legislation.

Step 2: Much federal legislative history research turns on knowing the bill number and/or the Public Law number assigned to the legislation. The Public Law number can be found in either <u>USCA</u> or <u>USCS</u>. Choosing one of those resources now, turn to the statute you used to complete Section A of this Assignment Sheet above. Look at the information contained in parentheses at the very end of the statute (just before any cross-references or annotated cases). If there is a Public Law number for the statute you have researched, please write it here: _____ . Public Laws are amended frequently, resulting in citations to multiple Public Law ("P.L.") numbers at the end of a statute. If you find this to be the case, write the first "P.L." number from the list. The first number references the original piece of legislation. Also, Public Law numbers were not routinely assigned before 1957. If your statute does not have a Public Law number at all, write the Chapter number here instead:

Step 3: In addition to listing the Public Law or Chapter number, <u>USCA</u> and <u>USCS</u> also list a cite to <u>United States Statutes at Large</u> in the parenthetical information immediately following the text of a statute. <u>United States Statutes at Large</u> contains all bills passed by Congress in chronological order by date of passage. Amendments are also entered by date of their passage (so you can't find all parts of an act in one place using <u>United States Statutes at Large</u> – what you can find, instead, is the original form of a bill or amendment filed at the time and in the form it was passed). In contrast, bills are codified in <u>USC</u>, <u>USCA</u>, and <u>USCS</u> by *subject,* not chronologically. Look again at the parenthetical information at the end of the text of your statute. Where in <u>United States Statutes at Large</u> would you find this statute as it was originally passed? (Write the cite):

Step 4: Parenthetical information in <u>USCA</u> and <u>USCS</u> also includes references to amendments. If your statute has been amended, what are the dates of those amendments?:

Step 5: Go to <u>United States Statutes at Large</u> in your library and look up the cite from Step 3 above. Find the first page of the Act. In most cases, the statute you used for Step 3 will be a very small section of a much larger Act of Congress. Be sure that you turn all the way to the beginning of the Act in its entirety – many Acts can be hundreds of pages long. TIP: At the top of the page on which your statute is published, you will see its accompanying Public Law ("P.L.") number. One way to know you're at the beginning of an Act is to keep flipping backwards until you see the Public Law number change (because no two Acts have been assigned the same P.L. number). Write the bill number here:

TIP: Bills introduced in the house carry the letters "H.R." in front of the bill number; bills introduced in the Senate are introduced by the letter "S". The vast majority of Public Laws will be introduced as a bill in one of these chambers and will carry one of these designations to indicate their origin.

TIP: Since 1975, <u>Statutes at Large</u> has included a summary of the legislative history of each law at the end of the text of the law. If you're doing legislative history research for a statute passed since that date (and you're curious), turn to the end of the text now and see if you can locate that summary.

TIP: Almost all research into legislative history can be done using the Public Law number or the bill number. Use <u>United States Code Congressional and Administrative News (USCCAN)</u> – published by West and cross-referenced in the historical notes of <u>USCA</u> – to find a variety of useful information ranging from tables tracing the status of a bill to Presidential messages proposing legislation. Of perhaps most significance are the collections of committee reports – often relied on by courts interpreting legislative intent – prepared when the bill was introduced in the House or Senate. Other kinds of documents that might be interesting to you when you conduct legislative history research in the future are records of floor debates (debates on the floor of the Senate or Congress) and public hearings that may have been held after the bill was introduced.

TIME-SAVING TIP: Often, legislative histories of major acts have been compiled already. If you can find a history that has already been published, you can save a lot of research time. References that can help you locate such compilations can be found in <u>Sources of Compiled Legislative Histories</u> by Nancy P. Johnson, which is carried in most large law libraries. Check your library's online catalogue for other titles that might help you find compiled legislative histories or ask a law librarian for additional resources.

ONLINE TIP: Lexis, Westlaw, and other fee-based services listed in Appendix A of the supplement to this workbook have all developed means for conducting legislative history research. Electronic resources are often the best way to search for the status of recently passed or recently proposed federal legislation. When conducting legislative history research online, always check for scope of coverage. Appendix A of the supplement to this workbook also lists free websites that provide useful access to legislative history documents. Most notably, THOMAS (http://thomas.loc.gov) (maintained by the Library of Congress) and GPO Access (http://www.gpoaccess.gov) (maintained by the Government Printing Office) are each a rich source of information about federal statutes and their historical development.

You have now learned at least a few of the many ways that you can conduct research into federal questions. You can use <u>USCA</u> and <u>USCS</u> to find a federal law on point, you know one way to find cases interpreting or applying that law, you know how to update your research to make sure it's current, and you know how to begin doing research into the legislative history of a statute.

Please note your actual time of completion (including background reading): _____ *hrs.*

MARSHALL, STORY & ASSOCIATES
ATTORNEYS AND COUNSELORS AT LAW
SUITE 101, THE JUSTICE BUILDING

⚖

THE LITIGATION DIVISION

To: New Associate
From: Assigning Partner
Re: Richard Roth [Client F] – File #03-2578

As a result of the misleading tape that the roommate sent to Richard's mentor, the military launched an investigation into the invention of Richard's computer controller. The military concluded that the controller was, in fact, created on government time using government material.

Based on this conclusion, the government has taken the position that it should own the patent to the controller. Richard received a certified letter from the U.S. Government this week informing him of its decision.

Richard believes that the government reached this decision based on erroneous impressions created by the roommate's tape. He also believes that he can demonstrate what actually occurred.

This is a critical issue that needs our immediate attention. For your next assignment, would you look into the federal administrative regulations concerning inventions and patents to see what policies control rights to inventions made by government employees. I believe those regulations have been promulgated by the U.S. Patent and Trademark Office under the Department of Commerce.

Please answer the following two questions: (1) if it can be demonstrated that Richard's invention was made on private time, is that enough to establish that the patent should not belong to the government; and (2) how long does Richard have to file an appeal to the government's decision?

▶▶ Turn to page 241 to begin your work for this assignment.

MARSHALL, STORY & ASSOCIATES
ATTORNEYS AND COUNSELORS AT LAW
SUITE 101, THE JUSTICE BUILDING

⚖

THE LITIGATION DIVISION

To: New Associate
From: Assigning Partner
Re: Ana Martinez [Client G] – File #03-2577

The research you have done on Ana's case has been very helpful to her, and she is becoming increasingly confident that she has entered an agreement that was unwise.

She would like to know if federal administrative regulations provide a way for her to request records concerning approval of new drugs. I believe the Food and Drug Administration, under the Department of Health and Human Services, may have promulgated such regulations.

We would appreciate your looking into this matter for her, and look forward to receiving your response.

▶▶ Turn to page 241 to begin your work for this assignment.

MARSHALL, STORY & ASSOCIATES
ATTORNEYS AND COUNSELORS AT LAW
SUITE 101, THE JUSTICE BUILDING

⚖

THE LITIGATION DIVISION

To: New Associate
From: Assigning Partner
Re: Christopher Smith [Client H], File #21-2206

     Now that I have a better understanding of the federal statutory law in this area, I am concerned because of the age of the car involved. It is my understanding that the Department of Transportation has published federal regulations establishing odometer disclosure requirements, but that these requirements may not apply to older cars. If the regulations don't apply, we won't be able to use the federal statutes to help Christopher regain his money.

     I would appreciate your taking some time to look into this matter for me. I believe you may need to begin your search with "Motor Vehicles" and related terms. Whether the news is good or bad, it is important that we understand the controlling regulations as we develop our strategies on Christopher's behalf.

▶▶ **Turn to page 241 to begin your work for this assignment.**

MARSHALL, STORY & ASSOCIATES
ATTORNEYS AND COUNSELORS AT LAW
SUITE 101, THE JUSTICE BUILDING

⚖

THE LITIGATION DIVISION

To: New Associate
From: Assigning Partner
Re: Carolyn Meyer [Client I] - File #21-2207

Now that I have a better understanding of the federal statutory law in this area, it seems to me that we need to gain a clearer understanding of how the statute has been interpreted and implemented through its accompanying federal regulations.

The attorney representing Carolyn's school called me this week and expressed his opinion that the school is free to exclude her from participation on the men's soccer team because soccer is a contact sport. It is his understanding that under the federal administrative regulations drafted to enforce the federal statutes concerning equal educational opportunities, a distinction has been drawn between the requirements for inclusion in contact versus non-contact sports. It is his further understanding that soccer is recognized in the regulations as a contact sport.

I would appreciate your expanding your research into the federal law in this area by turning now to the relevant administrative regulations that have been promulgated by the Department of Education. Is the school's attorney accurate in his understanding that soccer is a contact sport and that the school therefore can exclude Carolyn from the men's team without violating federal administrative law?

▶▶ Turn to page 241 to begin your work for this assignment.

MARSHALL, STORY & ASSOCIATES

ATTORNEYS AND COUNSELORS AT LAW
SUITE 101, THE JUSTICE BUILDING

⚖

THE LITIGATION DIVISION

To: New Associate
From: Assigning Partner
Re: Jeanne Martin [Client J] – File #21-2208

The research you provided concerning discriminatory rental practices was very interesting. Thank you for looking into that matter for Ms. Martin.

Based on the results of your research, Ms. Martin contacted Mr. Jordan to let him know that it was not acceptable for him to deny her twin brother access to an available rental based on his gender. Mr. Jordan was apparently very polite on the telephone, but stuck to his original refusal to rent to property to a man. His explanation was that he was not "hiding" any discriminatory practices, but rather openly advertised that the apartment in the large complex was available to women but not men. In his defense, he faxed a copy of a flyer he posted around campus advertising this apartment, and several others, for female undergraduate and professional students.

Ms. Martin has now called us to see if there is anything to Mr. Jordan's "defense." I understand that the Department of Housing and Urban Development has promulgated administrative regulations to implement the Fair Housing Act, and would appreciate your doing some research to discern if those regulations contain restrictions against advertising discriminatory rental practices.

▶▶ Turn to page 241 to begin your work on this assignment.

Assignment Sheet 3 *in Sequence of Assignments #2*
Researching Administrative (Government Agency) Law

Print Your Name:

Estimated Time
of Completion
(including recommended
background reading):
1.5 – 3.0 hrs.

(If you are doing this assignment as part of a class exercise, you may neatly write your answers directly on these sheets, staple all sheets together, and turn them in. If you prefer to write your answers separately using a computer, please be sure to number your answers to correspond to the appropriate questions before printing your responses).

Background Reading: To learn more about the resources and concepts introduced in this Assignment Sheet, read Chapter 7 of *Legal Research in a Nutshell* or a comparable chapter in a textbook listed in Appendix A of this workbook.

Background Information: We are all familiar with administrative agencies and routinely interact with them (e.g., the state Division of Motor Vehicles has rules about how to get your driver's license; the Food and Drug Administration has rules about what kinds of chemicals our produce can be sprayed with; the Federal Aviation Administration has rules that determine how close an airplane can fly to your home).

Because government agencies are not part of an elected body (they're not legislative) and are not part of our court systems, we sometimes fail to recognize that the rules they promulgate and their decisions about those rules are very much a part of our legal system. Knowing how to find both administrative regulations and administrative decisions interpreting and applying those regulations is a critical legal research skill. Here, your partner has asked you to find the answer to a specific regulatory question. By the time you finish this lesson, you will have an answer.

What You Will Learn. By the end of this assignment you will:

- Know how to find out the roles and functions of various federal agencies
- Be able to use the <u>Code of Federal Regulations</u> (CFR) to find a controlling federal administrative regulation
- Understand how to use the <u>List of CFR Sections Affected</u> (LSA) and the <u>Federal Register</u> to make sure a federal regulation is still current
- Understand how decisions of administrative law courts influence the application of administrative regulations
- Be introduced to resources to help you research state administrative regulations

The Research Process:
A. GETTING THE BIG PICTURE

It is valuable to get the big picture when doing administrative law research in order to identify what agencies may be drafting regulations that impact your client's situation. Your partner's memo has indicated that the question raised is controlled by a specific federal agency. The U.S. Government Manual has long been a useful tool for getting an overview of the roles and functions (and current status) of individual federal agencies. Go now to the online version of this manual at http://www.gpoaccess.gov/gmanual/index.html. Alternatively, if your law library has a print version of the manual, you may use that instead. In the space below, briefly describe this agency's mission (feel free to quote the Manual, but be sure to use quotation marks if you do):

TIP: Almost all federal agencies now maintain their own websites that include helpful information about the agency. In practice, when you know the agency that you believe is promulgating relevant regulations, you can go directly to that agency's website to learn more about its function and its regulations.

B. FINDING THE CONTROLLING REGULATION

Step 1: The place to begin your administrative law research is with the Code of Federal Regulations (CFR). The CFR, the official publication of federal rules and regulations, is the logical place to begin any regulatory research because the regulations are grouped there by subject. Just as the federal statutes you explored in Assignment Sheet 2 are grouped by Title and Section number in the United States Code, federal regulations are grouped by Title and Section number in the CFR. (Unfortunately, there is no correlation between the Title and Section numbers of federal statutes and their counterparts in the regulations.) **Go now to the location in your library where the CFR is shelved.**

Step 2: Find the "Index and Finding Aids" volume of the CFR at the far end of all the titles. The "Index and Finding Aids" volume is the index provided by the publishers of CFR to help you find the regulation you're looking for. If someone else has that volume out, as an alternative you can use a more detailed index provided by private publishers: the Index to the Code of Federal Regulations. This alternative index is almost always shelved immediately after the CFR. In any event, find one of these tools now (make sure you're using a current index) and use either the subject index or the agency index (since you already know the agency's name) to look for a regulation that is likely to answer the question or to contain a more detailed section that would answer the question. Write the Title, Chapter, and Part number of any regulations with potential here:

> **TIP:** Note that the most refined entry in the index is to "Part" numbers. When you get to the actual regulation, you will note that these "Parts" are further broken down into related "Sections." To find an answer to most legal questions, you will need to find a specific Section.

PLEASE PUT THE INDEX YOU USED BACK ON THE SHELF NOW FOR OTHERS TO USE.

Step 3: Find the volume in CFR that contains the Chapter, Title, and Part number you identified in Step 2 above. Go to the Table of Contents at the beginning of the Title and see if there are specific Section references that look even more promising. There is no easy way to skim for such relevant Sections. Just keep an open mind and look for what might be promising. List at least one relevant Section in the space provided:

Step 4: Turning to the text of the regulations, skim each promising Section entry (there may only be one) until you find the answer to your partner's question. In the space provided, please summarize what you think the outcome of your client's situation will be under the regulation and why.

Step 5: In the space below, write the proper citation for the regulation you have relied on (see Rule 14 of the Bluebook or Rule 19 of The ALWD Manual):

TIP: All administrative regulations are promulgated under the authority of some specific "enabling legislation." If you have the citation to a statute, you can often find cross-references to administrative regulations that have been drafted under its authority by checking for cross references in print copy or online versions of annotated codes such as U.S.C.S. or U.S.C.A. For purposes of this Assignment Sheet, we would like you to use the CFR to locate a regulation so that you become familiar with that resource.

ONLINE TIP: Searching for administrative regulations online is often a good choice, especially if you know narrow terms that would lend themselves well to a specific word search. Westlaw and Lexis both have databases covering the Code of Federal Regulations (CFR), and the text of regulations is also available free through GPO Access (http://www.gpoaccess.gov/index.html), which is maintained by the Government Printing Office. See Appendix A in the supplement to this workbook for additional fee-based and free resources that may help you locate (and update) administrative regulations. Westlaw and Lexis, as well as the GPO Access site, allow you to update regulations online.

C. MAKING SURE YOUR REGULATION IS STILL CURRENT

Step 1: Administrative regulations are constantly changing, so it is critical that you always check to make sure a regulation is current before you rely on it to answer a client's question. Begin your updating by checking the date on the front of the <u>CFR</u> volume where you found the regulation. You need to start your updating from this date. Write that date in the space below:

PLEASE PUT THE <u>CFR</u> VOLUME YOU HAVE BEEN USING BACK ON THE SHELF NOW.

Step 2: Go to the <u>List of CFR Sections Affected</u> (<u>LSA</u>) (usually shelved immediately after the <u>CFR</u>). Take down the volume with the most current date; check the page just inside the front cover. Write down the dates listed for changes in your title:

The <u>LSA</u> volume you just took down (the one with the most current date) will allow you to update your regulation through the last date listed on the inside front cover. Look inside the volume to see if the regulation you are working with has been mentioned/ changed/amended. The references you see are to pages in the <u>Federal Register</u> (a pamphlet-type publication). Has your regulation been changed in any way? If so, write below the page number in the <u>Federal Register</u> where you would find the text of the change:

> **BEWARE:** Note that <u>LSA</u> uses both the Title AND the Section number when listing changes to a federal regulation that have become final, but only lists <u>proposed</u> changes by Part number (presumably because a "Part" is a more general subdivision and many proposed changes are not yet refined enough to be arranged by Section number). Hence, when updating federal regulations, you need to stay alert to Part numbers even if you have a specific Section number you are researching.

PLEASE PUT THE <u>LSA</u> VOLUME YOU'VE BEEN USING BACK ON THE SHELF NOW.

Step 3: In Step 2 above, you noted any page references to the <u>Federal Register</u> that would contain changes to your regulation up to the date covered in the latest issue of the <u>LSA</u>. Now you need to make sure that no additional changes have occurred to the regulation since that date. To do so, **go to the location in your library where the Federal Register is shelved now.**

Look in the *most current issue* of every month not covered by the <u>LSA</u> (e.g., if you're doing research in September, and if the latest <u>LSA</u> update is through July 31st, you would check the <u>Federal Register</u> for the most current issue in August and also the most current issue available for September. Using this example, the last August issue would have entries for all of August, and the most current September issue would have relevant entries for September up to the date of the latest issue available. Thus, your research would be comprehensive up to that last date).

Select the issues you need and turn to the back where you will find a list of "CFR Parts Affected" in the Reader's Aids section. Look for your Title and Part number in each of the issues you have pulled. If you found any changes, list the <u>Federal Register</u> pages where you would find one of those changes here:

BEWARE: When doing administrative law research (as with statutory research), it is critical to know if a court has made a significant ruling on the regulation's meaning, application, or constitutionality. You can find this information in hard copy by using <u>Shepard's Code of Federal Regulations Citations</u> to shepardize the Title, Section, and/or Part number in the usual manner, or online using a variety of sources. <u>Shepard's Code of Federal Regulations Citations</u> can also lead you to law review articles and entries in <u>ALR</u> (<u>American Law Report</u>) that cite your regulation.

Step 4: If you found that your regulation has been altered since it was published in the <u>CFR</u>, go to the <u>Federal Register</u> pages you listed in Steps 2 and 3 above and see if the changes apply to your client's concerns. (The spines of volumes in the <u>Federal Register</u> do not list the page numbers covered within them. You have to open a volume to see if the pages you are looking for are contained within it). If the changes apply to your client's situation, use the space below and on the following page to write how you think they will affect your answer to your client's question:

TIP: From time to time, you may want to look up an old regulation to see what was in force at an earlier time. For example, if you are reading an old court case that refers to your regulation, you'd want to make sure the judges had been looking at a version of the regulation that was substantially similar to the current one when they made their ruling. Otherwise, the ruling might no longer be applicable. To check on an earlier version of a regulation, you could use the prior edition of CFR, which is often kept on the shelves in large law libraries even though the regulations have been revised. If you are working where there are no prior editions of the CFR available, you could find the original language of the regulation by looking at the beginning of the current regulation where the date and cite to the regulation's original entry in the Federal Register are given. Use that information to go back and read the original language printed in the relevant issue of the Federal Register.

Step 5: In the space provided here, please write a short paragraph answering the question raised in your partner's most recent memo.

D. LOOKING TO THE FUTURE

1. Completing Administrative Law Research

As with statutes, you can't study administrative regulations in a vacuum. Before you rely on the plain language of an administrative regulation, you may need to check for significant administrative law decisions and/or cases on point. Finding administrative law decisions (the quasi-judicial actions taken by agencies when they hear appeals about the meaning or application of their regulations) is beyond the scope of this assignment. In the years ahead, stay alert to the need to learn more about this kind of research. If you find yourself in a position where you need to find agency decisions about a regulation, consider any of the following options:

- Use a "looseleaf service" (which you can learn more about by reading Chapter 9 of the *Nutshell* or a comparable section in a textbook listed in Appendix A)
- Use <u>Shepard's United States Administrative Citations</u> in print form
- Use the Shepard's tool on Lexis
- Use the KeyCite tool on Westlaw
- Use an agency's website to check for listing of that agency's decisions

In addition to being aware of an agency's decisions about its regulations, you also need to consider how the regulation relates to its enabling statute and to the Constitution. An "enabling" statute is legislation that authorizes a specific government agency to promulgate regulations to forward the intent of the legislation passed. Administrative regulations are only valid if they are constitutional and within the scope of their enabling legislation. Hence, in-depth administrative law research requires careful attention to the boundaries set in the enabling statute, to administrative law decisions applying or interpreting the regulation, and also to federal and state court cases interpreting and applying the regulation and its enabling statute.

2. Conducting State Administrative Law Research

Each state organizes its own state administrative regulations using a system of the state's choosing. However, the principles of federal administrative law research generalize to any state or local agency. The actual process of conducting that research varies widely from state to state and from local government unit to local government unit. For example, the North Carolina Administrative Code has twenty-eight titles, which includes one for each of the major departments in the North Carolina executive branch of government. The titles are divided into chapters, subchapters, and sections as appropriate. If you are interested in doing additional administrative law research in your state, check with your law librarian. If you have the time, you might consider looking to see if your state has any regulations arising from the state statute you uncovered in Assignment Sheet 1.

TIP: States commonly maintain websites that provide easy access to information about the state's government, including legislation and administration regulations. Many state homepages can be found at <www.state.[insert U.S. Postal Service state initials here].us>. If you spend a short time searching a state government's website, you can often find a link to its administrative regulations and, with some luck, information about its administrative law process, links to the text of regulations, and information about pending regulations. Also, Appendix B of *Legal Research in a Nutshell* contains a comprehensive list of books and pamphlets to help you conduct research in individual states and there are many privately published books that explain the research process within a specific state. If you are interested in finding resources to help you conduct research specific to your state, ask your law librarian for assistance.

CONGRATULATIONS! You have now been introduced to the basics of administrative law research. You know how to find a federal regulation in the <u>Code of Federal Regulations</u> and how to update your research to make sure it is current.

Please note your actual time of completion (including background reading): ____ hrs.

MARSHALL, STORY & ASSOCIATES
ATTORNEYS AND COUNSELORS AT LAW
SUITE 101, THE JUSTICE BUILDING

⚖

THE LITIGATION DIVISION

To: New Associate
From: Assigning Partner
Re: Richard Roth [Client F] – File #03-2578

Although Richard's headaches concerning his invention are easing, he continues to have negative repercussions in his professional life from the roommate's action.

The roommate has now contacted his academic department head by phone. In his conversation with the department head, the former roommate said, "Your new graduate student, Richard Roth, is not to be trusted. He stole government information while serving as an Army Officer and he will discredit your graduate department if you allow him to stay." The roommate repeated this same message in a letter that he sent to the department head following their conversation.

Although Richard's department head has assured Richard that he gives no credence to the former roommate's remarks, Richard has decided that the former roommate's negative behavior needs to be stopped.

Richard would like to look at the legal avenues he might pursue to prevent such further communications to anyone by the former roommate. One possibility is to bring an action against the former roommate for libel or slander.

I have not been involved in a suit for libel or slander for many years, and I would appreciate your researching this topic for me. Looking only at the verbal remarks made during the telephone conversation with the department head, please see if a statement about a person's fitness to perform in his or her profession or trade constitutes slander under the common law in this state.

▶▶ **Turn to page 261 to begin your work on this assignment.**

MARSHALL, STORY & ASSOCIATES
ATTORNEYS AND COUNSELORS AT LAW
SUITE 101, THE JUSTICE BUILDING

⚖

THE LITIGATION DIVISION

To: New Associate
From: Assigning Partner
Re: Ana Martinez [Client G] – File #03-2577

Ana has received a response from the Food and Drug Administration and is now convinced that Dr. Townsend's new drug is a sham – and might even be dangerous.

Based on the information we have uncovered as a result of your research, it appears that marketing this drug, which has not yet received approval, would be illegal and probably against public policy as well.

Ana wants no further dealings with Dr. Townsend. She would like to have her contract with Dr. Townsend declared void, her $1,000 initial investment required by that contract returned to her, and any further obligations to pay additional funds cancelled.

While there may be many grounds for having this contract declared void (including, for example, fraud), I am fairly certain that the common law of this state would support voiding any contract made for an illegal purpose.

It would be helpful if you would do some research to confirm my initial reaction to this situation. Does the common law of this state hold a contract formed for an illegal purpose or against public policy to be void?

▶▶ Turn to page 261 to begin your work on this assignment.

MARSHALL, STORY & ASSOCIATES
ATTORNEYS AND COUNSELORS AT LAW
SUITE 101, THE JUSTICE BUILDING

⚖

THE LITIGATION DIVISION

To: New Associate
From: Assigning Partner
Re: Christopher Smith [Client H] - File #21-2206

I have been in contact with Susan Adams in our neighboring state to let her know that we are representing Christopher and his parents. I told her that Christopher would like to void this contract, have his money returned, and return the car to Susan. Unfortunately, Susan is not interested in returning the money and has contacted an attorney of her own in the town where she is attending school.

I then contacted Susan's attorney who says Susan does not feel that she is obligated to follow our state's odometer requirements because she does not live here anymore and also believes that she did not violate any federal laws concerning odometers. I have a conference call scheduled with Susan's attorney in two weeks. It seems to me that we should be able to negotiate a reasonable solution to this problem.

Quite apart from the statutory odometer issue, one legal theory I would like to rely on is the well-recognized principle that a minor cannot be held to a contract. As I remember the general rule from my days in law school, a contract with a minor (often called an "infant" in legal research jargon) is voidable (i.e., can be canceled) at the will of the minor (although I believe the contract would also be solid if the minor wanted to enforce it). In some states, however, the contract would not be voidable if it was for the purchase of a necessity (although I can't imagine that this car under these circumstances would be considered a necessity).

If we should have to end up going to court over this matter, it is my intention to file our action in our state's court system and to base at least part of our claim on Christopher's common law contract rights. Thus, I need to confirm our state's common law concerning the contract rights of minors to be sure my memory is serving me right before I enter negotiations with this out-of-state attorney. Also, knowing how our state courts have handled situations like this one in the past will help me assess the strength of Christopher's case.

Specifically, I would appreciate your looking into whether our state's common law recognizes that this contract could be canceled by Christopher, but not canceled by Susan. I appreciate the work you are doing on Christopher's behalf and hope we will be able to resolve this matter in the near future.

▶▶ **Turn to page 261 to begin your work on this assignment.**

MARSHALL, STORY & ASSOCIATES
ATTORNEYS AND COUNSELORS AT LAW
SUITE 101, THE JUSTICE BUILDING

⚖

THE LITIGATION DIVISION

To: New Associate
From: Assigning Partner
Re: Carolyn Meyer [Client I] - File #21-2207

Things have become more complicated for Carolyn at her school as a result of an incident that occurred at the beginning of this week. As I understand the facts, Carolyn was practicing soccer unofficially with a number of students from the men's soccer team after their official practice had been completed for the day. An out-of-state visitor to the school, Bill Styles, invited himself to join their game. Bill had been at school as a guest of another team member all week and had approached Carolyn on more than one occasion to tell her he thought she should stop "trying to be one of the boys."

During the unofficial game, Bill began to push Carolyn and to generally harass her. Although she moved away from him twice and asked him to stop once, he continued to bother her. Finally, for no apparent reason and while the ball was not in their vicinity, he kicked Carolyn hard in her left knee as they were leaving the field at the end of the game. His actions were particularly egregious since Carolyn is known to have had a recent knee injury and plays soccer only while wearing a brace on that knee. Carolyn, in turn, reached down, picked up her athletic bag that she had left at the edge of the field, and swung it at him, hitting him in the face. She hit him hard enough with the bag that he backed off immediately, his eye began to swell, and a friend had to drive him home.

Two days later, Carolyn's parents received notification from an attorney representing Bill and his family that they were suing Carolyn civilly for assault and battery. The Meyers have asked us to continue our support of Carolyn by looking into the feasibility of this claim and also what possible defenses Carolyn might have.

For this assignment, I would like you to look into what constitutes assault and battery in our jurisdiction. In addition, while you are doing your research, could you also look into whether Bill's claim might be defeated by an argument on our part that Carolyn was acting in self-defense.

▶▶ **Turn to page 261 to begin your work on this assignment.**

MARSHALL, STORY & ASSOCIATES
ATTORNEYS AND COUNSELORS AT LAW
SUITE 101, THE JUSTICE BUILDING

⚖

THE LITIGATION DIVISION

To: New Associate
From: Assigning Partner
Re: Jeanne Martin [Client J] – File #21-2208

I am happy to report that Jeanne Martin has settled her housing concerns. Both she and her brother have moved into new apartments and she reports being pleased with her new home.

Unfortunately, another legal difficulty has arisen for her. On the day she moved to her new apartment, her landlady offered to keep Ms. Martin's golden retriever so that the dog would not interfere with the move. Ms. Martin was grateful for the offer, particularly since her dog and the landlady's dog get along so well. To her surprise, however, when she returned to her old home to pick up her dog, the landlady refused to relinquish control of it. Rather, she said, "This dog belongs with its mother. You've never shown proper respect for it – you even left it here with me while you busied yourself with your move. I'm not giving you the dog back." It has been several days, and the woman steadfastly refuses to alter her position.

Ms. Martin, who is a fine pet owner, is understandably anxious to get her dog back as soon as possible. She has been told by local law enforcement officers that the police cannot reclaim the dog because the landlady acquired possession of it with her permission, rather than through a criminal act such as theft. Hence, they have advised Ms. Martin to look into a possible civil action against her former landlady to regain possession of the dog.

I would appreciate your looking into whether we could pursue a civil cause of action against the former landlady based on a theory of common law conversion. I have not handled a case involving conversion in some time, and would appreciate your checking specifically for the following information: (a) what would we have to show to establish such a claim; and (b) how specifically would we have to identify Ms. Martin's dog, who is a dead-ringer for the landlady's dog, if we decide to file a complaint against the landlady.

I will meet with Ms. Martin within the week, and look forward to sharing your research with her.

▶▶ Your work begins on the following page.

Assignment Sheet 4 *in Sequence of Assignments #2*
Finding Common Law

Print Your Name:

Estimated Time
of Completion
(including recommended
background reading):
4.0 – 5.0 hrs.

(If you are doing this assignment as part of a class exercise, neatly write your answers directly on these sheets, staple all sheets together, and turn them in. If you prefer to write your answers separately using a computer, please be sure to number your answers to correspond to the appropriate questions before printing your answer sheets.)

Background Reading: To learn more about the resources and concepts introduced in this Assignment Sheet, read Chapters 3 and 4 in *Legal Research in a Nutshell* or a comparable chapter in a textbook assigned by your professor. (See Appendix A.)

Background Information: The common law of your state controls the question raised by your senior partner. Re-read pages 18-19 in Chapter 3 of this workbook to learn more about the common law. To answer the question which has been raised, you will need to find judicial opinions from your state appellate courts that will show you how courts in this state have decided controversies like this one in the past. From time to time when you are doing common law research, you also need to know what courts in other states have held about similar problems. Such out-of-state cases can be helpful where there is no law on point in your state or where you want to try to persuade your court to change its view to be more like that of other states. Consequently, the exercises in this assignment will also teach you how to find what a court from another state might have decided about the common law question raised by your senior partner.

What You Will Learn. By the end of this assignment, you will:

- Know how to use an "annotated" digest ("West's <u>Digest</u>") to find cases
- Understand how to use West's Key Number System to find related cases by subject in all jurisdictions
- Understand how to use the American Law Reports (<u>A.L.R.</u>) to find common law cases and accompanying articles exploring legal issues raised in those cases
- Understand the importance of updating your common law research
- Know how to use "citators" to update your common law research (make sure it's still "good law") and to find additional cases and materials on the same subject

The Research Process:
A. FINDING STATE COMMON LAW USING WEST'S STATE DIGESTS

Step 1: Since you do not know the name or citation to a case on this topic yet, one good place to start is in West's <u>Digest</u> for your individual state. The official title of the volume you will want to use would be <u>West's [your state's name] Digest</u> (e.g., <u>West's North Carolina Digest</u>). The <u>Digest</u> is usually shelved at the end of your state's "reporters," although in some large libraries it is shelved at the end of your state's *regional* reporter instead. Remember, a "reporter" is what lawyers call the books containing the published opinions of a court. Go back to Assignment Sheet 1 if you want to review information about reporters. **Go now to the location in your library where the <u>Digest</u> for your state is shelved. (See TIP below.) When you have located your state's <u>Digest</u>, write its full name (as set out on the bindings for each volume) here:**

> **t** TIP: For whatever reason, Delaware, Nevada, and Utah do not have separate West <u>Digests</u> corresponding to their reporters. If you are doing research in one of those states, you should instead use the regional digest to find cases for that state.

Step 2: West's state and national digest system is a comprehensive research tool that provides a method for locating written court opinions that have been published in an area of law in which you need to find precedent. As you learned in Chapter 2, "Fundamentals of Legal Reasoning," you would want to find precedent on a topic when you need to know how a court in your jurisdiction has treated similar cases in the past – in that way, you will know what principles a court would apply in your case to reach a just result. The West digest system, which was initiated over a century ago and remains equally vital today, gave lawyers a tool for finding chronologically published cases by *subject*.

Under the West digest system, all opinions are divided into subjects that cover the legal "Topics" raised in the case. For example you would find all cases about home schooling grouped together, and this whole cluster of cases would be located as a sub-topic under the general "Topic" heading of "Schools." The trick, then, to finding cases that would shed light on how a court might treat the question raised by your partner is to figure out the general Topic and then any sub-topics under which the West <u>Digest</u> publishers have clustered cases resolving these types of controversies in the past. (For example, in the above hypothetical, there would have been nothing illogical about starting a search for cases dealing with home schooling by looking up the term "education." Eventually, though, you would have found that the West publishers have grouped the cases about home schooling under the Topic "Schools" instead.)

Finding where the West publishers have clustered your cases requires some brainstorming and guessing at first – the more research you do, the more familiar you will be with the terms Thomson-West uses to identify major legal "Topics" and sub-topics. For now, take down any volume of West's <u>Digest</u> for your state and look at the list of Topic headings (called Digest Topics) printed near the beginning of the volume. <u>In the space below, write the Topic heading that you think is most likely to cover our client's controversy:</u>

(Remember: Identifying the correct Topic in West's <u>Digest</u> is something of a hit and miss proposition at first. Don't get discouraged. Ask questions if your ideas aren't working). <u>If you find you want to explore more than one Topic heading, write additional Topics here:</u>

TIP: When using print materials, you can use the <u>Descriptive Word Index</u> to find promising Topic headings and subtopic headings. The <u>Descriptive Word Index</u> for each <u>Digest</u> system is generally shelved in close proximity to the <u>Digest</u> volumes. You can use this Index to find the "buzz words" which the West editors associate with the legal concept you're exploring.

Step 3: Once you have located a potential Topic heading, your next step is to narrow your search by locating appropriate sub-topics that may yield cases that have dealt with the same legal questions raised by your client. You will find appropriate sub-topic headings by pulling the volume of West's state <u>Digest</u> that contains the Topic heading you've decided to explore. As with encyclopedias, Topic headings are arranged alphabetically in the West Digest volumes. The first page of the Topic section includes a helpful summary of the concepts covered under that general Topic heading. Skimming those summaries is often a good way to get other ideas about where to look for relevant cases. Take down the volume containing a Topic heading you chose above.

Scan the sub-topic headings listed in the Table of Contents (called an "Analysis") on the first page of your Topic. In the space below, write down some sub-topic headings that look interesting:

You will note that the sub-topic headings in the Table of Contents are preceded by a little key icon followed by a number and perhaps further followed by a number in parentheses. These numbers are called "West Key Numbers" and are a rich source of legal research information. Carefully read Chapter 4 of *Legal Research in a Nutshell* or a comparable chapter from another legal research textbook covered in Appendix A for a detailed overview of how the Key Number system works. You can also check the "TIP" immediately below for an introductory explanation of the system. It is critical that you learn to use this system to be an efficient researcher. In the space below, write down the Topic heading, Key Number, and corresponding sub-topic heading that appears to have potential for further investigation:

TIP (The Key Number System): The West Key Number System is unique to the field of legal research and can be challenging to use at first. Because there is no parallel in non-legal research, it's hard to get your mind around it. Once you get a grasp of how the system works, however, it can be extremely useful to you.

The trick to understanding the West Key Number System is understanding how many different publications are distributed by Thomson-West, whose founder created the system. All these publications are interconnected by Key Numbers assigned by Topic so that you can move from one resource to another without having to go through indexes once you know a Key Number that is relevant to the question you're trying to answer. The Key Numbers are assigned to the West <u>Digest</u> "Topics" you are exploring in this assignment sheet. Thus, under the West Key Number System, let's say that you want to research a question about home schooling. The Topic and Key Number for that subject is "Schools 160.7."

continued on next page

Once you know that Topic name and its corresponding Key Number, you can turn to Schools 160.7 in any other state's <u>Digest</u> (which are all published by Thomson-West) and find annotations to cases addressing standards for home schools. The Key Number system is used in <u>C.J.S.</u> (originally published by West) and less extensively in <u>Am. Jur.</u> (recently acquired by West). You can also use Key Numbers when you do electronic research on Westlaw (but not on any other service provider).

ONLINE TIP: You can use the enormous power of Key Numbers in your online search as well as in hard copy. To begin from the "Welcome to Westlaw" main page or "Law School Classic" page, select the yellow-highlighted "Key Numbers" link from the top of the page. You will then find a number of options for using West Key Numbers to your advantage.

TIP (Headnotes): In addition to using Key Numbers to tie its many publications together, Thomson-West prints "headnotes" at the beginning of all cases that it publishes. Other publishers print similar "headnotes" at the beginning of cases they publish. A headnote is a short summary of a major point of law decided in a case. Each of these headnotes in any of the many Thomson-West Regional or State <u>Reporters</u> is assigned the corresponding Key Number dealing with the legal issue addressed in the headnote. Thus, if I were reading a case that raised a question about home schooling, the headnote (short explanatory paragraph) corresponding to that point would be numbered and would have the appropriate Key Number [Schools 160.7] printed next to it. These headnotes comprise the annotations that are cross-referenced in the <u>Digest</u> you are learning to use as a "finding tool." As you can see, once I find one case or even a <u>C.J.S.</u> entry on point, I'd have the "key" to finding any number of other cases on point simply by following the Key Number through other Thomson-West publications. With caution (see the BOMB immediately below), you can also use references to headnotes in the text of the opinion itself to focus your reading. In any case published by Thomson-West, references to a specific headnote (for example, Headnote 2) show up as a bracketed number in the margin of the text (for example, [2]) next to the area of the case from which the headnote arose.

BEWARE: Headnotes and Key Numbers are a great tool for legal researchers to use – in hard copy and online – to focus their search for cases that could be on point, but headnotes should *never* be used as a shortcut for actually reading a promising case. Headnotes are not part of an opinion – they are written by private editors working for the publishing companies that publish cases. Also, in general, headnote numbers are not universal among publishers. Rather, headnote numbers correspond with the subject-grouping system of each individual company.

ONLINE TIP: Headnotes can be used online as well as in print format to make your search for cases more efficient. West Key Numbers, which correspond with headnotes in cases published by Thomson-West, can be used extensively in online research on Westlaw and corresponding Thomson-West CD products. Cases found on Westlaw are hyperlinked by headnote Topic and Key Number to other cases and materials carried in the Westlaw databases. On Westlaw, use the Key Number feature to retrieve documents quickly using West Key Numbers. Lexis publications have their own headnote and Lexis has recently adopted an online legal topic grouping system (called the "LexisNexis Legal Taxonomy"). As of the time of the printing of this workbook, you could search for cases by headnotes or by subject area on Lexis by selecting "Search" on the homepage toolbar, and then using the "Search by Topic or Headnote" tab option. Note that, with a few exceptions for specific states [California, Montana, New Hampshire, New York, Ohio, Vermont, and Washington], the headnotes referenced on Lexis are increasingly less likely to be the same headnotes you'll see if you are reading a case published in a Thomson-West Reporter.

Step 4: Now that you have your Topic and Key Numbers, it is a simple matter to find cases that could be worth reading. Turn to the Key Number you want to explore in the section of "annotated" (summarized) cases which immediately follows the Table of Contents ("Analysis") in the state <u>Digest</u> you've been using. You will note that the cases under your Key Number are listed in reverse chronological order and by the court of decision. Thus, federal cases are listed first with the most current federal Court of Appeals cases appearing before earlier ones; federal Court of Appeals cases are followed by federal District Court cases in the same reverse chronological order. Likewise, the most recent state Supreme Court cases (if your state's supreme court is its highest court) are then listed in reverse chronological order, followed by the state's Court of Appeals cases (if your state has lower courts of appeal), in the same reverse chronological order. For this assignment, please locate an interesting case on point **that was decided in a state court before 1980** and write its name and the citation noted at the end of the annotation here (if there is no case cited earlier than 1980, skip this step):

Next, locate an interesting case on point **that was decided in a state court sometime in the 1990's or later** and write its name and the citation noted at the end of the annotation here:

Next, turn to the "pocket part" at the back of the entire volume to see if there are any very recent cases on point. Turn to the Topic and Key Number you've been using and write the name and citation of a very recent case on point here. (Note: if there is no current case in the pocket part on the key number you've been using, look for a related Key Number and write the name and citation for that case here, together with the new topic and Key Number):

Finally, you will need to check the "Cumulative Pamphlet" for updates. The Cumulative Pamphlet is a paperback book that includes updates beyond those that have been added through the pocket parts. In the Cumulative Pamphlet, find the Topic and Key Number you've been using and note here if you saw any additional updates:

> **TIP:** When doing common law research, it is often important to read an array of cases on a particular topic to see how the common law on point has evolved over time. While newer cases affirm the current state of the law, older cases help you establish what the law used to be and help you understand the reasoning behind a rule of law. If you are arguing for a change in the law or that the current law should not be applied to your situation, knowing how the law has evolved over the years can be critical. Also, when you read cases, keep in mind that you are not just reading to find a rule statement. Rather, you are reading each case to understand what rule this court applied to a specific set of facts and *why* the court decided as it did.

We have finished using West's <u>Digest</u> for your state for now. Please reshelve all volumes so that others may use them.

Step 5: The next step in searching for case law on point is to go to the actual decision itself and read it. <u>**Never**</u> rely on the <u>Digest</u> annotations by themselves to tell you what the law in any given area might be. Like the headnotes they duplicate, the annotations are merely the summarized opinion of an individual editor; they are not part of the opinion of the court. You may not agree with what the editor thought the holding of the case was or you may find that the annotation is not an accurate representation of the nuances of the case as they relate to your client's situation.

Choose one of the cases that you cited in <u>Step 4</u> above to read. To find that case, go to either your state reporter system (if your state has its own reporter system) or go to the regional reporter for your state if there is no state reporter system. If you are in a state reporter system, make sure you are in the reporter for the court that decided your case (for example, in North Carolina the N.C. Supreme Court cases are published in the North Carolina <u>Reports</u> whereas the North Carolina Court of Appeals cases are published in the N.C. Court of Appeals <u>Reports</u>). Most law libraries have several sets of reporters (either state and/or regional) that are easily located by call number or by following your library's key and/ or map to major resources.

Find the volume and page number of the case you have selected and read that case now.

TIP: As you learned in Assignment Sheet 1, the first number in a citation to a case refers to the volume number of that reporter, the letters between designate the reporter in which the case is published, the next number represents the page number in the volume where the case begins, and the date in parentheses represents the year the case was decided. Where you have a citation to a state reporter followed by a parallel citation to a regional reporter, you can find the case in either volume.

BEWARE: In some states, if you are looking for an extremely old case, you may be unable to find the case you want to read on the page where its citation indicates it should begin. That is because old cases were sometimes published in one format and, over the years, have been republished in a different format requiring repagination. For the sake of consistency, however, all citations to old cases still refer to the original, old page numbers. Where there is a mismatch of pages between the original publication and a newer edition, the publisher will put the original page numbers in parentheses alongside the text in the new publication. Thus, if you're looking for an extremely old case and find it doesn't begin on the page indicated by its citation, look along the outside margins for numbers in parentheses. These numbers are the page numbers from the original volumes and will correspond to the page numbers in the cite you have. Similarly, if you are looking at the regional reporter version of a case from a state that also has a state reporter, the regional reporter version indicates page breaks from the state reporter version in the margin of its text.

Step 6: <u>Good legal research requires good note-taking. While you still have the case that you have read open, please do a careful "brief" of that case in the space provided here.</u>

BEWARE (Not All Opinions Are Published): In the preceding Assignment Sheets, and immediately above, you have learned how to locate cases that have been published in state or regional reporters. Remember, however, that not all written opinions of a court are published. As you have learned, some courts elect to publish only select cases (those they believe have precedential value), sending all other written opinions only to the parties involved in the underlying action. Before the onset of widespread computer use, such cases were not widely accessible and many courts adopted rules disallowing or strictly limiting their use as precedent. Today, with multiple fee-based online resources and with many courts and governments maintaining internet websites, "unpublished" cases can be located through computer word searches. Thus, it has become important for lawyers to know what the rules of court are for the jurisdiction they are researching in – will a court there allow lawyers to rely only on published opinions, or may they cite unpublished opinions as well? If they may cite unpublished opinions, what is their ethical obligation to do a thorough search for them? For an interesting article chronicling the debate over the pros and cons of allowing access to unpublished opinions, see Thomas L. Fowler, <u>Unpublished Decisions: Should Precedent Be 'Managed' or Simply Followed?</u> J. N.C. State Bar 16, Summer 2002, at 16.

B. OTHER WAYS TO FIND COMMON LAW

1. Finding Cases Using the American Law Reports (ALR): In the first half of this Assignment Sheet, you learned to use the West's <u>Digest</u> for your state to find case law clarifying the question raised by your senior partner. You have also learned how to find cases interpreting statutes by using annotated Codes, and in the next Assignment Sheet you will learn how to use encyclopedias, periodicals, and treatises to find case law. Another good way to find cases (either at common law or where a court has applied or interpreted a statute) is through the **American Law Reports (ALR)**. If you are using a supplementary research textbook, you should go back and read the chapter covering <u>ALR</u> now (<u>see</u> Appendix A of this workbook for a list of such textbooks).

ALR is a finding tool that is very different from the West <u>Digests</u> you just learned to use in the first part of this Assignment Sheet, but is equally valuable and has many of the "big picture" advantages of a legal encyclopedia as well. <u>ALR</u> contains articles analyzing a selected case that has raised a distinct question of law. Each article discusses the legal ramifications of one case in detail, looking at how other jurisdictions have treated the question of law raised in that case. In addition to exploring a specific question of law in depth through one illustrative case, each ALR article also cites numerous cases from a variety of jurisdictions that have discussed the same or closely-related legal questions. You will learn how to use <u>ALR</u> by following Steps 1 through 4 below. ***Do not use <u>ALR</u> (lst) to complete this assignment – use a later series instead.***

Step 1: Go to the location in your library where <u>ALR</u> is located now.

Step 2: Using the six-volume <u>ALR Index</u> (and the pocket parts for updating), look for a topic heading which might yield a good discussion of the issue you are trying to research. In most libraries, this Index is shelved at the end of the <u>ALR</u> volumes themselves. (Note there is also an <u>ALR Quick Index</u> that you can use to complete this assignment if you choose.) Again, as with the West <u>Digest</u> system, this kind of index search takes creativity, patience, and at least some sense of serendipity. It gets easier the more experienced you are. Write the topic heading you chose here (note: if the first few topic headings you've chosen don't exist or don't have any annotated references to an <u>ALR</u> article on point, move on until you find one that does):

Step 3: Using the reference you found in Step 2 above, locate your article in the appropriate volume and <u>skim</u> it. Note that the publishers of <u>ALR 2d, 3rd, and 4th</u> print the main legal case being analyzed by the entry on the pages immediately <u>preceding</u> the page the index leads you to. <u>ALR 5th</u>, on the other hand, gives you a reference to all the cases covered in a particular volume and prints them together at the end of that volume. For this assignment, you will not have time to thoroughly read the article (called an "Annotation" by the editors of <u>ALR</u>). Rather, your time will be better spent familiarizing yourself with how <u>ALR</u> works and what it can do for you. In the space provided, please write the name and citation of the main case that is being discussed in your annotation and <u>briefly</u> summarize the gist of the annotation here.

Step 4: In the annotations section of the main volume you are using <u>and</u> in the pocket parts (for updating), look for cases from your state on point. Write the name and citation for one case from your state that you found here. (If you found none, find a case from a nearby state and write its citation here instead):

ONLINE TIP: In addition to being available in print copy, <u>ALR</u> is available on Westlaw and provides coverage from <u>ALR</u> lst through 6th as well as <u>ALR</u> <u>FED</u> first and second (exploring federal cases exclusively).

2. Finding Cases and Updating Your Research Using "Citators": A third method for finding relevant cases, and to also update your research to learn more about a case that you have found, is to use a legal "citator" as you did to update your statutory research in earlier lessons. Once you have found a case that addresses the legal question you are researching, a citator allows you to check for all of the following:

- Is your case available to read in more than one reporter?
- Does your case have any "prior history"? (i.e., did this case come before a deciding court at some point *before* the opinion you are holding was decided? For example, if you are holding the state Supreme Court opinion, had this case perhaps been heard at the state Court of Appeals earlier?)
- Does your case have any "subsequent history"? (i.e., did anything happen to your case at some point *after* the opinion you are holding was decided? For example, was the opinion you are holding appealed to a higher court?)
- Have courts referred to the case you are holding when writing other opinions (i.e., was your case used as precedent in another case)? If so, which of the many legal issues raised in your case (summarized as one or more headnotes) was addressed in the other case?
- If your case was referred to in another case, in what way did the second court make its reference? Did the second court rely favorably on your case, distinguish your case in some way, or reverse or disavow your case?
- Was your case cross-referenced elsewhere (for example, in a legal encyclopedia, in <u>ALR</u>, in comments to a statute, or in a journal article)?

Some of this information available in a citator is important for you to know in order to properly Bluebook the case you are holding in your hand (for example, the prior and subsequent history, and the parallel citation). Other parts of the information available in a citator helps expand your research, giving you other sources to explore as you deepen and broaden your understanding of the question you trying to answer. When you are using a citator to *expand* your research, it is important to recognize that it is an imperfect tool – many of the helpful aids (for example, those that address how the next opinion referred to your opinion) are based on subjective editorial decisions with which you may not agree and which may not be all-encompassing.

In this lesson, you will learn to use one or more citation tools (Shepard's online on Lexis, KeyCite online on Westlaw, or Shepard's in traditional print format) to update your common law research and to find additional cases on the common law topic your partner has asked you to research. Remember what Westlaw and Lexis screens change with some frequency. If you choose to search online, be sure to check the Errata section of www. LegalResearchWorkbook.com to make sure we have not modified our instructions below.

Step 1: In this section, you will be asked to update your research online using Westlaw, OR online using Lexis, OR in hard copy, using traditional print materials. While it's a good idea to learn how to use all three, you will not be required to do so here. If you have tried one of these tools in prior lessons, try using an alternate tool here. In the space below, please indicate how you plan to search for updates for the case you have read and briefed:

_____ I have my professor's permission and a Westlaw password, and will update online using Westlaw (**go immediately to Step 2 below**)

_____ I have my professor's permission and a Lexis password, and will update online using Lexis (**go immediately to Step 11 below**)

_____ I will update using traditional print materials (**go immediately to Appendix C in the back of this workbook**)

Step 2: Begin here only if you plan to update online using Westlaw. Update online using Westlaw only if you have a Westlaw password and your professor's permission to use it at this point in the semester. Go to Westlaw.com and log on using the password issued to you by your school. (If you inadvertently sign-on to lawschool.westlaw.com, click on the tab that says "Westlaw Research" to get to the correct homepage.)

Step 3: For this exercise, you will be using Westlaw's online citation tool, "KeyCite", to update the case you briefed earlier in this assignment. At the top of the Westlaw Research homepage, click on the hyperlink to "KeyCite." The next screen that appears provides a dialogue box on the left side for entering the case citation that you want to update, and also an abundance of useful information about the KeyCite feature itself on the right side of the screen.

Step 4: In the box provided on that initial screen, enter either the state or regional reporter citation (volume, Reporter, opening page) for the case you briefed earlier and hit "Go."

Step 5: The results of your search will show up on the right side of the next screen. That screen will show you the full name and citation to your case. Directly under the case name, in parentheses, you will find references to any additional reporters that print your case. In the space provided here, write the references to any additional reporters found in parentheses under your case name:

Step 6: Following any parenthetical references to other reporters, you will see any "prior history" or "subsequent history" of the case, as well as other related court documents. "Prior history" means any opinions regarding your case that were handed down prior to the present decision. "Subsequent history" is a term peculiar even in the legal research world, and is a little harder to understand because we generally think of "history" as something that has gone before. In law, "subsequent history" refers to things that happen to the case after the present opinion came down. In the space below, note the full cite to the case you are running the KeyCite search on, and indicate whether there is any "prior" or "subsequent" history on this case:

CITATION TIP: As you learned in Assignment Sheet 1, a "parallel" citation is a citation that identifies more than one reporter where a reader could find a case. In reference to state cases, a "parallel citation" is one that identifies the state reporter in which the case is published <u>and</u> the regional reporter in which the case is published. According to the 18th edition of <u>The Bluebook</u>, parallel citations should only be used when you are writing about a case in a document that will be submitted to a court in the state in which the case originates or when the local rules of court require parallel citations. For example, if you're citing a Georgia case to a Georgia court, you should use parallel citation form. Otherwise, you should omit the parallel citation, citing only the regional reporter followed by a parenthetical reference to the state court that decided the case. Read Rule 10.3.1 in the <u>Bluebook</u> to learn more about this rule. Under <u>The ALWD Manual</u>, you never use a parallel citation unless you are submitting a document to a court that has a local rule requiring parallel citations.

Step 7: While still on this first screen, look at the top left-hand corner. You may see a small green letter "C" there, directly under the small word, "KeyCite." If you see a green letter "C," rest your cursor on that green "C" and an explanation of its meaning will appear. You will see that the presence of a green "C" means that there are "citing cases" available for this case. If you do not see a green "C," enter a different case from earlier in this assignment until you find a case that does have a green "C" on the first screen. Click on the green "C."

Step 8: The screen that appears after you have clicked on the green "C" contains a great deal of additional valuable research information about your case. The cases that show up there are cases that have cited your original case. In other words, the judges who wrote those opinions relied in some way, or distinguished in some way, the case you are doing a KeyCite search on. Westlaw provides green stars that illustrate an editor's decision about how thoroughly the citing case treats your original case. One green star indicates fairly light treatment; the presence of four stars indicates that your case is discussed in great depth in the citing case. In the space below, write the cite to at least one case that cited your case and indicate whether there were stars associated with that cite that would show some depth of treatment of your original case in the citing case:

Step 9: In addition to giving you a heads-up as to how thoroughly the editor thinks a citing case treated your case, the Westlaw editor may also assign "status flags" to a case that has cited your original case. The available "status flag" cues are as follows: a red flag indicates your case may have been discredited on some point by the citing case; a "yellow flag" indicates that your case may have been discussed negatively on some point by the citing case; a "blue H" indicates that your case has been cited but without specific negative findings, and the "green C" you've already discovered indicates that the case citing your case has itself been cited elsewhere. (Note: you can always remind yourself about the meaning of a "status flag" on KeyCite by resting your cursor on it and waiting until an explanatory box appears.) In the space below, give the name and citation to a citing case that has a "status" flag next to it. If there is no "status flag" next to any of the cases that have cited your case, indicate that fact here instead:

READING TIP: Do not rely on the presence or absence of "status flags" to determine which cases to read. A good legal researcher recognizes that "status flags" on KeyCite represent the decision of editors employed by Westlaw. These editors are reading cases carefully, but are nonetheless reading them out of context. While it would be wrong to ignore a flag indicating negative treatment (because it might well be an indication that your case is no longer good law), it is equally wrong to assume that the presence of a red or yellow flag is a definitive statement on the value of your case – or that the absence of a red or yellow flag confirms that the case is still good law.

WESTLAW HEADNOTE TIP: Cases are complex and often resolve many legal questions in one opinion. As you have learned, these questions are often assigned headnote numbers in the West system. When you run a search using the KeyCite function to check to see if your case is good law, or to find additional related cases, you can narrow your search by looking for cases that have cited your case expressly on the headnote point that is of interest to you. The numbers introduced by a bold-face HN (for headnote) indicate that those particular West headnotes from your case appear also in the citing case. Finally, a rich purple quotation mark next to a citing case indicates that the case quotes the case that you are running your KeyCite search on.

Step 10: We do not have time in this assignment to ask you to read another case. However, if you were going to continue your research on this case, choose one case that you might read and, in the space below, explain why you chose that case (think about the status flags and depth of treatment stars assigned to the citing case, as well as the headnote tip above, when selecting what case you might read):

Go now to Section C on p. 280 unless you want to also update using Lexis following Steps 11-16 below.

Step 11: Begin here if you are going to update online using Lexis. Update online using Lexis only if you have a Lexis password and your professor's permission to use it at this point in the semester. Go to Lexis.com and log on using the password issued to you by your school.

Step 12: Using the tabs across the top of the Lexis homepage, click on "Shepard's" to begin your updating. As of the printing of this Workbook, you would be presented with a choice of asking for a "Report" that would include "Shepard's for Validation" (showing only the *future* history of your case as well as citations for cases in which your case has been cited AND that the Lexis editors have attached an explanatory signal to) OR for a Report that would include "Shepard's for Research" (showing both the *prior* and *future* history of the case as well as all cases that have cited your case). For this exercise, choose "Shepard's for Research."

Step 13: In the space provided on the Shepard's page, enter *either* the state or the regional reporter citation to the case you briefed earlier in this assignment. If you are uncertain as to what "format" to insert for your reporter, click on the hyperlink to "Citation Formats" immediately to the right of the box. Finally, click "check."

Step 14: The Lexis screen that appears first shows you, in a shaded box, a succinct summary of what information is available on Lexis about your case. The first thing you will see is a statement as to whether your case has any prior history or subsequent history. Does it?

Step 15: The summary also includes visually helpful icons called "treatment letters" followed by the number of cases that fall into any of the relevant categories. Possible "treatment letters" include: a red stop sign (symbolizing actual negative treatment – such as a reversal), an orange square with the letter Q (symbolizing a questioning of your case), a yellow triangle (symbolizing possible negative treatment), a green diamond with a plus sign (symbolizing favorable treatment, such as direct reliance on your case), a blue circle with an "A" included (symbolizing discussion of your case), a blue circle with an "l" (indicating that your case is cited but no treatment letters have been assigned).

Does your case have any "treatment letters" associated with it? If so, what letter appears and how many citing cases or other sources are associated with that letter?:

Treatment letter: _____

Number of Cases indicating such treatment: _____

Step 16: Next, scroll below the shaded summary box. You will find references to the cases involved in any prior and subsequent history, followed by cases that have cited your case (in priority order, starting with the highest court in your jurisdiction and moving, then, to other jurisdictions). We do not have time in this assignment to ask you to read another case. However, if you were going to continue your research on this case, choose one case that you might read and, in the space below, explain why you chose that case (think about the treatment letters assigned to the citing case and the headnote tip below when selecting what case you might read):

LEXIS HEADNOTE TIP: Cases are complex and often resolve many legal questions in one opinion. As you have learned, these questions are often assigned headnote numbers in the West system. LexisNexis has developed a similar system and now assigns its own Lexis headnote numbers to all current cases. LexisNexis editors have also reached back and have assigned Lexis headnote numbers to all prior federal cases and a substantial number of state cases. When you run a search using the Shepard's function to check to see if your case is good law, or to find additional related cases, you can narrow your search by looking for cases that have cited your case expressly on the headnote point that is of interest to you. The numbers introduced by a bold-face HN (for headnote) indicate that those particular LexisNexis headnotes from your case appear also in the citing case. The LexisNexis headnotes referenced in citing cases show up in the shaded summary box on the first screen when you do a Full Search using Shepard's online. You can also click on the "show headnotes" feature to get a drop-down box that will highlight the content of those headnotes.

BEWARE: The presence of a "treatment letter" is a useful aid in your search. However, treatment letters are only a help – not a substitute for reading a case yourself. You cannot assume that the editors who read the case and assigned a letter have the last word on the meaning of the case. Additionally, you cannot assume that treatment letters are attached to every relevant case – they are not. If you find a treatment letter, be grateful and use it to search further. If you do not find a treatment letter, you cannot assume definitively that there is no negative (or positive) subsequent history.

C. FINDING CASES FROM OTHER STATES

You have learned several ways to locate cases in your state. Before we move on, it is important that you also be able to find cases outside of your state. Thus, for your final task in this Assignment Sheet, we would like you to use the West Key Number system using print materials to see how the state of Georgia handles the area of common law raised by your senior partner. (Note, if your original research is in the state of Georgia, try looking up a Florida case following Steps 1 through 4 below to see how that state handles this topic.) Remember, Georgia has a whole separate state court system and can do whatever it wants in this area of the law (assuming it's consistent with federal constitutional and statutory law). The law of Georgia may or may not be the same as the law of your state on this topic. To complete this final assignment, follow Steps 1 through 4 below.

Step 1: Annotations of cases for the state of Georgia are found in the regional digest for the southeastern region. The official title of that regional digest is West's <u>South Eastern Digest 2d</u> (note the space between "South" and "Eastern" if you are using an on-line catalogue to find this title). **Go there now.**

Step 2: Using the West Topic and Key Number you uncovered earlier in this Assignment Sheet, find an annotation for a case from Georgia in West's <u>South Eastern Digest 2d</u> that you think might be worth reading. Write the name and citation for that case as it appears at the end of the annotation here:

> **TIP:** Note that the publishers of the digest series cite the regional reporter first, followed by any state reporter (e.g., <u>West v. Slick</u>, 326 S.E.2d 601, 313 N.C. 33 (1985)). That is unusual. In your own legal writing, <u>The Bluebook</u> and <u>The ALWD Manual</u> direct you to cite the state reporter first when using a parallel cite, followed by the regional reporter. Hence, you will see the state reporter first in almost all written work about a law if there is a parallel cite (e.g., <u>West v. Slick</u>, 313 N.C. 33, 326 S.E.2d 601 (1985)). Hang in there; all this becomes easier with time and practice.

Step 3: The annotated case you just found using the <u>South Eastern Digest 2d</u> is printed in its entirety in the <u>South Eastern Reporter</u>. Using your library's cataloguing system, locate that volume now (you may find it near the <u>South Eastern Digest 2d</u> you just used). Find your case in the Reporter and skim the headnotes. Does it look to you like the common law of Georgia on this topic is the same as the common law of your state?

Step 4: If you wanted to see if this Georgia case was still good law, what resources could you use? (Hint: See Section B(2), <u>Step 1</u> of this Assignment Sheet above):

Please reshelve all books now.

Summary and Writing Assignment: Take a few minutes and think about what you have learned about your state's common law principles governing the question raised by your senior partner. On a separate piece of paper, please write a <u>short</u>, *informal* memo to your senior partner answering the question raised in Memo 4 using the limited information you've uncovered to this point.

To write this short memo, follow the business heading format you've seen modeled in your partner's memos in this workbook. In legal writing, as in all writing, think about who your reading audience is. In our case, pretend your reading audience is your assigning partner and address your memo to that person. Most people who read law are busy readers, so try to write simply and with as much clarity as you can muster. It's often best to begin by repeating the question you have been asked so that you can make sure everyone is on the same wavelength. Follow your paraphrase of the question with your answer to that question, being sure to cite the authority that led you to conclude what you have (so far) about the law.

As you write your answer, try to be as logical and clear as possible – state any controlling legal principles as you understand them (followed by a citation to the material that led you to your understanding of that rule); explain what happened in your client's case as it relates to that rule; draw a conclusion. To avoid inadvertently plagiarizing, be sure to use quotation marks around language that is a direct quote. Remember: you have only done a little bit of research here – not enough to find an irrefutable response, but only enough to get some beginning ideas. Your "partner" will understand the limitations of this assignment when reading your memo. Use this writing exercise to let your professor know what you think at this point about your client's legal question.

Congratulations! You have now completed your Assignment Sheet on common law and have learned some additional ways to find case law on a given common law topic in your state. You have also learned how to cite a case properly in your state, how to update your research to make sure the case you're using is still followed in your jurisdiction, and how to find a case on the same topic in another state. **To learn more about how to do case law research electronically, read the** ONLINE TIP **on the following page.**

*Please note your actual time of completion (including background reading):*_____ *hrs.*

ONLINE TIPS for Case Law Research: Once you have completed the supplement to this workbook and have your professor's permission to use electronic resources, you can begin to explore the many fee-based and free services that can help you locate cases and update case law research online. As you think about integrating electronic resources into what you already know about finding cases in hard copy, consider the tips below:

- See Appendix A in the supplement to this workbook for a list of free websites and fee-based services that you will find helpful as you expand your online skills.

- As you have learned, some courts allow lawyers to use "unpublished" cases (cases not printed in the official reporters) as precedent under restricted circumstances. Some do not. **Know the rules of court in the jurisdiction you are working in so you know if you should be looking for such cases or not.** Unpublished opinions are available to the individual lawyers who litigated the case decided (the court sends these opinions to those lawyers), and when you practice in a particular area you will learn to watch for news about such cases. For those not involved in the litigation itself, such cases can often be obtained directly from the court. You can find such cases by doing a "whole text" search online using key terms as you will learn to do in the supplement.

- Note that free internet sources for finding case law (for example, states' Supreme Court websites) generally do not include the kind of enhancements (use of headnotes, Key Numbers, <u>Shepard's</u> editorial analyses, hyperlinks, etc.) that are contained on the fee-based search engines such as LexisNexis and Westlaw. Similarly, reduced fee services generally have fewer enhancements, and sometimes no enhancements than their for-fee counterparts.

- Online databases often do not have full scope coverage. Always check your resource to see how far back cases are covered and whether coverage is comprehensive or includes only select cases.

- The importance of considering accuracy, economy, and efficiency when deciding what resources to use cannot be overemphasized. For many students, using online resources is the most convenient way to do their school-based research (and sometimes the most economical as well). It is therefore tempting to abandon hard copy research and gravitate to electronic resources. In practice, however, the choices will be more varied, and there will be a cost (often high) associated with electronic research. It is therefore critical to know how to use all available resources well so you can make wise choices as you search for law in the future.

Marshall, Story & Associates
Attorneys and Counselors at Law
Suite 101, The Justice Building

⚖

The Litigation Division

To: New Associate
From: Assigning Partner
Re: Richard Roth [Client F] – File #03-2578

    I met with Richard Roth to discuss his case, and learned that the roommate has engaged in conversations with others in which he quotes the remarks he made earlier to Richard's department head. Apparently the roommate believes that because he is not making additional comments, but rather only repeating former comments, that he is insulated from additional liability.

    As a general rule, I believe the roommate is wrong and that a speaker is responsible for any republications he or she chooses to make of a prior slanderous remark.

    The roommate is now represented by counsel, and I will be meeting with that lawyer this week to discuss possible mediation of this case. Without doing specific research in our jurisdiction yet, I would like to know in general if I am correct about republication of prior remarks that constitute libel and slander.

    For your final assignment on Richard's behalf, would you do some general research to see if a person who makes repetitious republications of a slanderous remark may be liable for having repeated those same remarks again. In addition, would you please see if the topic of libel and slander has been examined lately in legal journals and find an article that might expand our knowledge in this area.

▶▶ Turn to page 295 to begin your work on this assignment.

MARSHALL, STORY & ASSOCIATES
ATTORNEYS AND COUNSELORS AT LAW
SUITE 101, THE JUSTICE BUILDING

⚖

THE LITIGATION DIVISION

To: New Associate
From: Assigning Partner
Re: Ana Martinez [Client G] – File #03-2577

I plan to meet with Ana at the end of the week and would like to give her some general advice about her case. The research you have done to date has been extremely helpful.

Although I will not go into details at this time about trial strategies, if it comes to that, I would like some additional information for my own records.

I am curious as to whether Dr. Townsend's initial representations to Ana that he was a physician and that the drug he had invented was already approved might constitute fraud.

For your last assignment on this case, could you do some general research to determine what generally has to be shown to establish a common law action for fraud?

▶▶ **Turn to page 295 to begin your work on this assignment.**

MARSHALL, STORY & ASSOCIATES
ATTORNEYS AND COUNSELORS AT LAW
SUITE 101, THE JUSTICE BUILDING

⚖

THE LITIGATION DIVISION

To: New Associate
From: Assigning Partner
Re: Christopher Smith [Client H] - File #21-2206

Your research to date has convinced me that we have a strong case against Ms. Adams. During my conference call with Ms. Adams' attorney, however, it seemed to me that she was not so sure. Rather, she seemed to think that much of the legal theory upon which I am basing negotiations is peculiar only to our state.

I have a second conference call scheduled with her attorney next week. At that time, I'd like to have some more general background information about voiding contracts with infants/minors. Specifically, I would like to know how other states would handle Christopher's contract rights in the unlikely event that the car is considered a necessary purchase (a "necessity"). Would he still lose the whole $4,900 he paid for this car which he has now been told is worth only $1,000 at best?

Finally, in an effort to settle this matter out of court, I anticipate a request by Ms. Adams' attorney that we submit to voluntary mediation. Please see if you can find a recent law review article on the subject of mediation so I can familiarize myself with both the concept and the process. Again, I am most appreciative of the work you are doing for Christopher and am confident that we will be able to mediate a settlement that will work for him.

▶▶ Turn to page 295 to begin your work on this assignment.

MARSHALL, STORY & ASSOCIATES
ATTORNEYS AND COUNSELORS AT LAW
SUITE 101, THE JUSTICE BUILDING

⚖️

THE LITIGATION DIVISION

To: New Associate
From: Assigning Partner
Re: Carolyn Meyer [Client I] - File #21-2207

Your research to date has been very interesting and I appreciate the effort you've put into it.

For your last assignment on Carolyn's behalf, I please look into whether our state's position on assault and battery, as well as the question of self-defense as a way of defeating that claim, is an isolated perspective or one that is generally shared. I would like to reassure myself that this area of law is relatively stable across most states.

I will look forward to learning more about this area of law in general.

▶▶ **Turn to page 295 to begin your work on this assignment.**

MARSHALL, STORY & ASSOCIATES
ATTORNEYS AND COUNSELORS AT LAW
SUITE 101, THE JUSTICE BUILDING

⚖

THE LITIGATION DIVISION

To: New Associate
From: Assigning Partner
Re: Jeanne Martin [Client J] – File #21-2208

Your research to date has been very helpful, and has raised an additional concern on my part that I would like to clear up before making final decisions about drafting a complaint to help Ms. Martin regain possession of her dog.

As I understand your research, conversion is a cause of action that allows a property owner to regain possession of personal property. I would like to confirm that a pet, such as this retriever, is considered "property" in the eyes of the law. For your final assignment on Ms. Martin's behalf, I would appreciate your doing some general research to assure me that a dog is considered property and could be reacquired through an action based on the theory of conversion.

In addition, I am curious to know if the topic of conversion has been the study of much academic work. Please also see if you can find a journal article on the subject of conversion that might be enlightening.

I will look forward to finding out what you learn in general about this question.

▶▶ **Turn to page 295 to begin your work on this assignment.**

Assignment Sheet 5 *in Sequence of Assignments #2* **Using Secondary Resources**	Estimated Time of Completion (including recommended background reading): 2.5 – 4.0 hrs.
Print Your Name:	

(If you are doing this assignment as part of a class exercise, you may neatly write your answers directly on these sheets, staple all sheets together, and turn them in. If you prefer to write your answers separately using your computer, please be sure to number your answers to correspond to the appropriate questions before printing your answer sheets.)

Background Reading: To learn more about the resources and concepts introduced in this Assignment Sheet, read Chapter 2 of *Legal Research in a Nutshell* or a comparable chapter in a textbook assigned by your professor. (See Appendix A.)

Background Information: Your partner has asked you to look into a question of law that is general in nature. In such a situation, and also in situations where you are asked a more specific question but don't yet know a lot about the topic the question covers, secondary sources are a good place to get started. In legal research, secondary sources are a rich source of information on a variety of legal topics and also can often point you directly to primary law that may have an impact on the question before you. Re-read pages 21-22 and page 24-25 in this workbook for more information on the importance of using secondary sources.

What You Will Learn. By the end of this assignment, you will:

- Be able to identify two leading legal research encyclopedias
- Find and update information in a legal encyclopedia
- Identify your state encyclopedia, if there is one
- Recognize the significant value of legal treatises
- Recognize the origin and purpose of Restatements
- Be alert to a number of online options for finding secondary sources

The Research Process:
A. USING LEGAL ENCYCLOPEDIAS

Introduction: Print copy legal encyclopedias are easy to use because they are akin to the general encyclopedias you have seen for years and are set out in relatively simple terms. Unlike legal periodicals (which you'll learn about later in this Assignment Sheet), they are not generally used as persuasive secondary authority (although you will still see an encyclopedia cited in a court opinion from time to time). Instead, encyclopedias are tools that introduce you to general concepts and lead you to further research. The two national encyclopedias, <u>Corpus Juris Secundum</u> (<u>C.J.S.</u>) and <u>American Jurisprudence 2d</u> (<u>Am. Jur. 2d</u>), are very similar, but it's a good idea to be able to use both. Like using the <u>World Book Encyclopedia</u> and <u>The Encyclopedia Britannica</u>, researching in both legal encyclopedias might enable you to pick up something from one that you didn't find in the other. In this assignment, you will get to try your hand at both.

1. <u>Corpus Juris Secundum (C.J.S.) and American Jurisprudence 2d (Am. Jur. 2d)</u>

Step 1: Although <u>Am. Jur. 2d</u> and <u>C.J.S.</u> perform pretty much the same function, you will find that they differ in some respects. Over time, you may develop a preference for one over the other, or you may find more thorough coverage of a particular subject in one or the other. Choose one of these encyclopedias to begin your research. Write the name of the encyclopedia here:_____, then **go to the location of the encyclopedia you chose.**

ONLINE TIP: Although many resources can be found online and in hard copy, issues of cost, convenience, and scope of coverage are critical factors lawyers must consider when deciding whether to search online or to use traditional books. In addition, studies indicate that many readers browse more comfortably using actual books rather than online materials. Recognizing this challenge, both Westlaw and Lexis have recently added online browsing features such as Tables of Contents, Indexes, and search tools that allow readers to move backwards and forward online. By 2008, online access to <u>Am. Jur.</u> and <u>C.J.S.</u> will be restricted to Westlaw. You can locate alternative secondary source materials on Lexis by clicking on the "Search" tab at the top of the Lexis homepage, choosing the "Search by Source" option, and then clicking on the link provided for Secondary Legal Sources. On Westlaw, you can locate additional secondary source materials on the Law School homepage by clicking on the links listed under "Secondary Source" grouping. On the main Westlaw homepage, click on the "View Westlaw Directory" hyperlink. Using secondary resources to get oriented to a new topic is important when you are doing research online as it is when you are using hard copy materials.

Step 2: Determine which major area(s) of law your client's case falls under. Often, identification of a proper area of law where you can begin researching isn't obvious. In this case, however, you're lucky because your senior partner has already identified the legal issues that he or she would like you to investigate. As a rule in legal research, however, you need to be flexible and creative in thinking of a variety of possible terms that will lead you to the area of the encyclopedia that will discuss what you're interested in. Look back at your partner's memo for guidance. Next, list one or two terms to begin with here:

TIP: As you have learned to do in earlier assignmens, keep the "5 W's" that you may have learned about in a beginning journalism class (who, what, when, where, and why) in mind as you generate search terms in legal research. In a legal context, applying these concepts helps you think about the parties or things involved (minor child, teacher, dog, etc.), the type of action or conflict (battery, robbery, trespass), when the action occurred (vacation, workday, off duty), where the action occurred (bank, school, playground) and why the action occurred (malice, self-defense, mistake, protection of property). Generating synonyms broadens the chance that you will find the law in a place where editors or publishers have also catalogued the information.

Step 3: Find the multi-volume General Index located at the end of the entire set and look up the terms you listed in Step 2 above. (Note that there are also individual Topic indexes at the end of each individual Topic.) The General Index and the individual Topic Indexes contain *Topic* and *Section* numbers that will lead you to the main volume that will contain entries related to the search terms you've generated. You will find the Topics published alphabetically in the main volumes (like other print copy encyclopedias you may have used); Sections are sub-parts of the larger Topics. Spending a few extra minutes with the General Index is often a wise investment of time. The Index can help you narrow your search quickly and will also refer you to other subject areas (Topics) you hadn't even considered. In the space below, write down the references and corresponding Section numbers to at least three entries you found in the General Index that look like they might relate to your partner's question:

Please return the General Index to the shelf now so that others may use it.

Step 4: In the main set, find the text for the references you noted in Step 3 above. Read the entries in the text. Choose one of these entries and, in the space provided, summarize the general law on the point it addresses and describe how it relates to our client's problem. If the Sections you have read do not appear to be on point, read the following "BOMB" and "TIP" and repeat Steps 1 through 3 until you find a section that does.

BEWARE: Occasionally the sections cited in the General Index are incorrect or confusing. If the Sections your search has led you to seem incorrect, consider using the individual index at the end of each Topic to find a Section you want to read. See the **TIP** below for more ideas on how to find the information you want in the encyclopedia.

TIP: The General Index and the individual index for each Topic are both good resources for finding an encyclopedia Section to read. Each Section, of course, is a sub-division of a larger Topic. It is often helpful to look at the Table of Contents (called an "Analysis") that appears at the beginning of every Topic if you are having difficulty finding an entry on point. This is a good habit to get into even when you think the more narrow Section you've found is directly on point. You may find related Sections listed that would yield additional ideas for further research.

Use this space to summarize the general law on the point your Section addresses and describe how that law relates to your client's problem:

Step 5: In the space below, write the correct <u>Bluebook</u> or <u>ALWD</u> citation to the section you have summarized (see Rule 15.8 of <u>The Bluebook</u> or Rule 26 of <u>The ALWD Manual</u> for an example of how to cite to <u>C.J.S.</u> and <u>Am. Jur. 2d</u>):

DO NOT RESHELVE YOUR ENCYCLOPEDIA VOLUME YET.

Step 6: In addition to being good sources of general background information, <u>C.J.S.</u> and <u>Am. Jur. 2d</u> entries are also a good source for locating relevant case law (court decisions) from a wide variety of jurisdictions. You have learned other ways to find case law in Assignment Sheets 1, 2 , and 4 of this Sequence of Assignments. While you still have the encyclopedia open to the Section you summarized above, look at the bottom of the page for references to relevant case law. Find an entry to a case on point and write the citation exactly as it is printed there in the space below (note that the way the publisher has printed this citation may or may not be in compliance with the way <u>The Bluebook</u> or <u>The ALWD Manual</u> recommends that you cite the case if you write about it in the future. Always check your citation manual for proper citation form if you're writing an important document):

Taking your best guess based on the citation to the state reporter in which the case is published, what state do you think the case is from?

Step 7: Law changes rapidly and you want the most recent information you can find to be sure there are no significant changes in the principles you're uncovering. To update your research in legal encyclopedias, turn to the "pocket part" at the end of the volume you are using. In the pocket part of the volume you have been using, look up the Topic and Section you just summarized. Are there any changes to the text?:

Are there any new cases listed? If so, list at least one here:

Step 8: Turn now to the encyclopedia you have <u>not</u> been using. Write the name of that encyclopedia here: _____. In this other encyclopedia, find a Section closely related to the one you've been working on. Read that Section and put its complete cite here (be sure to check the pocket part, too):

Did you learn anything new from this entry?:

You may now reshelve all national encyclopedia volumes before moving on to the next section of this Assignment.

2. <u>State Encyclopedias</u>

Many states have their own encyclopedias that serve the same purpose as a national encyclopedia, but are focused solely on that state's law. When you are dealing with a question such as this one that will almost surely fall under the domain of your state court system, there is often no reason to begin your research with a national encyclopedia if your state has a local one. If your state does not have its own encyclopedia, you may move on to the next section now. If it does, take a few minutes to become familiar with that encyclopedia. Write a paragraph in the space below comparing your state's position on the topic you are researching with what you learned from the national encyclopedias.

B. FINDING ARTICLES IN LEGAL PERIODICALS

Introduction: The most widely regarded legal periodical articles are those found in "law reviews." A "law review" is a major academic journal. Law reviews are published by all of the leading law schools in the country. The University of North Carolina School of Law, for example, publishes The North Carolina Law Review.

There are many specialized law school journals as well. At UNC, for example, we also publish The North Carolina Journal of International Law and Commercial Regulation, the journal of The Banking Institute , The Journal of Law and Technology, and The First Amendment Law Review. As a rule, periodical articles shed new light on a subject (whereas the encyclopedias you have just used do not raise questions about existing law nor challenge cases in depth). Such articles can be used effectively by lawyers to try to persuade a court to reconsider its prior position in a particular area of law. This part of your Assignment Sheet is designed to help you find an article in a law school journal or other periodical on the subject raised by your partner's memo.

ONLINE TIP: Online research has led to the birth of new scholarly sources, beyond traditional law school journals. The Social Science Research Network (SSRN) is one such source. If your law school subscribes to SSRN, you will have access as a law student to some of the works in progress of many recognized scholars who post online at www.ssrn.com for scholarly comments from colleagues. Blogs are also a prevalent source of background information and scholarly comment about the law, with blogs of well-recognized experts being more credible than institutionally generated blogs or blogs of authors who are less well-established. A number of sources are available to search for available law-related blogs. Try BlawgSearch <blawgsearch.justia.com> or Google Blog Search <blogsearch.google.com>.

BEWARE: Accessing copies of journals in print format has been a mainstay of competent legal research for decades. Today many journals can also be accessed online. If you search for a journal article online using free or fee-based services and databases, be aware of possible limitations in years of coverage. You may miss important historical perspectives unintentionally.

Step 1: To complete this section of your assignment, you may use EITHER hard copy research techniques or online research techniques to locate an article on point. You should use the method that is consistent with your professor's wishes and that is supported by the materials in your law library. In the space below, indicate whether you will use an electronic (online) index or a print (hard copy) index to locate a journal article:

_____ I will be searching a print index

_____ I will be searching an online index

_____ I will be searching both an online and a print index

If you are searching a print index, or plan to search both in print and online, go immediately to Step 2 below. If you are searching online only, go immediately to Step 5 below.

Step 2: <u>(begin here and proceed through Step 4 only if you're searching using a print index):</u> When you are using hard copy research techniques, legal periodicals can be found by using <u>either</u> the <u>Index to Legal Periodicals and Books</u> or the <u>Current Law Index</u>. Often it is beneficial to search both. **Go to the location in your library where these resources are shelved.**

Step 3: Choosing one or the other of these resources, take down the latest volume that you can find on the shelf. Using any of the search topics you found profitable in Section A (Encyclopedias) above, find a reference to one interesting article and write its citation here, following the **CITATION TIP** below. (Note, if you are not able to find an article on point in the most recent volume, go back chronologically until you are successful – or try a broader or a more narrow search term.):

CITATION TIP: Check out Table T.13 in your <u>Bluebook</u> or Appendix 5 of <u>The ALWD Manual</u> for a complete listing of proper abbreviations for almost all widely used legal periodicals. In general, see Rule 16 of <u>The Bluebook</u> or Rule 23 of <u>The ALWD Manual</u> for directions on how to properly cite periodical.

BEWARE: Each volume of the <u>Index to Legal Periodicals and Books</u> and of the <u>Current Law Index</u> only contains references to articles published during the time noted on the binding of that volume. Hence, to find older articles, you have to pull older volumes down (one at a time), which tends to be tedious.

Step 4: Once you have located an article using a hard copy index, you can try your hand at using an online index by following Steps 5-7 below, or you can proceed immediately to Step 8. **Before proceeding, please return all volumes of the <u>Index to Legal Periodicals and Books</u> or the <u>Current Law Index</u> so that others may use them.**

Step 5: (begin here and proceed through Step 6 only if you are searching using an online index): LegalTrac is an online periodical index that is available in most academic libraries. You can search LegalTrac a number of ways (by keyword, subject, author, title, etc.) to find an article of potential interest. Begin first by finding the link to LegalTrac through your library's online catalogue.

ONLINE TIP: Your library may or may not provide access to LegalTrac. If your library does not provide access to LegalTrac, ask a librarian or search your library's online catalogue to see if an alternate online periodical index is available. Be cautious with online indexes. Many databases cover only recent articles. LegalTrac itself only indexes articles published since 1980 and for some periodicals its coverage is even more reduced. For articles published before 1980, you could use the print version of the <u>Index to Legal Periodicals and Books</u> or the <u>Current Law Index</u>. HeinOnline is another excellent tool (available by subscription) for online retrieval of law-related journal articles (and other materials as well). HeinOnline has made a point of providing full coverage for many journals, dating back often to the beginning of a journal's publication. You can check your school's online catalogue to see if HeinOnline is available to you.

Step 6: Once you are on the LegalTrac homepage, choose "search by keyword." In the space below, write down a keyword or several keywords that might yield profitable results for you. After you have entered your keyword search terms, hit "search" (not browse).

How many articles did your search yield? (The number of articles yielded will show up under the tab for the kind of journal (e.g., academic journal, magazine, book, etc.) searched.) _____

To familiarize yourself further with LegalTrac, repeat your search, choosing to search by subject instead. In what way were your results different in this search?

Step 7: In the space below, write the name and citation to a particular article that looks like it would be useful in your research for your client:

Step 8: Even in this day of widespread access to computers, it is useful to know how to find an article in print copy. Studies show that most readers vastly prefer to read a print version of a long document than an online version, and that many readers often get more out of what they read in print than what they read online. In most law libraries, periodicals are shelved alphabetically. Go to the location in your library where periodicals are shelved. If the article you want to read is in a very current journal, ask for it at the Circulation Desk.

Once you have a title and author for an article, you may locate it now in hard copy. (Alternatively, you may locate the article online, but only if online access is permitted by your professor). Ask your professor or a law librarian if you need further direction.

Once you have located the article you would like to read, skim it and summarize the author's main points in the space that follows:

Step 9: If you were a practicing attorney, in what way might this article have been useful to you as you considered the question raised by your partner about your client?

C. OTHER KINDS OF SECONDARY RESOURCES

Legal encyclopedias and legal periodicals (journal articles) are only two of the many kinds of secondary sources that are indispensable sources of information about the law. Chapter 2 of *Legal Research in a Nutshell* sets out several important additional resources. Read that chapter or a comparable chapter in one of the textbooks listed in Appendix A to learn more about the many other secondary resources available for your use.

1. Treatises and Hornbooks: Perhaps the most significant of these other secondary resources are legal treatises and hornbooks. A *legal treatise* is a definitive treatment of a particular area of law, often containing several volumes, which includes both text and references to cases and other primary resources. A *hornbook* is a similar respected scholarly work, but often printed in only one volume and often targeted to law students. Both treatises and hornbooks are generally viewed as being more scholarly and reliable treatments of a subject than is an encyclopedia. A treatise is frequently written by a recognized expert in a given field, usually a law professor, and is often cited in court opinions. A hornbook, by contrast, is generally shorter and more to the point. Like a treatise, however, it is generally written by a recognized expert in the field and is an excellent source of general scholarly information on a given topic. There are both national treatises and state treatises on many broad legal topics.

If you have time, you should look for a treatise that covers the general area of law that addresses your partner's question (for example, if your question concerns the tort of slander, look for a *treatise* on Tort Law; if your question concerns breach of contract, look for a *treatise* on Contract Law, etc.). Use the index or table of contents of the treatise you have found to identify a relevant section and see what you can learn about how the resource might be helpful to you. *If you are a law student, you will find that a treatise or hornbook can also help clarify complex areas of law that you are studying in class.*

> **(t) TIP:** You can use your library's online catalogue to find treatises on almost any legal topic, or ask at the reference desk of your law library for recommendations about the most widely recognized treatises in the area you are researching. Additionally, faculty members who teach in a defined area of law often have specific treatises that they recommend to students. Many law libraries keep national and state treatises on reserve at their reference desks.

2. Restatements: Restatements are another important secondary source that can help you understand trends in the law. *Restatements* are collections of summaries of the common law (or, in some cases, predictions of what the common law rules may become) that have been drafted by leaders in the legal community through the American Law Institute.

These "restatements" of the law are frequently relied on by judges to clarify the common law in their jurisdiction as they try to resolve a particular case in controversy, but a Restatement of the law is NOT primary law itself. There are Restatements available on a wide variety of common law topics (e.g., the Restatement on Contracts, the Restatement on Torts, etc.). If you have time, you should look through a Restatement and see how it could help you learn more about the topic your senior partner has asked you to explore. If you are a law student, you may remember having seen references to Restatements in your casebooks and perhaps even cited within cases contained in your casebooks.

ONLINE TIP: Both Westlaw and Lexis carry databases that give you access to leading hornbooks and treatises, as well as the Restatements. Check with each service to see specifically what materials are searchable.

D. TYING IT ALL TOGETHER

Now that you've had a chance to read a number of secondary resources addressing the subject raised by your senior partner, it would be helpful to synthesize what you've learned. Please use the space provided to write a paragraph addressing your partner's question. As you write your paragraph, bear in mind that the purpose of this assignment was more to learn how to use the research materials than to find a reliable answer at this preliminary stage of research. It is a good habit in legal writing to make sure that your reader is focused from the beginning on the exact legal question you are addressing. With that goal in mind, be sure to clearly identify the question you are answering at the beginning of your paragraph.

Congratulations! You have just completed your last assignment sheet in this part of the workbook and have learned how to access valuable legal information through secondary resources.

Please note your actual time of completion (including background reading): _____ *hrs.*

Appendix: A

Table of Cross-References
for Supplementary Reading

The following textbooks are included in the chart on the following two pages, with cross-references noted for specific chapters and sections that correspond to the assignments in this workbook. Books are listed alphabetically by authors' last names.

Updated Sources

- Robert C. Berring & Elizabeth A. Edinger, <u>Finding the Law</u> (12th ed. 2005)

- Robert C. Berring & Elizabeth A. Edinger, <u>Legal Research Survival Manual</u> (2002)

- Morris L. Cohen et al., <u>How to Find the Law</u> (9th ed. 1989)

- Morris L. Cohen & Kent C. Olson, <u>Legal Research in a Nutshell</u> (9th ed. 2007)

- Roy M. Mersky and Donald J. Dunn, <u>Legal Research Illustrated</u> (8th ed. 2002)

- Christina L. Kunz et al., <u>The Process of Legal Research</u> (6th ed. 2004)

- Roy M. Mersky & Donald J. Dunn, <u>Fundamentals of Legal Research</u> (8th ed. 2002)

- Amy E. Sloan, <u>Basic Legal Research</u> (3rd ed. 2006)

- Larry L. Teply, <u>Legal Research & Citation</u> (5th ed. 1999)

	Introductory Material	Encyclopedias	Common Law	State Statutes	Federal Statutory Law	Admin. Law	Online
Berring & Edinger Finding the Law	Chapter 1	Chapter 10	Chapters 1, 2, 3 (Citators), 4	Chapters 5 & 6; Appendix B	Chapters 5 & 6	Chapter 8	Integrated throughout
Berring & Edinger Legal Research Survival Manual	"A Note on Sex, Drugs, & Rock n Roll"; Chs. 1, 4 & 11	Chapter 1	Chapters 2 & 3	Chapter 5	Chapter 5	N/A	Integrated throughout; see generally pp. 9-10
Cohen et al. How to Find the Law	Chapters 1 & 18	Chapters 11, 12 & 13	Chapters 2, 3 & 4; App. B, C	Chapters 5, 6 & 7; Appendix B	Chapters 5, 6 & 7	Chapter 8; App. B, D	Integrated throughout
Cohen & Olson Legal Research in a Nutshell	Chapter 1	Chapter 2	Chapters 3 & 4; Appendix A	Chs. 5 & 6; Appendix B	Chapters 5 & 6	Chapter 7	Integrated throughout
Mersky & Dunn, Legal Research Illustrated	Chapters 1 & 2, App. D, F	Chapters 7, 16, 17, 18	Chs. 3, 4, 5, 6, 7, 15 (Citators); App A	Chapter 11, App. A	Chapters 9, 10; pp. 138-144; 162	Chapter 13	Chapter 21, App. E
Johnson et al. Winning Research Skills							
Kunz et al. The Process of Legal Research	Chapters 1, 2, & 18	Chapters 3-8	Chapters 9 & 10	Chapters 11 & 12	Chapters 11 & 12	Chapters 13-15	Integrated throughout
Mersky & Dunn Fundamentals of Legal Research	Chapters 1 & 2; Appendix H	Chapters 16, 17 & 18	Chs. 3,4, 5, 6, 7 & 15 (Citators), App. D, E	Ch. 8 & 11, Appendix B	Chapters 8, 9, 10	Chapter 13	Chapter 22, Appendix G
Sloan, Basic Legal Research	Chapters 1, 2, 11	Chapter 3	Chapter 4; 5 (Citators)	Chapter 6	Chapters 6, 7	Chapter 8	Chapter 2, 10; Appendix A

A Sample Student Brief for <u>Gideon v. Wainwright</u>[1]

<u>Gideon v. Wainwright</u>, 372 U.S. 335 (1963)

Parties:
Petitioner: Mr. Gideon
Respondent: Mr. Wainwright, Corrections Director for the State of Florida

(In many appeals, the parties would be a plaintiff v. a defendant or the State v. a defendant. The parties are called "petitioner" and "respondent" here because the case came up on appeal by way of a petition for certiorari).

Procedural History:
(1) criminal trial in Florida state court for felony breaking and entering - guilty

(2) habeus corpus petition filed by Gideon with Florida Supreme Court - denied

(3) petition for certiorari granted by the U.S. Supreme Court (i.e., the U.S. Supreme Court agreed to hear the case – see 370 U.S. 908) - reversed the Florida conviction

Facts:
Petitioner (defendant Gideon) was charged in Florida with breaking and entering a poolroom with the intent to commit a misdemeanor (which is a felony offense in Florida) and was tried in Florida state court without an attorney. At that trial, he asked to be provided with an attorney because he could not afford one. He was told it was not the policy of the State of Florida to appoint counsel to represent him. He replied, "The United States Supreme Court says I'm entitled to be represented." He conducted his own defense, was found guilty, and was sentenced to five years in prison. Again representing himself, he appealed his conviction to the Florida Supreme Court and lost. He then wrote the U.S. Supreme Court which heard his case.

Question:
Is a criminal defendant who cannot afford an attorney entitled to have one appointed for him or her in a state court?

---

[1] The story of how this case came before the United States Supreme Court is eloquently presented by Anthony Lewis in his well-known book, <u>Gideon's Trumpet</u>. Anthony Lewis, <u>Gideon's Trumpet</u>, (Vintage Books 1989). If you are interested in our legal system and how one "case in controversy" can set policy for the entire country, you will find this book to be enjoyable to read.

Holding:
Yes – an indigent criminal defendant is entitled to have counsel appointed for him or her in both state and federal criminal trials.

Rule of Law:
The United States Constitution guarantees that all criminal defendants are entitled to be represented by counsel, whether they stand accused in a state or a federal court, and where they cannot afford to hire an attorney, one must be appointed for them.

Reasoning:
Relying on a long line of cases, the court reasoned that the Fourteenth Amendment of the U.S. Constitution obligates all states to recognize and protect any "fundamental" rights guaranteed in the original Bill of Rights. Although the U.S. Supreme Court has long recognized that appointment of counsel for indigent criminals in *federal* cases was constitutionally mandated, it originally determined that the representation by counsel guarantee of the Sixth Amendment was not sufficiently fundamental to warrant its imposition on the states through the Fourteenth Amendment (see Betts v. Brady, decided in 1942, where the court determined that an indigent criminal defendant in state court was NOT entitled to be represented by appointed counsel). This Court now believes that decision was incorrect and is abandoning that precedent. Upon reconsideration of the question of whether indigent criminal defendants are entitled to have counsel appointed to represent them, this court determined that the guarantee of right to counsel found in the Sixth Amendment of the United States Constitution is sufficiently fundamental to warrant its imposition on all the states. As Justice Black, writing for the Court, stated, "The right of one charged with crime to counsel may not be deemed fundamental and essential to fair trials in some countries, but it is in ours."

Other Thoughts: (It's a good idea to take notes on your personal reactions to a case)

Appendix: C

Updating Using Shepard's in Print Format

Background Information: Citators (whether used online or in hard copy) are tools that are a critical part of accurate, thorough legal research. You can (and should) use a "citator" for three purposes:

(1) to confirm that the primary resource material (case law, statutory law, administrative regulation) has not been over-ruled, reversed, or in some other way discredited. Without checking in a citator for this information, you might well build all your analysis on material that is no longer "good law." Such reliance on outdated or discredited information is a disaster in the legal field;

(2) to find both the prior history and future of a case you have in your hand. This information is necessary to get a full sense of what happened to your case before it got to the court that decided the opinion you are holding, and also to find out what happened to the case after this opinion was written. Some of this information is also an important part of proper citation format – what information you have to write down so that others can find the same case in the future; and

(3) to expand your search for related material once you have found some primary law that impacts the legal question for which you are seeking an answer. Citators provide you with a myriad of cross-references to other primary authority (cases, statutes, and administrative regulations) and secondary sources (treatises, encyclopedias, law review articles, etc.) that have made reference to the primary law you have found.

Although most legal researchers find it more convenient and accurate to update and expand their searches using one of the online citators available through Westlaw (KeyCite) or Lexis (Shepard's online), there may be times when you would need to rely on the traditional hard copy method of searching Shepard's Citators in print copy. This Appendix will teach you how to update and expand your research using a traditional hard copy of Shepard's Citators.

- To complete your Assignment Sheet on Common Law , go now to Part I below.

- To complete your Assignment Sheet on State Statutory Research, go now to Part II below.

- To complete your Assignment Sheet on Federal Statutory Research, go now to Part III below.

Part I: Updating Cases and Expanding Your Search for More Cases Using Hard Copy (Print) Materials

Step 1: To use <u>Shepard's</u> in print to find cases on point, you have to already know a case to use to get your foot in the door. (Happily, you have learned how to use the West's <u>Digest</u> in Part A of the assignment on Common Law research to find such a case.) Turning back to the case you briefed earlier in that assignment sheet, and write its citation here:

Step 2: <u>Shepard's</u> has a volume labeled "<u>[your state's name here] Citations, Case Edition</u>" for every state. These volumes are generally fairly thick and are bound in red with gold writing on the spine. You can usually find the <u>Shepard's</u> volume for your state's case law in close proximity to your state reporter system (usually at the end) or in close proximity to your state statutes. [Occasionally, additional copies of <u>Shepard's Citations, Case Edition</u> for your state will also be housed at the reference desk.] For this exercise, we want you to find the <u>Shepard's Citations, Case Edition</u> for the Reporter that contains your state's published cases. **Go to one of these locations now.**

Step 3: Find the first <u>Shepard's</u> volume that contains the citation for your case (look on the spine to see which cases are included in that volume and select the book that contains the Reporter referenced in your citation. Use a citation to the state Reporter if you can. In <u>Shepard's</u>, **make sure** you're in the section covering the court that decided your case – i.e., your state Supreme Court or your state Court of Appeals if you have more than one appellate court in your jurisdiction). Take the book down and look for the Reporter volume number of the case you listed above (the first number listed after the case name in a parallel citation). Volume numbers are listed at the top left or top right of the pages as in a dictionary or in the yellow pages of the telephone book.

When you find the right page, look for the column on that page that lists the exact volume number of the case you are shepardizing (stated in bold face as **Vol. x** in the first column containing entries for that volume).

Next, find the first page of your case as it appears within that column (the first page of your case is listed in the citation immediately after the abbreviation for the reporter the case is published in). In <u>Shepard's</u>, page numbers are centered in bold face in columns below the volume number.

Directly under the page number on which your case begins, you will see a case citation in parentheses. That is the "parallel citation" for your case (a "parallel citation" is the citation to a second reporter that also publishes the case). There will not be a parallel citation if you're in a state that only uses a regional reporter. If you're using a state reporter, write the full parallel citation (including the case name and the date) here. [If you're using a regional reporter only, see Rule 10.3.1 in The Bluebook or Rule 12 of The ALWD Manual for directions on how to properly cite your case in the absence of a parallel citation and write that citation here instead]:

CITATION TIP: According to the 18th edition of The Bluebook, parallel citations should only be used when you are writing about a case in a document that will be submitted to a court in the state in which the case originates. For example, if you're citing a Georgia case to a Georgia court, you should use parallel citation form. Otherwise, unless your local court rules provide otherwise, you should omit the parallel citation (citing only the regional reporter with a parenthetical reference to the state court that decided the case) as directed by Rule 10.3.1. Under The ALWD Manual, you never use a parallel citation unless you are submitting a document to a court that has a local rule requiring parallel citations. For purposes of this exercise, write the citation in the step above as if there is a local court rule requiring that you use parallel citations when possible.

Step 4: Look back at the page in Shepard's that you are using. Believe it or not, all the numbers that follow under the parallel citation refer to cases (or academic articles, or annotations to statutes) that cite your case. All of these cases, to one degree or another, are relying on your case as authority for something. Hence, they may or may not be useful cases to read in your effort to learn more about the common law on the point you are researching. If the new case is citing your case on the point you are researching, you would want to read it. If the new case is citing your case for an entirely different reason (say, on a point of civil procedure unrelated to the legal topic you're trying to learn about), you may not want to invest the time to read it.

When using Shepard's, it is not unusual to find fifty cases or more that have cited your case (and hence might be potentially important to read). To prioritize which of these cases to read first, you can use a small letter symbol which can be spotted from time-to-time to the left of a page number to help you narrow down which case may be of the greatest interest to you. These letter symbols indicate how the case that cites yours ruled. (For example, if there's a small 'r' next to the case listed in Shepard's, that case reversed some aspect of the case you were shepardizing. That would be a case you'd almost surely want to read.)

Look through the first few pages of any <u>Shepard's</u> volume for a list of the abbreviations and their meanings – in this instance, you'd want the list called "ABBREVIATIONS-ANALYSIS (cases)." In the space below, write down a specific reference that has a superscript letter to the left of it for the case you are sheparadizing (if the case you are shepardizing doesn't have one, look around the same page to spot a reference to another case with a superscript and write it here instead):

BEWARE: The page numbers used in <u>Shepard's</u> to indicate a resource that has cited your case are NOT the same page numbers you would use in proper citation form for the case. Rather, those page numbers lead you directly to the place <u>in the opinion</u> where your original case is cited. Go to the actual reporter volume on the shelf and pull the case to find where the case begins (and hence what page number to use) if you, in turn, want to read or cite to this second case which your <u>Shepard's</u> search uncovered. Note also that you need to pull the case from the actual reporter and look on the first page of the case to find the date to use for a proper parallel citation. If you want to practice, you can write the full parallel citation for the case you just found here:

TIP (how to use headnotes as you shepardize in print): Look back at the TIP on page 265 of this workbook concerning headnotes. As you learned, for every case published in a West reporter in any jurisdiction, Thomson-West places "headnotes" (synopses of important legal rules or principles) that summarize the main points of law in a case at the beginning of that case. These headnotes are numbered consecutively in the order that the points were raised in the opinion. In the West system, headnotes are selected because there is information in the case that corresponds with a West Key Number.

Using these headnote numbers has traditionally been another way to help prioritize which cases you want to look up when the case you are searching in <u>Shepard's</u> yields an unwieldy number of citing cases.

continued on next page

In print volumes of <u>Shepard's,</u> the West headnote number from the original case (corresponding to the headnote numbering system for the publisher of that reporter) was traditionally marked as a superscript just to the right of the Reporter cited in <u>Shepard's</u>. Thus, going back to the Schools 160.7 (home schooling) example used in the main volume, let's say I found and read a case in which this Key Number (160.7) was assigned to headnote #5 of that case. Later, when I shepardized that case, I saw another case listed with a small "5" just to the right of it. That would mean the case I uncovered in <u>Shepard's</u> was addressing the topic summarized in headnote #5 of my original case – in our illustration, Key Number 160.7 (home schooling). I would want to take the time to read this new case that Shepard's has helped me locate because it, too, has at least one point to make about home schooling and it has cited my case on that point. If, on the other hand, I found another case in Shepard's listed with only a small "3" immediately to the right of it, I might not be as interested in reading that case. What the "3" would tell me is that the case I just found is citing my original case *on the point made in headnote #3 of my original case.* If the *only* thing my original case was useful for was the point covered under headnote #5 (about home schooling), I might not have found this second case profitable to read, and might have chosen to look at other cases instead.

We live in a time of rapid change in the publishing world. <u>Shepard's</u> is no longer published independently but, rather, is now published by LexisNexis. Lexis, in turn, produces its own headnotes -- totally distinct from the West headnotes that are tied to the West Key Number System and that appear in West publications. Since early 2006, Lexis has begun phasing out all references to West headnote numbers in its print and its online <u>Shepard's Citators</u>. With a few jurisdictional exceptions (California, Montana, New Hampshire, New York, Ohio, Vermont, and Washington), you will find either no headnote references or only Lexis headnote references in <u>Shepard's</u> online and in print. References to West headnotes (but not to Lexis headnotes) and to the West Key Number System are still a core part of the Thomson-West publishing system and can be found on Westlaw.

Step 5: Using the abbreviations table at the <u>front</u> of your Shepard's volume as a guide, explain how the case you found in Step 4 above relates to the original case you were sheparding (in other words, does the court in the second case overrule your earlier case, agree with your earlier case, etc.):

Would this be a case that you would want to read if you were researching the issue of past consideration in more depth? _____ (yes or no). Why or why not?

Step 6: Remember, updating is always an important (although often tedious) part of doing accurate legal research. To accurately and completely update your search in <u>Shepard's</u>, you need to repeat this process (find the volume and page number for the original case you're searching) in all the red, gold, and white paperback volumes of <u>Shepard's</u> placed on the library shelf. These paperback pamphlets contain updates to the entries in the hardback version of <u>Shepard's</u> you've been working in and using them will give you the completely updated information about the statute you've been researching. For the sake of brevity, we will not ask you to update your case now unless you would just like to. However, skipping this step when you are researching a real legal issue is a <u>very bad idea</u>.

Imagine that you have failed to update your search of a case that you think summarizes everything your senior partner or a judge needs to know on the topic. Imagine next that the partner shows you the case in the latest supplement and it has a small "o" next to it. What would the discovery of such updated information mean about the reliability of the case you were planning to use?:

Step 7: In addition to helping you determine if the case you have found is still "good law" and helping you find additional cases to read related to the point you are researching, <u>Shepard's Citators</u> can also help you discover whether the case you are reading has any "prior history" (i.e., was it heard in an appellate court earlier, before the court wrote the present opinion) and its "subsequent history" (a sort of peculiar term that lawyers use when they mean whether the case reached an appellate court again *after* the present opinion was written.) You can find references to prior and future history directly under the parenthetical reference to the case's parallel cite to another reporter. Does your case have any prior or subsequent history? If so, indicate here a cite to any preceding or later opinions stemming from this case:

> **TIP:** Shepard's is a great finding tool for lots of resources in addition to cases. Note that ALR annotations, legal encyclopedias, and law review articles are listed along with cases in each volume. Also, there is a useful Shepard's volume called the Case Name Citator that can help you find the citation to a case if all you know is the case name. Thus, if I wanted to read Brown v. Board of Education, I could find the case by checking in Shepard's U.S. Citations - Case Name Citator. There is a similar Case Name Citator for each individual state. Finally, note that all these same volumes which you've explored for finding and updating state cases in state reporters are available for state cases reported in the regional reporters and for federal cases as well.

STOP HERE and return to Part C of your common law assignment in the main body of the workbook. Please reshelve any Shepard's volumes now so that others may use them.

Part II: Updating and Expanding Your State Statutory Research Using Hard Copy (Print) Materials

Introduction: Shepard's Citations offers a series of print citators similar to the Shepards [state] Citations, Case Edition that you learned to use in Part I of this Appendix. The print citator for each state's statutes provides you with a method for ensuring that your statute has not been amended or repealed, and also for point you to related materials such as cases that have cited your statute, law review articles that have discussed your statute, state Attorney General's opinions discussing your statute, etc. In this section of Appendix C, you will learn how to use Shepard's to learn more about the statute you have uncovered in response to your client's legal problem.

Step 1: Shepard's Citations for your state's statutes is usually found in close proximity to the statutes themselves. As with all Shepard's volumes, it is bound in dark red with gold writing on the binding. **Go to location in your library where the Shepard's Citations for your state's statutes is shelved now.**

Step 2: Find the volume that lists "statutes" on the spine. Turn to the Table labeled "Abbreviations-Analysis (Statutes)" near the front of that volume and note that there are a number of treatment symbols that the publishers use to let you know how an entry under your section relates to that section. For example, if you see an "A" directly to the left of an entry under your statute, you know that the statute has been amended. The citation listed next to the "A" when you search for your statute's entry in Shepard's will be the amendment. Similarly, if a case reference is listed under your statute, there are symbols that tell you how that case relates to your statute. For example, if a "U" appears next to the case entry, you know that case found at least part of your statute to be unconstitutional. In the space below, explain what it would mean if you saw the letter "R" next to an entry when you search your statute in Shepard's:

Step 3: In Shepard's, turn to the Chapter in which your statute is codified. For example, if you were going to shepardize N.C. Gen. Stat. § 75-1.1, you would be looking for Chapter 75 in Shepard's North Carolina Citations - Statutes. You would look for Chapter 75 by scanning the top right or left corners of the pages (as if you were looking for dictionary entries). Once you found the page where Chapter 75 is located, you would scan the columns on that page for the specific reference to the section you are sheparding (in this example, § 75-1.1). The chapters are listed in bold print and are centered in the column in which they first appear, and the sections are listed in numerical order beneath. If your section has subsections (e.g., 50-19(a)), each subsection will be dealt with separately as well. Follow these same steps using the statute that you analyzed in your Assignment Sheet for State Statutes. In the space below, write down at least one entry you found for your statute and describe what that entry means (note that if there are no entries for your statute, flip through the volumes until you find a statute that does have related entries and use that statute for the rest of this exercise. If you switch statutes, write down the cite to the new statute so your professor will know which statute you are sheparding):

Step 4: To make sure your search is completely up-to-date, you now have to turn to the paperback versions of your state's <u>Shepard's Citations</u> for statutes. These paperback versions will give you the completely updated information about the statute you're researching. To use these volumes, find the gold paperback version that begins with the date that the hardback volume stops. Check out your Chapter and Section number in it. Continue this process through all the paperback versions (moving from the gold to red to white, if available) until you have checked all possible dates for any changes that may have had an effect on your statute. (Note that the white volumes cover only very recent revisions to the law and are not always on the shelves because the most recent information has already been incorporated in the red volumes.) Did you find any changes?:

STOP HERE and return to your State Statute Assignment Sheet now.

Part III: Updating and Expanding Your Federal Statutory Research Using Hard Copy (Print) Materials

Step 1: To update the federal statute you are using, you will use <u>Shepard's Federal Statute Citations</u>. **Go to the location in your library where this volume is shelved.**

---

t TIP: <u>Shepard's Federal Statute Citations</u> does NOT include references to judicial opinions from a state court on a federal statute nor does it include references to law review articles concerning a particular federal statute. If you were interested in knowing if a particular state court has considered a particular federal statute, you would need to use the <u>Shepard's</u> volume for that state. To find law review articles that have cited the federal statute you are interested in, use <u>Shepard's Federal Law Citations in Selected Law Reviews</u>.

Step 2: In <u>Shepard's Federal Statute Citations</u>, look for the Title of your statute. Title numbers are listed on the top right and left corners of each page. Next, again using the top right and left corners of each page (like a dictionary or telephone book), find the page that addresses your section number. Section numbers are listed in bold face in the center of the columns. Finally, look for any subsection numbers that apply to the statute you're researching.

Step 3: In the space provided below and on the next page, write down at least one entry you found under your statute and describe what that entry means. (Remember from your earlier work in Assignment Sheet 3 (State Statutes) that the small letters to the left of an entry indicate some special action taken. Turn to the Abbreviations and Analysis table near the front of the <u>Shepard's</u> volume to find out what those abbreviations mean.):

Step 4: To make sure your search is completely up-to-date, you now have to turn to the paperback versions of <u>Shepard's Federal Statute Citations</u>. These paperback versions will give you the completely updated information about the statute you've been researching. To use these volumes, find the gold paperback version that begins with the date that the hardback volume stops (these paperback versions are shelved immediately to the right of whatever <u>Shepard's</u> volume you're using). Check out the Title and Section number in the gold paperback volume and note any references to your statute. Continue this process through all the paperback versions which are available on the shelf (moving from gold to red to blue, if available) until you have checked all possible dates for any changes which may have had an impact on your statute. Did you find any?:

TIP: The publishers of <u>Shepard's</u> print the latest updates in white paperback supplements in state volumes, but in blue paperback supplements for federal volumes.

Don't forget that whenever you use <u>Shepard's</u>, you have to update through all the available yellow, red, and blue (or white) volumes to make sure your research is still accurate.

Please return the <u>Shepard's</u> volume you have been using to the shelf now, and then return to Part IV of your Federal Statute Assignment Sheet to learn how to search for Federal Legislative History.

Appendix: D

How Statutes Come Into Being

The passage of a statute is a long, arduous process. Understanding the process of how a statute comes into being is important because it helps a researcher know what type of information might be available as the researcher tries to unravel the mystery of a statute's past. The textbooks listed in Appendix A have good information about the process of passing legislation. For our present purposes, let's take a brief look at just the federal process.[2]

As with all legislation, a federal statute is first conceived of as a wish or an idea – a concept for action.[3] The concept (which can come from any number of sources ranging from a single individual, to a special interest group, to the President) must be "sponsored" by a member of the House or Senate. Once an idea has a sponsor, that legislator introduces it as a proposal (put in writing as an "introduced print"). Most often, a proposal takes the form of a bill. Bills are numbered at inception. If the bill is introduced in the House, it is assigned a number beginning with "H.R." If it is introduced in the Senate, its bill number is preceded by the letter "S." A proposed bill can only survive a maximum of two years – the length of a term of Congress. If it is not passed into law by that time, it must be re-introduced at the next term to be considered (and would receive a new number).

Once introduced, the bill is assigned to committee where it is frequently reassigned to a subcommittee. Sometimes public hearings are held (at the subcommittee level if a subcommittee is involved, and then again at the committee level if the bill is passed back to the main committee). The committee must then decide whether to submit (report) the bill back to the full chamber where its sponsor originally introduced it. If the bill is reported, it is often accompanied by a committee report. These committee reports are among the documents sometimes considered by courts faced with the task of interpreting a statute at a later date.

Once in the chamber, the bill may be the subject of debate – another possible source of information about the legislative intent behind a bill's passage. Ultimately the chamber must vote. If the bill passes, it moves to consideration by the opposite chamber where it again is assigned to a committee or committees. Once it emerges from that committee, the bill can again be the subject of floor debate. In the end, this second chamber can pass the bill as is, can defeat the bill as is, or can amend the bill and send it back to the first chamber for reconsideration.

---

[2] For a cogent and detailed explanation of the federal legislative process, see Appendix K of Christopher G. Wren & Jill Robinson Wren, The Legal Research Manual (2d ed. 1986). If you are interested in learning more about a particular state's legislative process, you may find information on that state's homepage (most of which can be found at www.state.___.us) (inserting the U.S. Postal Service initials for the state)).

[3] I first grasped the notion of an "idea" being the seed of all legislation from Wren & Wren, supra n. 6, and recommend their clear explanation of the legislative process to you.

After the bill has been passed by both chambers, it moves on to the President's Office where it becomes law if the President signs it, fails to veto it within a prescribed period of time, or if both chambers override a veto by a two-thirds vote. The bill is immediately assigned a number (generally preceded by a designation of P.L. for "Public Law" and the number of the term of Congress that it was passed under). Eventually, this "slip law" is republished in the "session laws" and then ultimately in final codified form.

Index

K

KeyCite Citations

L

M

O

P

Q

R

S

W